STAR-SPANGLED EDEN

ALSO BY JAMES C. SIMMONS

The Novelist as Historian:
Essays on the Victorian Historical Novel

Truman Capote: The Story of His Bizarre and Exotic Boyhood
(with Marie Rudisill)

The Secrets Men Keep (with Ken Druck)

Passionate Pilgrims:
English Travelers to the World of the Desert Arabs

The Big Book of Adventure Travel

Americans: The View from Abroad

Castaway in Paradise: The Incredible Adventures of
True-Life Robinson Crusoes

STAR-SPANGLED EDEN

19th Century America Through the Eyes of
Dickens, Wilde, Frances Trollope, Frank Harris,
and Other British Travelers

JAMES C. SIMMONS

CARROLL & GRAF PUBLISHERS, INC.
NEW YORK

First Carroll & Graf edition 2000

Carroll & Graf Publishers, Inc.
A Division of Avalon Publishing Group
19 West 21st Street
New York, NY 10010-6805

Library of Congress Cataloging-in-Publication data is available.
ISBN: 0-7867-0734-8

Manufactured in the United States of America

For the Gillette family:
Lori and Christopher, Anna Celia and Christopher, Jr.

❦ Acknowledgments ❦

This book profited greatly because a number of people graciously agreed to critique an earlier draft of the manuscript. Special thanks go to Professor William Rogers of the Department of English at San Diego State University; Professor John Reardon of the Department of English at Miami University, Oxford, Ohio; Professor Martin Shockley of Denton, Texas; and Dr. Barbara Newman of the Department of Political Science at Ohio State University, Columbus, Ohio.

Also, a nod to one of England's greatest historians, who has had an enduring influence on the kind of historiography I write. I am a historian in the grand tradition of Thomas Macaulay, who insisted more than 150 years ago that with proper research and an attention to the small details of place, action, and character, formal history could be written to read as easily and effortlessly as the finest historical romance.

And, finally, heartfelt thanks to my copy editor, Nancy Gillan, for her usual splendid job.

ॐ Table of Contents ॐ

"And how do you like our country, sir?" asked Mrs. Hominy.
"Very much indeed," said Martin, half asleep. "At least–that
is–pretty well, ma'am."
"Most strangers–and partick'larly Britishers–are much surprised
by what they see in the United States," remarked Mrs. Hominy.
"They have excellent reason to be, ma'am," said Martin. "I never
was so surprised in my life."

—Charles Dickens, Martin Chuzzlewit

STAR-SPANGLED EDEN

❦ Introduction ❧

No country of the world so stimulated the imagination of the British people in the nineteenth century as its former colonies, the United States of America. The great American social and political experiment utterly captivated the British public, and a peaceful invasion began as the British came in droves to explore the politics, the society, and the character of the United States. "America was the China of the nineteenth century—described, analyzed, promoted, and attacked," historian March Pachter has observed. "What had been a somewhat obscure, occasionally romanticized backwater of colonial exploitation became, virtually overnight, a phenomenon to be investigated, a political and moral experiment to be judged."

Countries have a habit of becoming metaphors. America has probably stood for more things to more people than any other nation in human history. Many nineteenth-century British visitors began their journey here as a quest for the New Eden, otherwise known as the Promised Land or the Golden Land. The French traveler Alexis de Tocqueville struck a common chord when he called America "a laboratory of the future" and wrote after his 1831 visit: "Never before has a people found for itself such a happy and fruitful basis of life." Although republicanism, democracy, and the industrial revolution did not begin here, America nonetheless was the first country given over entirely to new social ideas and technological innovation and, as such, often

1

the first to show the benefits and suffer the shocks of change.

For most of these British visitors, we Americans were a strange and inexplicable lot. They quickly perceived that we exhibited characteristics not shared by our cousins back in England. We had become virtually a different people. The nineteenth-century Londoner who remarked, as many did, that he felt more at home in Paris than Chicago was only mirroring a belief that Americans had been transmuted into a different species from the English pioneers who had planted their civilization at Jamestown and Plymouth three centuries before.

"The moment I set foot in the United States I felt that I had got amongst a new people," observed the Reverend David Macrae soon after his arrival in New York in 1867. "It is very remarkable that a country still in its infancy should already have produced so distinct a type of man. . . . An American is everywhere recognized. You know him by his speech; you know him by a certain ease and grandeur of manner, which is inspired by the greatness of his country and his personal share in its government; you know him by his features—the long sharp face, the eagle eye, and the pointed chin."

(Why this transmutation? The more perceptive visitors in the nineteenth century understood that many of the national characteristics they branded as uniquely American were products of the generations of pioneering needed to settle the continent.)

The 50 years between 1830 and 1880 saw a crucial transformation of America from primitive frontier to modern industrial state. These five decades were a time of swift industrialization, explosion in knowledge, immigration, vast population growth, urbanization, geographical expansion, and the greatest armed conflict ever to occur on American soil.

The eight British men and women selected for this book

all came to America for different reasons. Each had a set of experiences utterly unlike the others. Their discoveries of the physical and social realities of America often led in turn to personal discoveries of uncharted and unsuspected worlds within. Most returned to England profoundly changed by their exposure to the American people, institutions, and landscapes.

Each of the eight visitors was a mirror reflecting American society at a particular time in its history. Together their travels provide a rich social and political history from the outside in, so to speak, of 50 of our most critical years. From George Ruxton, caught up in the forces of Manifest Destiny, through Oscar Wilde's witty cross-country lecture tour, each of these travelers intimately reflects a major theme of American history.

"The people of the United States are like persons surrounded by mirrors," wrote the American Charles Sumner in 1838, noting the numerous books produced by English travelers to America. "They may catch their likeness from every quarter, and in every possible light, attitude, and movement.... Turn we as we may, we catch our reflected features. The vista seems to lengthen at every sight."

Today, more than 150 years later, the mirrors are still with us. And now, as then, the first question many Americans ask visiting foreigners continues to be, "Well, what do you think of us?"

Part

§ **1** §

Jacksonian America

The inauguration on March 4, 1829, of General Andrew Jackson as the seventh president of the United States will always remain part of the folk legend of American history. Some 10,000 people had gathered in Washington to see their idol. "Persons have come five hundred miles to see General Jackson," Daniel Webster marveled. "And they really seem to think the country is rescued from some dreadful danger." Chief Justice John Marshall administered the oath. Afterward, President Jackson mounted his horse and rode leisurely at the head of an enormous crowd of followers to the White House for a planned reception. The crowd thronged into the East Room. All order quickly dissolved. The people surged toward the bowls of rum punch. Windows shattered. Fights broke out. Noses were bloodied. Ladies fainted. The crowd of well-wishers pushed President Jackson out a rear door and forced him to take refuge in the nearby Gadsby's Hotel. Only a quick removal of the punch bowls and food tables to the lawn saved the mansion from further damage. Conservatives shuddered over what appeared to be the start of another French Revolution. "The reign of King Mob seemed triumphant," a fearful Justice Joseph Story recalled later.

A new era dawned with the inauguration of Andrew Jackson, the courageous soldier boy of the American Revolution, hero of the War of 1812, and celebrated Indian fighter who had vanquished the fierce Creeks on the Tennessee frontier and the Seminoles in Florida. His election represented the triumph of the

American faith in the Horatio Alger dream of upward mobility. Affectionately known as "Old Hickory," Jackson was born in a log cabin on the Carolina frontier and rose to the White House by way of the Hermitage Plantation near Nashville. (In 1832 Henry Clay coined the phrase "self-made man" to describe those who had gained their wealth through enterprising, patient, and diligent labor. Roughly one-fourth of the rich men in the United States in the 1830s had inherited their wealth; the others had acquired it through their own hard work.) Whereas in England leaders took pains to hide their lower-class backgrounds lest they be socially stigmatized, American leaders boasted of their humble origins. For many decades after Jackson's election, birth in a log cabin was almost a requirement for political success.

When Alexis de Tocqueville journeyed through America in 1831 and 1832, he marveled, "This people is one of the happiest in the world." The country was awash in prosperity. Its population stood at 13,000,000 in 1831. *The Encyclopedia Americana* of 1832 published the following description of the American people in the Jacksonian era:

> The population of no country in the world ever enjoyed the necessities and comforts of life in such abundance as that of the United States. The high state of wages, the great demand for labor of all kinds, the plenty of provisions, the cheapness of land, and the lightness of taxes, connected with the absence of all restrictions upon industry, and the character of the institutions, would naturally produce such a result. It has been computed that a laborer can earn as much in one day as will furnish bread and meat to himself, wife, and four children for three days nearly. . . .
>
> Where the means of subsistence are so easily procured, no person able to work need be in want; but there must be some in all countries who, from age, bodily or mental infirmities, are unable to support themselves: the number of these, how-

ever, is small, and comfortable provision is made for their
support by state legislation. . . . A beggar is rarely seen in any
part of the country.

Americans in the era of Jacksonian Democracy were a thrifty,
industrious, self-reliant, optimistic people suffused throughout
with an unshakable faith in democracy and individual freedom.
"In their eyes, the United States was a great evangelist, sounding
the trumpet of freedom, leading the way along a path that Old
Europe, sooner or later, would have to follow," historian Glyndon
G. Van Deusen observed in *The Jacksonian Era.* "Exhilarated by
the conviction that America was the pioneer in forging a new era
for mankind, Americans in the Jacksonian period undertook a
variety of experiments that were designed to broaden the area of
freedom. They tested new religious faiths and philosophies that
ranged from spiritualism and Mormonism to transcendentalism
and Unitarianism. Some tried to establish religious or quasi-reli-
gious Utopias. Others undertook socialistic and communistic
experiments that were supposed to bring in their train freedom
from want and from social maladjustment. Devoted humanitari-
ans ministered to the deaf, the blind, and the insane; penal reforms
were instituted; secular education was widened and its quality
improved; a temperance movement gathered headway. There were
crusades for peace, for women's rights, and for the abolition of
slavery. America was offering a challenge to the rest of the world,
the challenge of a free society seeking a better way of life."

Under Jacksonian Democracy, for the first time, "the spirit of
equality" gave rise to a new social structure. "There reigns an
unbelievable outward equality in America," de Tocqueville noted.
"All classes are constantly meeting, and there does not appear the
least arrogance resulting from different social positions."

A major factor behind this harmony was that farmers in
America owned their land, unlike in England, thus avoiding the
caste clashes between landlords and tenants, which proved such
a fertile source for vexation in the British countryside. Jackson
made the Presidency expressive of the democratic spirit of

equality sweeping the land. Any visitor to Washington could get an invitation to the White House's social functions simply by making a request.

The erosion of cultivated manners in public life and the disappearance in many arenas of gentlemanly standards of courtesy and moderation in social intercourse caused considerable dismay among men and women of letters and lovers of culture. They watched in horror as a newly elevated breed of Jacksonian Americans made their vulgar presence felt in Congress, state legislatures, and numerous public forums across the country, engaging in noisy quarrels while spitting disgusting streams of yellow tobacco juice in every direction.

Jacksonian America was full of an unruly energy that never ceased to amaze foreign visitors. "No sooner do you set foot on American ground than you are stunned by a kind of tumult," de Tocqueville wrote. "A confused clamor is heard on every side, and a thousand simultaneous voices demand satisfaction of their social wants. Everything is in motion around you."

Nothing better illustrated this "confused clamor" than the American elections. One George D. Prentice penned a lengthy account for *The New England Weekly Review* of a rowdy election in Kentucky in 1830. This bacchanalian display was repeated hundreds of times over elsewhere in the country:

> An election in Kentucky lasts three days, and during that period whiskey and apple toddy flow through our cities and villages like the Euphrates through ancient Babylon. . . . In Frankfort, a place which I had the curiosity to visit on the last day of the election, Jacksonianism and drunkenness stalked triumphant—"an unclean pair of lubberly giants." A number of runners, each with a whiskey bottle poking its long neck from his pocket, were busily employed bribing voters, and each party kept a dozen bullies under pay, genuine specimens of Kentucky *alligatorism,* to flog every poor fellow who should vote illegally. . . .

I barely escaped myself. One of the runners came up to me, and slapping me on the shoulder with his right hand, and a whiskey bottle in his left, asked me if I was a voter. "No," I said. "Ah, never mind," quoth the fellow, pulling a corncob out of the neck of the bottle, and shaking it up to the best advantage. "Jest take a swig at the cretur and toss in a vote for Old Hickory's boys. . . ." Here was a temptation to be sure; but after looking alternately at the bottle and the bullies who were standing ready with their sledgehammer fists to knock down all interlopers, my fears prevailed and I lost my whiskey.

The above account of the election also illustrates another major feature of Jacksonian America: its fondness for alcohol, especially whiskey. In the 1830s Americans consumed more than five gallons of liquor per capita annually, the highest rate in our history. Two popular prejudices insisted that water be shunned as a carrier of disease, while drinking tea was regarded as unpatriotic because most tea was imported from England. Beer did not become popular until after the great German migration began in mid-century. That left whiskey as the beverage of choice for most people. In 1810, Louisville, Kentucky, shipped 250,000 gallons of whiskey up the Ohio River. By 1822 the volume had swelled tenfold to 2,250,000 gallons. Upon learning that most crime in America could be traced back to the overconsumption of alcohol, de Tocqueville asked a Philadelphia man why Congress did not put a stiff tax on all whiskey. Because, he was told, that would cost the legislators their seats, if not provoke a rebellion. One result was the founding of the American Society for the Promotion of Temperance in 1840, which soon could claim more than four million members.

A keen interest in wealth and business was also pervasive throughout an American society embarked upon a strenuous pursuit of material gain. The entrepreneur became a popular hero, as mercantilist notions of political economy began to yield the economic stage to a rising laissez-faire capitalism. "There is probably no people on earth for whom business constitutes pleasure and industry amusement, in an equal degree than with the inhabitants of the United States of America," Francis J. Grund, an 1837 British visitor, reported. "Business is the very soul of an American; he pursues it, not as a means of procuring for himself and his family the necessary comforts of life, but as the fountain of all human felicity; and shows as much enthusiastic ardour in his application to it as any crusader ever evinced for the conquest of the Holy Land, or the followers of Mohammed for the spreading of the Koran."

By and large, Jacksonian America had little time for the pursuit of the cultural side of life. Newspapers were the principal reading matter for most Americans. (The state of New York boasted 239 in 1831, with 54 in New York City alone.) The president's own contempt for literature and the arts reflected the fundamental bias of the vast majority of his supporters, particularly in the Western states. The jackass as a symbol for the Democratic Party, newly formed in 1828 to support Jackson, was first used by the Whigs as a satiric thrust at the reputed ignorance of Old Hickory; it was a sign of the times that the party not only joyfully accepted this emblem but has retained it for more than 170 years.

The abundance of land and resources in the western regions of the country and the development of democratic institutions kept American society open and fluid during the Jacksonian years. Tocqueville saw America as "a land in motion." Thousands upon thousands of restless Americans turned their backs on the East and its security and headed into the trans-Appalachian West, drawn by the promise of cheap land and a new life. A popular story of the time had Henry Clay, on his way to give a speech, stopping for a time in Cumberland Gap. "Why do you linger?" someone asked. "I am listening to the tread of the coming millions," he was supposed to have replied. Unlike the later frontiers of Oregon and California, the Midwest was easily accessible by steamboats, barges, keelboats, and flatboats. The Erie Canal opened to traffic in 1825, and its horse-drawn barges offered to folks from the New England states ready access to the Great Lakes region. Ohio's population mushroomed from 230,760 in 1810 to

937,637 in 1830; in that same period Indiana's grew from 24,520 to 341,582 and Illinois's from 12,282 to 157,575. In 1820, the Midwest with its two million settlers boasted more people than all of New England.

Virtually every foreign visitor to America's shores at this time commented upon the incredible energy of its people. "Time to an American is everything and space he attempts to reduce to mere nothing," the Englishman Captain Frederick Marryat observed during his 1837 visit. "'*Go ahead*' is the real motto of the country; and every man does push on, to gain an advance of his neighbour. The American lives twice as long as others; for he does twice the work during the time he lives."

And Michel Chevalier insisted during his 1833 visit that the typical American is "devoured with a passion for locomotion. He cannot stay in one place; he must go and come, he must stretch his limbs and keep his muscles in play. When his feet are not in motion, his fingers must be in action. He must be whittling a piece of wood, cutting the back of his chair, or notching the edge of the table, or his jaws must be at work grinding tobacco."

The American economy of the period exhibited a similar sort of energy. The Erie Canal became known shortly after its opening in 1825 as the "Eighth Wonder of the World." The 363-mile-long canal connected the Great Lakes and the Atlantic Ocean and became the most important American transportation artery of its time. Freight rates plunged ninety percent; business boomed along its length. Tens of thousands of pioneers boarded the canal packet boats for the first stage of their trip to the western frontier. "The Erie Canal rubbed the Aladdin's Lamp," one contemporary observer wrote. "America awoke, catching for the first time the wondrous vision of its own dimensions and power."

Frances Trollope, Fanny Kemble, and Charles Dickens would, over the course of a few years, make their own discoveries about this new American man, who embodied the values of Jacksonian Democracy. The encounters would often prove unpleasant and shatter many of the visitors' most cherished ideals.

Chapter

§ 1 §

Frances Trollope: America's Nemesis

In late March 1832 bookstores throughout England began displaying a new book with the innocent title *Domestic Manners of the Americans*. Its author, Frances Trollope, had just celebrated her fifty-third birthday. This was her first book. It recounted in graphic detail her stay of 25 months in Cincinnati, then the largest city on the northwestern American frontier. Mrs. Trollope proved to be a shrewd, if prejudiced, observer whose style was laced throughout with an acid wit. "I do not like Americans," she confessed. "I do not like their principles. I do not like their manners. I do not like their opinions." Mrs. Trollope unequivocally insisted that the American experiment was a giant step back toward barbarism, an unruly triumph of the mob.

Domestic Manners quickly became that rarity of the publishing business, a bona fide phenomenon. No other travel book on America has ever generated so much controversy. In the United States an outraged citizenry bought up copies as fast the publishers could print them. A British Army officer in New York City in 1832 viewed the commotion with utter disbelief. "The Tariff and Bank Bills were alike forgotten, and the tug of war was hard, whether *Domestic Manners* or the cholera, both of which had burst upon them simultaneously, should be the more engrossing topic of conversation," he wrote home. "At every table d'hote, on board every steamship, in every stage coach, and in all societies, the first question was, 'Have you read Mrs. Trollope?'"

No English citizen since King George III enjoyed such notoriety in America as did Mrs. Trollope. She was lampooned, parodied, travestied, and caricatured everywhere, until she became a folk character. A British tourist in New England later encountered her likeness in a traveling menagerie. "This exact likeness turned out to be the figure of a fat red-faced *trollop,* smoking a short pipe, and dressed in dirty flannel and worsted and a ragged slouched hat," he wrote. "'This,' said the showman, 'is the purty Mrs. Trollope, who was sent over to the United States by the British lords to write libels against the free-born Americans.' The figure excited a good deal of attention and was abused in no measured terms." And *trollope* in America became a universal slang term of reproval to be hurled at ill-mannered and uncouth brethren. "A trollope! A trollope!" American theater audiences shouted whenever a gentleman parked his feet on the edge of his box.

And yet Mrs. Trollope had not come to America expecting to judge it harshly. Indeed, in late 1827 when she sailed from the British shores for New Orleans, her heart was full of hope. America was for her a promised land where anything might be possible. Severe times had overtaken her own family. Her husband was nearly bankrupt. In America she hoped to recover his losses. She was then a true believer in the American dream of happiness and freedom for all men. Within two years she had been totally disillusioned. What had soured her dream?

2

Frances Trollope was born on March 10, 1779, near Bristol, England, the third of four children. Her father was the Rev. William Milton, an eccentric country clergyman who dabbled with inventions. (His pride and joy was a set of dinner plates with silver strips embedded in them to eliminate the screeching noise of knives against porcelain.) In 1784 his wife died, leaving him the dominant influence in the lives of his children. In 1801 he remarried and relocated to a small country parish. Frances Milton's education was desultory and typical of the period for girls in her situation: singing and playing the pianoforte, a smattering of languages, and some art lessons.

In 1803 her brother Henry took a position in London at the War Office and moved with his two sisters into a house in the Bloomsbury section. Beau Brummel and George, Prince of Wales, dominated London's high society, a world of stylishly dressed men and women who devoted their days to clothes, parties, witty conversation, and sexual intrigues. Frances Milton's days were a whirl of theatrical performances, card parties, museum visits, small dinner parties, and balls. In 1808 her brother introduced her to Thomas Arnold Trollope, a 34-year-old barrister, the younger son of a baronet, and a man with "expectations." They were opposites—she vivacious, witty, extroverted; he reserved, stolid, and taciturn. Yet in spite of their differences they fell in love and were married on May 23, 1809. The marriage was ill-fated. In that happy honeymoon period Mrs. Trollope could never have foreseen that ahead lay bankruptcy and sorrow. Her family's salvation was to depend entirely on her courage and faith.

Mrs. Trollope quickly settled into her new career of housewife and mother. In the next nine years she gave birth to seven children, including Anthony, in 1815, who would establish himself as one of England's most beloved novelists. Their comfortable middle-class establishment included a nurse, several servants, and a liveried footman. Thomas Trollope's law practice in Lincoln Inn prospered. This, plus the expectation of a large inheritance from a favorite uncle, prompted him in 1813 to lease a farm of 160 acres near Harrow, an hour's ride from his London office. He soon started construction on a handsome new house, a stately brick mansion of four stories with several chimneys. He underestimated the costs and then was horrified to learn that his uncle, the source of all his expectations, had unexpectedly married a young woman. Their first child appeared the following year, dashing nephew Thomas's hopes for a large inheritance. "That farm was the grave of all my father's hopes, ambition, and prosperity, the cause of my mother's sufferings, and those of her children, and perhaps the director of her destiny and ours," his son Anthony observed years later in his *Autobiography*.

To make matters worse, Thomas Trollope's London law practice slowly unwound. His arrogance, coupled with a quarrelsome manner, offended both his clients and colleagues. His reputation as a dour, sullen, and rude-mannered man quickly spread. Soon he found himself without a practice. One consequence was a marked deterioration in his health. The Trollope family's standard of living underwent a slow but steady decline.

Mrs. Trollope did what she could to stem the ebb of the family fortunes, displaying a mix of common sense and fortitude. She simply refused to dwell on losses and adjusted to each new crisis by doggedly forging ahead. She studied farming journals to learn the latest techniques, kept the house in order, read Dante while hemming her sheets, and gave parties that delighted others. Her daughter-in-law remembered her in later years: "She had admirably good sense, much genuine humour, great knowledge of the world, and a quick appreciation of others' gifts, and above all, a character of the most flawless sincerity and a warmly affectionate heart." She, not her husband, proved the dominant force within their family.

Mrs. Trollope had long considered herself something of a radical in her political persuasion. Her drawing room at Harrow soon developed a reputation as a sympathetic refuge for anyone fleeing persecution. "She used to be such a Radical that her house . . . was a perfect emporium of escaped state criminals," her good friend novelist Mary Russell Mitford recalled. "I remember asking her at one of her parties how many of her guests would have been shot or guillotined if they had remained in their own country."

One of these was a young, handsome artist, Auguste Hervieu, a 33-year-old refugee from monarchist France. Most of his life had been spent in the lonely pursuit of art and revolution without the benefit of family or funds. His father, a professional soldier, had died during Napoleon's retreat from Moscow. The young Hervieu was forced into exile in 1823 after his complicity in a plot to overthrow Louis XVIII was discovered. He was sentenced in absentia to a fine of 15,000 francs and five years in prison. He eventually found refuge in the Trollope household as the children's art tutor.

In 1823 Mrs. Trollope made her first visit to Paris, where she met General Marie Joseph Paul Lafayette, the venerable hero of the American Revolution, and his ward, Frances Wright. This wealthy Scotswoman would soon shape Mrs. Trollope's fortunes in a direction she could never have foreseen. A person of strong character and fanatical idealism, Miss Wright at 28 enjoyed a large fortune with which she indulged her enthusiasms for such revolutionary causes as socialism, free love, and women's rights. Thomas Adolphus Trollope, the oldest son, remembered her as "a very clever woman . . . handsome in a large and almost masculine style of beauty, with a most commanding presence."

In 1824 when General Lafayette embarked upon his triumphant tour of the United States, Miss Wright was at his side. She developed a special interest in slavery and purchased a small plantation called Nashoba fifteen miles from Memphis, Tennessee. There she set up a utopian community where she hoped to solve the problem of American slavery. Her Negroes would earn their emancipation while special schools would teach them the survival skills necessary for a new life outside the United States. Upon her return to France she invited the Trollopes for an extended visit at General Lafayette's splendid chateau. (Another guest there was American novelist James Fenimore Cooper.) From the first Mrs. Trollope had been enormously attracted and somewhat overwhelmed by the younger woman. A reformer, world traveler, and published author, Miss Wright seemed to have done it all. By contrast Mrs. Trollope's own life at Harrow appeared barren of excitement and achievement. Her youngest son was in school. She yearned for a new direction in her life. Frances Wright's scheme at Nashoba seemed to promise just that.

At Harrow Mr. Trollope's financial problems multiplied while his health deteriorated still further. Early in 1827 he informed his wife that they must give up their spacious mansion at Harrow for the cramped confines of a cottage remote from London. In the meantime Miss Wright had returned to America and sent glowing letters of her progress at Nashoba. "Our people are now singing in chorus," she wrote. "We have a tolerable fiddle among them, and I shall bring . . . a flute for another. We have already a large room where they dance twice a week, and so heartily after a day's hard work of hewing and chopping that I could wish myself one of them. Thus far I am amazed at our success. We were told of difficulties and apprehended many. Truly as yet we have found none worthy of the name." To Mrs. Trollope, struggling with marital disillusionment and major financial problems, faraway Nashoba seemed like an Eden newly carved out of the wilderness.

In 1827 Miss Wright returned to England in the hopes of gaining new recruits for her plantation in Tennessee. "The more I see of the old world the less I feel inclined to remain in it," she advised her friends the Trollopes. "But I should like to rescue out of it a few rational beings who are too good for it and would be much happier in the woods." She desperately wanted a female companion to accompany her to Nashoba. "Must I return without a bosom intimate?" she pleaded. "Our little circle has mind, has heart, has right opinions, right feelings. . . . Yet I do want one of my own sex to commune with and sometimes to lean upon in all the confidence of equality and friendship."

Miss Wright and Mrs. Trollope had another lengthy visit outside Paris at the Lafayette estate. The ardent reformer pressed her friend to return to Nashoba with her. She suggested that Mrs. Trollope's son Henry and companion Hervieu also come along to assume teaching positions in the commune. At last Mrs. Trollope gave in. She convinced her husband that a year or two in the American woods with three of their children (Henry, age 16; and Cecilia and Emily, ages eleven and nine) would resolve many of their most pressing financial problems. Her mind made up, Mrs. Trollope quickly packed and with a servant and maid in tow joined Miss Wright in London. She looked forward to her adventure with great excitement. She knew next to nothing about the country ahead. At the time of her birth, the American colonies had been in revolt against England; they had united and written their Constitution while she was a young girl. Except for Frances Wright and her companion General Lafayette, Mrs. Trollope had talked to almost no one who had actually spent time in America. And the young Scotswoman had applauded unstintingly the energy, integrity, hospitality, cleanliness, and polite manners of the American people.

On November 4 the small group boarded a ship bound for New Orleans. After seven weeks of sailing they reached the mouth of the Mississippi River on Christmas Day and found themselves in the middle of a barren landscape of "mud banks, monstrous bulrushes, and now and then a huge crocodile luxuriating in the slime." For two days they traveled up the wide river past flat mud banks devoid of any features except an occasional hut and stunted tree. On December 27 their ship docked at New Orleans, and they set their legs on solid ground for the first time in almost two months. Mrs. Trollope felt like an explorer entering an uncharted land. "At our public schools America (except perhaps as to her geographical position) is hardly better known than Fairy Land," she wrote later in *Domestic Manners*. "And the American character has not been much more deeply studied than that of the Anthropophagi. All, therefore, was new, and everything was amusing."

3

Before railroads came to dominate the American landscape in the post–Civil War years, New Orleans was the hub of the great Mississippi Valley. Vast quantities of grain, cotton, furs, and tobacco flowed from the Rocky Mountains and the Alleghenies into the city on steamboats, flatboats, and barges. In the minds of the Americans New Orleans was a great, rich, romantic city. And as long as water travel had been dominant, it remained so—a joyous, epicurean metropolis whose French character fitted well into the Jacksonian culture of the agrarian West.

After settling into a hotel, Mrs. Trollope ventured out to explore the sights and sounds of America. In 1827 New Orleans was still more French than American in many ways. The language was equally divided between French and English. She thought the city had all the appearances superficially of "a French Ville de Province." But it possessed an exoticism no French city could match. She marveled at "the grace and beauty of the elegant Quadroons, the occasional groups of wild and savage looking Indians, the unwonted aspect of the vegetation, and the huge and turbid river with its low and slimy shore." The sight of her first slave, a young black girl sweeping the steps of her master's house, made a profound impression on her. A dedicated abolitionist, Mrs. Trollope gave her imagination free rein to invent little romantic miseries for each of the numerous slaves she saw.

On January 1, 1828, the small band of British travelers boarded the steamboat *Belvidere* for the passage to Memphis. Mrs. Trollope deplored the condition of their cabins—"I would infinitely prefer sharing the apartment of a party of well conditioned pigs." She spent long hours on the deck intently watching the river traffic. Accustomed to the neatly tamed rivers of the English countryside, she was utterly unprepared for the desolation and savagery of the lower Mississippi River and the culture along its banks. The *Belvidere* carried in deck passage 200 flatboat crewmen returning to Kentucky. They were her introduction to the rough-mannered frontiersmen so common along the river. Her initial feelings were mixed. She thought the Kentuckians "noble-looking and extremely handsome." Yet she also found them "a most disorderly set of persons, constantly gambling and wrangling, very seldom sober, and never suffering a night to pass without giving practical proof of the respect in which they hold the doctrine of equality."

American manners—or their absence—grated upon Mrs. Trollope almost from the first. Nowhere was this more apparent than in the ship's dining room. For her meal time quickly became major ordeals:

> The total want of all the usual courtesies of the table, the voracious rapidity with which the viands were seized and devoured, the strange uncouth phrases and pronunciation; the loathsome spitting, from the contamination of which it was absolutely impossible to protect our dresses; the frightful manner of feeding with their knives, till the whole blade seemed to enter into the mouth; and the still more frightful manner of cleaning the teeth afterwards with a pocket knife, soon forced us to feel that we were not surrounded by the generals, colonels, and majors of the old world; and that the dinner hour was to be anything rather than an hour of enjoyment.

Mrs. Trollope began to have doubts, too, about her companion Frances Wright. "I was a very poor creature during the voyage and persuaded myself repeatedly that it was my weakness that made me deem Fanny too eccentric," she wrote home in one letter. "I saw her sitting upon a coil of rope in the steerage, reading to a sailor occupied in patching his breeches . . . some of the wildest doctrines of equality and concubinage that pen ever traced on paper. Writing such and reading them aloud were her chief occupation during the voyage. And I often recurred to the idea that had tormented us at Paris that she was not in her right senses."

Steamboats were an unexpected novelty to Mrs. Trollope. Nothing remotely like them existed in Europe. "They are the stage coaches and fly wagons of this land of lakes and rivers," she marveled. Steamboats were the invention of Robert Fulton, a Pennsylvania-born civil engineer. His boat, the *Clermont,* made history in August 1807 when it steamed at five miles per hour up the Hudson River. Four years later the *New Orleans* became the first steamboat to operate on the Mississippi River and ushered in an era of rapid industrial and agricultural development along the entire Mississippi and Ohio river valleys. (One of the early steamboats named each of its cabins after a state, thus giving the term "stateroom" to the English language.) In 1827 the *Tecumseh* set a record when she traveled from New Orleans to Louisville in eight days and two hours. By 1827 the waters of the Mississippi and Ohio rivers teemed with more than 175 steamboats. Most were between 100 and 150 feet in length and cost about $7,500 to build. Steamboat travel was relatively inexpensive. A cabin-class ticket for the passage between New Orleans and Pittsburgh cost about $50. (That same trip in a flatboat with none of the creature comforts ran $6.) The average lifespan of a steamboat was less than five years. Travel on a steamboat was far more dangerous than a long ocean voyage to China. Explosions, mid-river collisions, and groundings on sandbars were daily risks to be endured. Accidents were frequent and often resulted in a horrendous loss of life. On April 25, 1838, the steamship *Moselle*, crowded with 260 passengers, was backing away from the wharf at Cincinnati when her four boilers exploded simultaneously. Pieces of bodies rained down in Kentucky half a mile away. "One hundred and fifty souls were ushered into eternity," one local newspaper editor wrote.

Furnishing wood to steamboats was a common industry along the rivers, fuel amounting to thirty percent of their operating costs. A cord of cut wood sold for $2.50. The *Belvidere* made daily stops to collect wood. Mrs. Trollope was appalled at the isolation, squalid lifestyle, and poverty of the woodcutters and their families. Most lived in ramshackle huts atop tall piles at the river's edge. "Their complexion is of a bluish white that suggests . . . dropsy; and the little ones wear the same ghastly hue," she wrote later. "A miserable cow and a few pigs standing knee-deep in water distinguish the more prosperous of these dwellings. On the whole, I should say I never witnessed human nature reduced so low, as it appeared in the woodcutters' huts on the unwholesome banks of the Mississippi."

The *Belvidere* slowly pushed its way up the river toward Memphis. Mrs. Trollope noted one of the most common sights of river travel in the 1820s, the lurid glare of burning forests, which often illuminated the river at nighttime and sent great clouds of smoke swirling over their heads. New settlers in the virgin wilderness cleared land for farming simply by burning the forests away. The waste appalled Mrs. Trollope. But the fires marked a major difference between England, where men were many and land scarce, and the American frontier, where men were few and land was abundant. Flagrant wastefulness was already established in 1828 as a national American trait. "Wastefulness came naturally to the frontiersman," historian Ray A. Billington has observed. "Who would think of preservation amidst overwhelming abundance? In his eyes nature's riches were so plentiful that their exhaustion was beyond comprehension. Why protect trees in a land where they grew by the billions? Why preserve soil when a move to virgin fields was cheaper than fertilizer?"

The *Belvidere* arrived in Memphis at night in a heavy rain. Wet and exhausted, the little group made its way to a hotel near the riverfront. There Mrs. Trollope had her introduction to the democratic spirit prevailing in Western inns. She quickly learned that the frontier refused to sanction any distinction between "first-class" and "second-class" service. Tradesmen, plantation owners, generals, deckhands, farmers, and congressmen all ate side by side at long tables and received the same treatment. The next day Mrs. Trollope made clear her desire to take her meals in her room; but Miss Wright quickly discouraged her, saying that the lady of the house would take the request as a personal affront. Mrs. Trollope was horrified to discover that she had to eat her meals with fifty other guests around an enormous table with her servant William seated directly across from her.

The following morning Mrs. Trollope's group piled their trunks and boxes into a carriage and set out for Nashoba along a crude muddy roadway studded with stumps, with an impenetrable forest looming on either side. In the late afternoon they reached their destination. Mrs. Trollope sat in the carriage in stunned disbelief and looked around at the rude clearing with its small collection of crude cabins. "Every idea I had formed of the place was as far as possible from the truth," she recalled with a shudder in *Domestic Manners*. "Desolation was the only feeling—the only word that presented itself." Shocked and bewildered, Mrs. Trollope, Hervieu, and her children explored the small settlement. The cabins proved crude two-room affairs with dirt floors and only a smattering of rough furniture. The several whites living there were pale, thin, and chronically ill from the poor climate.

The eloquence of Frances Wright had brought them all these many thousands of miles from England. Her mind's imagination had transformed the little log cabins with their dirty, half-clad Negro tenants into a splendid hall with columns and arcades. Miss Wright appeared genuinely surprised that her guests should find anything disagreeable in the arrangements of her colony. She "stood in the midst of all this desolation with the air of a conqueror," Mrs. Trollope noted, and dined upon corn bread and a glass of rainwater, smiling with a complacency that made her guest think of Peter the Hermit eating acorns in the wilderness.

Fearful for her children's health, Mrs. Trollope determined at once to leave Nashoba. But her money was exhausted. She had to wait ten days while Miss Wright's trustees made arrangements to lend $300 so she could relocate her family in more agreeable surroundings.

On January 26 Mrs. Trollope led her group back to Memphis. On February 1 they embarked on the steamboat *Criterion* for Cincinnati, after New Orleans the most important city west of the Allegheny Mountains. In Memphis she had heard numerous stories of Cincinnati's beauty, wealth, and unequaled prosperity. She was much too dedicated an abolitionist to relocate in a Southern state, and Cincinnati seemed to offer the nearest and most convenient place of refuge. England was clearly beyond reach. But, she reasoned, a skillful use of the $300 she had borrowed might lead to a new life in Cincinnati.

Mrs. Trollope's spirits lifted as the *Criterion* left the muddy waters of the Mississippi for the clearer Ohio River. The shore scenery presented a greater variety than before. Virgin forests hung in solemn grandeur from the cliffs. Settlements were frequent. In Kentucky the vast tracts of rich pastureland impressed her. On February 10 they arrived in Cincinnati, a city of some 20,000 inhabitants situated on the south side of several hills that rose gently from the river's edge. Mrs. Trollope's first impression was that the city's skyline "wanted domes, towers, and steeples." But the wharf, with its 15 steamboats tied up, impressed her. She and her group checked into the Washington Hotel. Cincinnati would be her home for the next 25 eventful months.

4

Although only recently carved out of the wilderness, Cincinnati had grown far beyond a frontier post of log cabins and mud paths. In 1828 it was a center for western migration, the steamboat capital of the Ohio Valley, and well on its way to becoming the economic colossus of the entire Midwest. Several thousand people a month passed through the city on their way to Ohio, Indiana, Michigan, and Illinois. Immigrants poured into Cincinnati at such a rapid rate that not even the construction of 1,400 new homes the preceding year proved sufficient. The city boasted nine steam-engine factories and nine cotton mills. It supported 12 newspapers, 34 charitable organizations, 23 churches, 40 schools, two colleges, and a medical school. The city's one theater was reputed to be the finest in America, after New York's and Philadelphia's.

In 1828 Cincinnati was already the manufacturing center of the Ohio Valley. Its factories annually exported more than $2,500,000 of tools, furniture, clocks, paper, hats, books, whiskey, and flour. Early farmers in southern Ohio discovered that corn thrived in the soil; but getting their corn to distant markets proved difficult. They solved the problem by walking their crops to market on pig's feet, thus forming the basis for one of Cincinnati's largest industries—meat packing. The city soon was shipping so much pork and lard that others referred to it as "Porkopolis," much to the indignation of its citizenry. (In 1837 two Cincinnati merchants, candle-molder William Proctor and soap-boiler James Gamble already grown wealthy from the by-products of pigs, married sisters and merged their businesses. Within a few years Proctor & Gamble was a household name in the American soap industry.) As many as 20 large steamboats at once often tied up at the city's wharf. The city was so dominant that river men sometimes called the Ohio the Cincinnati River. The Ohio River valley reminded the early German immigrants of their Rhine valley back home. Soon thousands of Germans were arriving. (By 1841, 28 percent of the city's population was German and Cincinnati had taken on a distinctly German flavor.) In 1831 Timothy Flint, the editor of the Cincinnati magazine *Western Monthly Review*, observed with satisfaction that the city presented "a picture of beauty, wealth, progress, and fresh advance, as few landscapes in any country can surpass."

After settling into temporary quarters in the Washington Hotel, Mrs. Trollope set about exploring Cincinnati. The sight of three-story brick-and-mortar buildings cheered her after many weeks of crude log buildings. She likened the place to Salisbury in size and population but "without even an attempt at beauty in any of its edifices and with only just enough of the air of a city to make it noisy and bustling." She noted with interest the large number of free Negroes on the streets, most of whom lived in a section of the city known as Little Africa. Main Street, the city's principal thoroughfare, was the only one entirely paved. Most of Cincinnati had been built around a system of squares. On the south the city fronted up against the Ohio River ("a beautiful feature"). But to the north it abutted against a series of steep, timber-covered hills, which, she thought, gave life in Cincinnati a certain claustrophobic air.

The newness of Cincinnati constantly amazed her. "Freshly risen from the bosom of the wilderness," the city had been carved out of raw frontier only a generation earlier. The most obvious vestiges of the frontier—the log cabins, buckskin jackets, and Indian raids—had vanished. But Mrs. Trollope soon discovered, to her horror, that the behavior of many of the city's inhabitants still exhibited the coarseness, expediency, rugged individualism, restlessness, nervous energy, crude manners, and fanatical devotion to equality characteristic of life in the West. Mrs. Trollope quickly came up against the leveling influence of the frontier on Jacksonian democracy. She, in turn, was always much too British to accept as a fundamental difference between America and England a social code that merged groups rather than set them apart.

Mrs. Trollope soon arranged to rent a house. However, settling her domestic arrangements proved a major challenge. Simply finding servants on the frontier became an unanticipated nightmare in a land where illiterate farm girls thought themselves too proud to work for a lady. "Hundreds of half-naked girls work in the paper mills . . . for less than half the wages they would receive in service," she complained. "But they think their equality is compromised by the latter." Her first girl lasted only a few days and then left in a sulk after Mrs. Trollope refused to let her eat at the family table. "I guess that's 'cause you don't think I'm good enough to eat with you," she pointedly informed her employer. "You'll find that won't do here." Mrs. Trollope quickly learned that on the frontier Americans of both sexes felt equal, acted the part, and resented both menial tasks and menial titles.

Finally, Mrs. Trollope and her group were settled into a house that was both "neat and comfortable." But life in Cincinnati lacked many of the amenities she had taken for granted in London. Her house had no pump, cistern, or drain. And no dustman's cart stopped regularly to collect the garbage.

"What," she demanded of her landlord, "are we to do with our refuse?"

"Your help will have to fix them all into the middle of the street, but you must mind, old woman, that it is the middle," he informed her. (Her landlord was the first, but not the last, to address her as "old woman." So she would become known around Cincinnati, much to her distress.) "I expect you don't know as we have got a law that forbids throwing such things at the sides of the streets. They must all be cast right into the middle, and the pigs soon takes them off."

Cincinnati was one giant pigsty. The ubiquitous pigs, thin-backed and dirty, rooted about in every quarter of the city, fattening themselves on the mounds of garbage until they themselves disappeared into the many slaughterhouses. (Cincinnati was not the only American city employing a leave-it-to-the-pigs system of garbage removal; Mrs. Trollope later discovered that even in New York City vast numbers of the animals roamed freely along the streets.) In one of the most vivid passages of *Domestic Manners* she complained:

> It seems hardly fair to quarrel with a place because its sta-ple commodity is not pretty, but I am sure I should have liked Cincinnati much better if the people had not dealt so very largely in hogs. The immense quantity of business done in this line would hardly be believed by those who had not witnessed it. I never saw a newspaper without remarking such adver-tisements as the following:
> "Wanted, immediately, 4,000 fat hogs."
> "For sale, 2,000 barrels of prime pork."
> But the annoyance came nearer than this. If I determined upon a walk up Main Street, the chances were five hundred to one against my reaching the shady side without brushing by a snout fresh dripping from the kennel. When we had screwed our courage to the enterprise of mounting a certain noble-looking sugar-loaf hill that promised pure air and a fine view, we found the brook we had to cross at its foot red with the stream from a pig slaughter house. . . . Our feet on leav-ing the city had expected to press the flowery sod, [but] literally got entangled in pigs' tails and jawbones.

New revelations came with each passing day. After the pollu-tion of the large English cities, the clarity of the American air was a real joy. ("By day and by night this exquisite purity of air gives a tenfold beauty to every object," Mrs. Trollope noted enthusiastically. "I could hardly believe the stars were the same.") The abundance, cheapness, variety, and quality of food available in the Cincinnati markets also impressed her. Not once in her 25 months in the city did she ever see a beggar. She attributed the general prosperity to the low rate of taxation, which "unquestionably permits a more rapid accumulation of individual wealth than with us." It also meant that Americans were eternally in pursuit of the dollar. She met Nick, a dirty ten-year-old urchin, who had enough initiative to run his own chicken business. "I asked him how he managed his business," she reported. "He told me that he bought eggs by the hundred and lean chickens by the score from the wagons that passed their door on the way to market. He fatted the latter in coops he had made himself and could easily double their price." Nick, she discovered, was already worth a small fortune.

One day Mrs. Trollope made an excursion into the wilderness lying north of Cincinnati to visit a pioneer farm. The man had cleared several acres in the dense forest and planted corn. He had put his house on a hillside so steep the family needed a ladder to gain entrance. Nearby were several sheds for the cows, pigs, horses, and chickens; a small garden; and an orchard of fruit trees. The farmer's wife invited her English guest inside their two-room log cabin. Three small children played while she worked a handmade spinning wheel. Mrs. Trollope questioned her at length about her life as a pioneer wife, and discovered the family was almost totally self-sufficient. "The woman told me that they spun and wove all the cotton and woolen garments of the family and knit all the stockings," she noted in amazement. "Her husband, though not a shoemaker by trade, made all the shoes. She manufactured all the soap and candles they used and prepared her sugar from the sugar-trees on their farm. All she wanted with money, she said, was to buy coffee, tea, and whiskey, and she could 'get enough any day by sending a batch of butter and chicken to market.'" Mrs. Trollope applauded their "backwood's independence" but thought there was "something awful and almost unnatural in their loneliness."

Mrs. Trollope was appalled at "the total and universal want of manners, both in males and females." Sometimes it was something as trivial as the American manner of eating watermelons: "The huge fruit is cut into half a dozen sections of about a foot long and then, dripping as it is with water, applied to the mouth, from either side of which pour copious streams of the fluid, while, ever and anon, a mouthful of hard black seeds are shot out in all directions, to the great annoyance of all within reach."

More bothersome to Mrs. Trollope was the lack of privacy and the "violent intimacy" her American neighbors forced upon her. They addressed her as "Frances" (or even worse, "Fanny") asked a barrage of pointedly personal questions, and even invaded her house without a proper invitation.

(This curiosity of Westerners was universally remarked upon by foreign visitors, yet few understood its source. The pioneer's lonely isolation on the thinly settled frontier made him embarrassingly curious and inquisitive toward all strangers, whereas the island of England, long densely populated, evolved the opposite characteristic among its people, making them reserved and cautious.)

Not even president-elect Andrew Jackson was spared these displays of "brutal familiarity" when he stopped briefly in Cincinnati in early 1829 on his way to Washington. A large crowd of enthusiastic supporters greeted him at the wharf. His bearing impressed Mrs. Trollope; she thought he looked like "a gentleman and a soldier." His wife had recently died, and the general was still in mourning. Suddenly an unkempt fellow with long, greasy hair accosted the president-elect.

"General Jackson, I guess?"

The General bowed assent.

"Why they told me you was dead."

"No!" he replied emphatically. "Providence has hitherto preserved my life."

"And is your wife alive, too?" the man persisted.

General Jackson slowly shook his head.

"Aye, I thought it was the one or t'other of ye," his supporter said and then turned away.

The "want of refinement" never ceased to shock Mrs. Trollope. In her view, Cincinnati was a cultural wasteland peopled by dull oafs without the vaguest knowledge of the finer arts. In its drawing rooms, she noted, "the gentlemen spit, talk of elections and the price of produce, and spit again." One evening she tried in vain to discuss English literature with a man reputed to be "a scholar and a man of reading." He had read a little of the poetry of Byron. But when it came to the other English poets and dramatists his ignorance was only exceeded by his arrogance. She asked him about the poems of Alexander Pope.

"He is so entirely gone by that in *our* country it is considered quite fustian to speak of him," he replied haughtily.

"But what of his poem, *The Rape of the Lock*?" Mrs. Trollope insisted.

"The very title!" he muttered, indignantly shaking his handkerchief.

"And Dryden?"

He dismissed the question with a smile as if to say, "How the old woman twaddles!"

"And Shakespeare, sir," Mrs. Trollope persisted.

"Shakespeare, Madam, is obscene, and, thank God, *we* are sufficiently advanced to have found it out! If we must have the abomination of stage plays, let them at least be marked by the refinement of the age in which we live."

Thus ended the dialogue. "That was the most literary conversation I was ever present at in Cincinnati," Mrs. Trollope recalled later. Americans, she quickly discovered, read newspapers, not literature. Then, as now, they had an insatiable thirst for news. (In 1840, Ohio had one paper for every 9,264 persons.) "I have seen a brewer's dray-man perched on the shaft of his dray and reading one newspaper while another was tucked under his arm," she noted. Once she asked a milkman why he "wasted" so much time reading newspapers. "And I'd like you to tell me how we can spend it better," he replied sharply. "How should free men spend their time, but looking after their government and watching them fellers as we gives offices to, [making certain they] doos their duty and gives themselves no airs?"

Cincinnati's highly ranked theater provided additional disappointment for the Englishwoman. She thought the acting admirable. (The manager and several of the cast were English.) But the performances were sparsely attended, and she was often the only woman in the orchestra section. When she asked about the absence of women, she was advised that "the larger proportion of females deem it an offense against religion to witness the representation of a play." The crude behavior of the men in attendance outraged her. She complained:

> Men came into the lower tier of boxes without their coats; and I have seen shirt sleeves tucked up to the shoulder. The spitting was incessant. And the mixed smell of onions and whiskey was [overpowering]. The bearing and attitudes of the men are perfectly indescribable. The heels thrown higher than the head, the entire rear of the person presented to the audience, the whole length supported upon the benches, are among the varieties that these exquisite posture-masters exhibit. The noises, too, were perpetual and of the most unpleasant kind. The applause is expressed by cries and thumping of the feet instead of clapping. And when a patriotic fit seized them and "Yankee Doodle" was called for, every man seemed to think his reputation as a citizen depended on the noise he made.

Poor innocent Frances Trollope. How much more shocked she would have been had she understood the true nature of the theater in America at this period. One of the best-kept secrets of American social history is that until the Civil War the entire third tier of seats in most theaters was customarily reserved for the exclusive use of prostitutes. The nineteenth-century actress Olive Logan

lashed out at "that dark, horrible, guilty 'third tier'" with "its brutal exhibition of faces." Entire populations of nearby brothels
often showed up well in advance of curtain time, entered the theater through a separate door, and filled the third tier. Throughout
the performance men from other parts of the theater made their
way to the upper tier to arrange dates for later in the evening. A
bar was often located nearby to serve the prostitutes and their
clients, no doubt contributing to the rowdy atmosphere. Yet this
same third tier was all that stood between many a legitimate theater and sudden bankruptcy.

But of all this Mrs. Trollope remained blissfully ignorant. And
in an age growing increasingly prudish, no gentleman was about
to take this rather formidable Englishwoman to one side and
explain the truth to her. Nor was she ever aware how her attendance at the theater scandalized the proper ladies of Cincinnati
society.

The exposure to rude manners coupled with a general lack of
social deference put Mrs. Trollope in a constant state of shock
during her stay in Cincinnati. A well-bred English lady stranded in
a strange and ill-bred land, she saw herself as the ambassadress of
a civilized and genteel society. As Emerson remarked in *English
Traits*, "English believes in English." Against the frontier society,
with its careless notions of unregulated behavior, she preached a
message of good breeding. "All the freedom enjoyed in America,
beyond what is enjoyed in England, is enjoyed solely by the disorderly at the expense of the orderly," she concluded. Her mistake
lay in a failure to recognize the culture of western America for
what it was—a stage in the development of a country out of the
raw wilderness. Refinements never flourish on a frontier, and the
prevalent regression toward the primitive that she observed was
only temporary.

Within a few weeks of her arrival in Cincinnati, Mrs. Trollope
had exhausted the last of the Nashoba loan. When her husband
refused to send money for a return passage to England for her
group, she determined to make her own way. For the first time in

her life she was utterly on her own. Her son Henry placed an advertisement in the *Cincinnati Gazette* for his services as a Latin tutor at a charge of 50 cents per hour. There were no takers. (Hardly a surprise in a frontier community where utilitarianism was the rule of thumb by which all knowledge was measured.) Auguste Hervieu, on the other hand, opened his own academy of fine arts and accepted several young ladies as his pupils. Soon he was at work on a huge historical canvas, *The Landing of Lafayette at Cincinnati.*

Mrs. Trollope discovered her own opportunity at the Western Museum. Founded in 1820 by a group of public-spirited citizens for the display of specimens of natural history and archaeology, the museum in 1828 was entirely under the management of a naturalist from New Orleans, Joseph Dorfeuille. The museum's collection included 100 mammoth bones, 500 stuffed birds, 200 fishes, 1,000 fossils, 325 botanical specimens, the tattooed head of a New Zealand chief, and one "elegant church organ." Dorfeuille soon realized that the people of Cincinnati had little scientific curiosity about biology and archaeology. So he quickly reshuffled his collection to include two-headed pigs, four-legged chickens, and a variety of life-size wax figures of celebrated historical personages. None of this worked.

The Western Museum stood on the brink of bankruptcy in 1828 when Frances Trollope approached Dorfeuille with a business proposition. She suggested that the museum was failing to attract attention because its exhibits lacked novelty. What she proposed was an entirely new attraction, unlike any ever seen before in the Ohio Valley—an oracle, shrouded in mysterious decorations, who would speak in several languages and answer questions from the spectators. Under her supervision, her son Henry, who spoke several languages, would provide the voice for the oracle while Hervieu would manage the decorations. Mrs. Trollope was confident about the outcome. Had she not staged numerous dramatic productions in her Harrow drawing room? Dorfeuille agreed. On April 12, 1828, she placed the following announcement in the *Cincinnati Gazette*:

The proprietor of the WESTERN MUSEUM is now able to tender to the public, the gratification of receiving the responses of the Invisible Girl. As he has spared no expense in preparing this most interesting philosophical experiment, relies upon his fellow citizens for a fair demonstration of a disposition to remunerate him for an attempt to present to the world a subject in which science and taste have been equally consulted.

In addition to the pleasure to be expected from the mysterious responses of the Invisible Girl herself, it is fair to state that her chamber of audience has been fitted up in such style, as to afford great interest to the classical and refined mind. In this the proprietor of the Museum has been aided by the taste and skill of one of the most accomplished artists who has ever visited our country. The room is made to resemble one of those theatres of probations, in the Egyptian Mysteries, in which the candidate for initiation was subjected to his incipient trials: the genius and pencil of Mr. Hervieu have given to it an effect truly impressive. . . . In the centre of the room is a cloud, perfectly pervious to the sight, from which a female arm projects, holding gracefully a small glass trumpet; the whole is entirely unconnected with any part of the wall or ceiling. . . .

Parties of 12 persons, and no more, can be admitted at a time to the presence of the Oracle—and each visitor allowed to propound three questions. . . . The profoundest silence is to be observed during the delivery of the responses.

"The Invisible Girl" was a smashing success. Mrs. Trollope had given the people of the Ohio Valley their first taste of the occult. Henry Trollope provided the voice for the oracle, finding a use at last for his smattering of Latin, French, German, and Spanish. "The Invisible Girl" sold out each of its performances until Dorfeuille closed it after eight weeks to prepare for a new and more spectacular attraction, a tour through Dante's Inferno. Once again Hervieu handled the decorations and transparencies, while a second artist, Hiram Powers, shaped an array of wax figures. As before, Mrs. Trollope supervised the construction. Called "The Infernal Regions," the exhibit opened in July and generated more excitement than anything in Cincinnati's brief history. One visitor described the scene at length:

> In the center is seated his Infernal Highness "as large as life." This diabolical personage sits on a throne of darkness of sufficient elevation to give him a commanding view of the abyss on either side. His body is clad in a sable robe, which, however, discloses the all-essential appendage—a "cloven foot." In his left hand he holds a pitchfork . . . while his right is pointed towards an inscription directly in front, "Whoever enters here leaves hope behind!" His head is adorned with a huge crown, and his face...is woefully ornamented with a hoary beard, made of horses' tails! To give importance to this King of Hell, his neck is so constructed as to admit of his giving a nod of recognition to the spectator; and his glaring eye-balls are made to roll most horribly by means of some machinery in the room below.
>
> On the right hand of the devil . . . is seen one department of this hell, which is denominated the hell of ice; a most heretical place, where the damned, instead of being burned in fire and brimstone, are frozen in eternal death! This department is filled with wax figures representing persons of all ages and conditions . . . .
>
> On the left of the devil . . . is the hell of fire. In this department are seen the skeletons of persons, thrown into various positions. The sockets of their eyes . . . are filled with some bright substance resembling fire; presenting to the eye one of

the most loathsome and disgusting scenes that imagination can betray! While the heart is pained with beholding these representatives of misery, the ear is saluted with a subterranean noise, produced by some instruments of discord in the apartment below, resembling the imaginary groans of the damned. Taken all together, it presents a scene well calculated to alarm weak minds. . . .

Within weeks the word had spread the length of the Ohio Valley that a "great and glorious revival" was under way in Cincinnati. "The Infernal Regions" was doing more to win souls to God than any minister on the tent circuit. Local papers reported that numerous sinners, after paying their 25-cent admission, experienced a sudden conversion upon looking on the face of Satan and hearing the groans of the poor damned souls in hell. ("The Infernal Regions" continued to be a popular attraction for over a quarter of a century. When Artemus Ward visited the city in 1861, he pronounced it "the best show in Cincinnati.")

No records remain to tell us to what extent Mrs. Trollope, Hervieu, and Henry shared in the profits of these two popular attractions. But in May she moved her family into a much larger house in a more fashionable part of the city.

Throughout her stay in Cincinnati Mrs. Trollope continued to observe the manners of its residents, keeping a detailed journal of her impressions. She enjoyed her first Fourth of July festival, the most popular of the American holidays. Firecrackers popped, cannons boomed, bands played, parades marched, and orators gave patriotic speeches.

And in that first summer Mrs. Trollope also experienced her first presidential campaign. The supporters of the incumbent president John Quincy Adams and General Andrew Jackson waged one of the most unruly and vile campaigns in American history. The election of 1828 was not fought over great issues. Instead both sides spread the most outrageous and slanderous lies. Adams was charged with turning the White House into a gambling den because he had installed a billiard table. Jackson's supporters even accused him of serving as a pimp to the emperor of Russia. Adams's people struck back, charging Jackson with adultery, seduction, murder, theft, and treason. One editor of an important Whig paper trumpeted: "General Jackson's mother was a COMMON PROSTITUTE, brought to this country by British soldiers! She afterward married a MULATTO MAN, with whom she had several children, of which number GENERAL JACKSON IS ONE!!!" When the votes were finally counted, the general had won 56 percent of the popular vote and carried all the Southern and Western states.

Mrs. Trollope was particularly interested in the role of women in American society. Using "the lynx-like eye of the female," she carefully documented what she called "the lamentable insignificance of the American woman." Everywhere she saw a society characterized by a rigid segregation of the sexes. "In America, with the exception of dancing, which is almost wholly confined to the unmarried of both sexes, all the enjoyments of the men are found in the absence of the women," she observed. "They dine, they play cards, they have musical meetings, they have suppers, all in large parties but all without women."

Mrs. Trollope was quick to point out the stultifying impact of such separations upon American women:

> Whatever may be the talents of the persons who meet together in society, the very shape, form, and arrangement of the meeting is sufficient to paralyze conversation. The women herd together at one part of the room and the men at the other. But, in justice to Cincinnati, I must acknowledge that this arrangement is by no means peculiar to that city or to the western side of the Alleghenies. . . . The ladies look at each other's dresses till they know every pin by heart; talk of Parson Somebody's last sermon on the day of judgment, on Dr. T'otherbody's new pills for dyspepsia, till the "tea" is announced, when they all console themselves together for whatever they may have suffered in keeping awake by taking

more tea, coffee, hot cake, and custard. . . . The American
people will not equal the nations of Europe in refinement till
women become of more importance among them.

Other visitors had commented upon this striking separation of
the sexes in American society. ("In no country has such constant
care been taken as in America to trace clearly distinct lines of
action for the two sexes and to make them keep pace one with the
other, but in two pathways which are always different," de
Tocqueville observed with approval. "American women never
manage the outward concerns of the family, or conduct a business,
or take a part in the political life.") But Mrs. Trollope was the first
to analyze its debilitating effects. "Throughout her book, [she]
documented a hostility to women lying under the surface of
American life," her biographer Helen Heineman states. "In her
view, those arrangements limited the potential social development
of both sexes. Without a coming-together for enrichment, communication, and sharing of experiences, there could be no society
worthy of the name."

One obvious result was the extraordinary timidity many
American women exhibited in the company of men. Mrs.
Trollope collected a variety of anecdotes to illustrate the almost
pathological fear of men and sex many women demonstrated. A
young German gentleman "of perfectly good manners" confided that he had been ostracized by a leading Cincinnati family
because he had indiscreetly used the word "corset" in mixed
company. An Englishwoman who ran a boarding school for
young girls told of a 14-year-old pupil who suddenly became
hysterical upon finding a man in the school's parlor; she "put
her hands before her eyes and ran out of the room, screaming,
'A man! A man! A man!'" And when a small signpost in the
shape of a Swiss peasant girl holding a scroll asking people not
to pick the flowers appeared in a public garden in Cincinnati,
local women were outraged to discover a pair of ankles peeking
out beneath her dress. They demanded the artist immediately

extend the girl's petticoat, "giving bright and shining evidence before all men of the immaculate delicacy of the Cincinnati ladies."

The American woman in 1828 was, in the words of social historian Barbara Welter, held a "hostage in the home." Society judged her by the extent to which she embodied the four cardinal virtues of domesticity, piety, purity, and submissiveness. Fame, fortune, and achievement counted for little if a woman was judged deficient in the first four.

A nighttime camp meeting of some 2,000 persons in Indiana was a real revelation for Mrs. Trollope. She had already noted that religion provided the American woman with perhaps the sole outlet for her energies beyond the home. At the revival she suddenly understood that the religious enthusiasm of the women there was often thinly disguised sexual energy, frustrated from finding any sort of healthy release in a domestic situation. This daughter of an Anglican minister watched in stunned disbelief as illiterate spellbinders fired the crowd's enthusiasm. ("When I hear a man preach," Abraham Lincoln once said, "I like to see him act as if he were fighting bees.") Scores of women worked themselves into a frenzy. "Above a hundred persons, nearly all females, came forward, uttering howlings and groans so terrible that I shall never cease to shudder when I recall them," she recalled later. "They appeared to drag each other forward, and on the word being given, 'let us pray,' they all fell on their knees. But this posture was soon changed for others that permitted greater scope for the convulsive movement of their limbs; and they were soon all lying on the ground in an indescribable confusion of heads and legs."

Mrs. Trollope saw the popularity of the kind of religious fanaticism common on the frontier as yet another indication of the extent to which American society had warped its women. "I think that it is from the clergy only that the women of America receive that sort of attention which is so dearly valued by every female heart throughout the world," she argued in *Domestic Manners*.

"With the priests of America, the women hold that degree of influential importance, which, in the countries of Europe, is allowed them throughout all orders and ranks of society, except perhaps the very lowest."

The American woman had her choice. Either she defined her life according to the restrictions of the "cult of true womanhood," or she went outside the home and sought other rewards. The latter option risked almost certain social banishment. Mrs. Trollope first experienced this soon after her arrival in Cincinnati when she attended a lecture by her former friend Frances Wright. The Scotswoman's appearance on a public platform excited "the most violent sensation." Men lectured; women, never. (Miss Wright's whirlwind campaign for female equality and emancipation from the "slavery of marriage" concluded tamely enough. While in Cincinnati she fell in love with a French teacher of languages and married him. She died in 1852, a respectable married woman to the end.)

The clearly drawn lines between the sexes eventually proved Mrs. Trollope's undoing. Almost from her first day in Cincinnati she caused eyebrows to be lifted. She arrived with little money and no letters of introduction. Instead of a husband at her side, she was almost always accompanied by a young, attractive French artist. Her manner was brusque and patronizing. In a society that measured persons first by their exteriors, there was little about Mrs. Trollope to recommend her. Timothy Flint, a Cincinnati editor and her close friend, admitted she had "a short, plump figure with a ruddy, round Saxon face of bright complexion . . . [and] an appearance singularly unladylike, a misfortune heightened by her want of taste and female intelligence in regard to dress."

Mrs. Trollope's appearance, dress, manner, and business activities at the Western Museum all marked her clearly as a woman who deviated from "the cult of true womanhood." Furthermore, she was energetically independent in a society that demanded total submissiveness of its women. That made her dangerously unfeminine in the eyes of the local population. To her horror, the woman who counted the great General Lafayette among her good friends found herself snubbed and ignored by the best families in Cincinnati. "Her manners were bad and she had no refinement," one dowager recalled years later. "After seeing how she behaved in the market, no one could think of asking her inside a drawing room."

And so Mrs. Trollope never had access to the first families of Cincinnati. Such local dignitaries as Samuel Foot, the uncle of Harriet Beecher Stowe; Judge Jacob Burnet, a United States senator; David K. Estes, and his wife, the son-in-law and daughter of William Henry Harrison; Nicholas Longworth, the lawyer, patron of the arts, and pioneer in grape culture; and Dr. Daniel Drake, a pioneer in medical education, all closed their doors to her. "The elegance of the houses, the parade of the servants, the display of furniture, and . . . the luxury of their overloaded tables would compare with the better houses in the Atlantic cities," her friend Timothy Flint observed. "But none would welcome or receive her, save in four respectable families and they were not families that gave parties."

Mrs. Trollope's violation of the pattern of American female domesticity eventually forced a confrontation that brought down upon her disgrace, bankruptcy, and scandal. It all began innocently enough in the summer of 1828 as she watched the crowds pour into "The Infernal Regions." The great success of her first two projects pleased her enormously. In each instance she had correctly gauged the tastes of the local citizenry and reaped a financial bonanza. She was now ready for a daring new speculation, far more ambitious than these first two ventures. The idea began as a shop selling little vanities and the needlework of the women in the city. But this quickly expanded in her imagination to an elaborate *Arabian Nights* edifice housing a shop for fancy English goods, a coffeehouse, an ice-cream bar, an art gallery, and a grand ballroom offering dramatic productions, concerts, and poetry readings. She never doubted that this combination of pleasure dome and center for the cultural arts would dazzle the good people of Cincinnati and be a great financial success. Her plans called for her son Henry to take over its management, while she and her two daughters returned to England to enjoy their new-found prosperity in a more civilized setting.

Mrs. Trollope fixed upon her bazaar with a missionary zeal. It would be her Brighton Palace where the "backwoodsmen" of Cincinnati would assume an aura of refinement and pay her courtly tribute. Its civilizing influence would be felt throughout the city. And it would strike a blow for female liberation, providing a place where women could come together outside their homes. "The ladies are too actively employed in the interior of their houses to permit much parading in full dress for morning visits," she had complained. "There are no public gardens or lounging shops of fashionable resort, and were it not for public worship and private tea parties, all the ladies of Cincinnati would be in danger of becoming perfect recluses." Her bazaar, she hoped, would correct this deficiency.

In the early autumn of 1828 Mr. Trollope and his oldest son arrived in Cincinnati. His wife quickly won him over to her scheme. They planned to use a recent inheritance from her father to cover the costs. She sent him back to England with a lengthy shopping list of fancy goods she needed to stock her store.

Mrs. Trollope bought an empty lot for $1,655 and set about supervising the construction of her bazaar. The residents of Cincinnati watched in disbelief as a most unlikely structure slowly rose above the surrounding shops and warehouses. Originally patterned after the Egyptian Hall in Piccadilly, Mrs. Trollope's bazaar ended up an eclectic jumble of architectural styles reflecting an imagination steeped in the Oriental fantasies of Lord Byron. In a lengthy description in the *Cincinnati Chronicle* she explained "the parts." The front wall looking south toward the river boasted as its chief feature an Egyptian colonnade formed of four massive columns, each three stories high and modeled after those "in the temple of Appollinopolis at Edfu." The wall facing Third Street was "taken, in part, from the Mosque of St. Athanase in Egypt" and consisted of "three large arabesque windows with arches, supported by four Moorish stone pilasters with capitals." Overhead soared "gothic battlements, each of which supports a stone sphere." The bazaar's crowning glory was its cylindrical superstructure, a rotunda 28 feet in diameter, 18 feet in height, and topped with a large Turkish crescent.

The interior of Mrs. Trollope's structure reflected the style of the exterior. She promised in the prospectus that the bazaar itself would offer "every useful and useless article in dress, in stationery, in light and ornamental household furniture, chinas and more pellucid porcelain, with every gew-gaw that can contribute to the splendor and attractiveness of the exhibition." Directly behind the bazaar was "an elegant SALOON where *Ices* and other refreshments will lend their allurements to the fascinations of architectural novelty." Nearby would be "an EXHIBITION GALLERY that is at present occupied by Mr. Hervieu's superb picture of LAFAYETTE'S LANDING AT CINCINNATI." The dominant fixture of the second floor was the ballroom, the cultural heart of the edifice, heavily decorated by Hervieu in the style of the Alhambra in Granada, Spain. "The architecture is a mixture of Saracenic and Gothic," Mrs. Trollope promised. "The ornaments are . . . accurate imitations of the brilliantly coloured tiles so much used in the Alhambra." Female figures representing the Muses of dancing and music topped the windows. On the third floor visitors had their choice of an art gallery inside the rotunda and "a fine promenade, commanding an extensive view of the city and surrounding country." The entire building was lighted with gas, the first structure in Cincinnati to use this means of illumination.

For years the bazaar dominated the Cincinnati skyline. In 1838 the British traveler Harriet Martineau visited the city and reported at length upon Mrs. Trollope's emporium. "This bazaar is the great deformity of the city," she noted. "From my window at our boarding house it was only too distinctly visible. It is built of brick and has Gothic windows, Grecian pillars, and a Turkish dome. It was originally ornamented with Egyptian devices which have, however, all disappeared under the brush of the whitewasher. . . . They call it 'Trollope's Folly.'"

The project proved an unmitigated disaster. "Everything from the time you left us went wrong, inspite of exertions—nay, hard labour, on our part that would pain you to hear of," a disheartened Mrs. Trollope wrote to her husband and son back in England. Unscrupulous contractors swindled her out of hundreds of dollars. "She was snuffed like carrion by every rogue within cheating distance," one local resident observed. "Every brick in her Babel cost her three prices." She made the mistake of paying in advance for the installation of the gas pipes, only to have the contractor abscond with the money. An even greater problem developed when she opened the crates of goods her husband had shipped from England and discovered to her horror that he had ignored her instructions and sent only cheap merchandise. One Cincinnati editor looked over the items for sale in the bazaar and later scoffed that her plan was "to trade in knick-knacks with the simple inhabitants of the New World, much as in the old days people sailed for the West Coast of Africa to exchange beads and buttons for ivory and gold."

There was another, less obvious reason for the failure. "Unfortunately, Mrs. Trollope tried to accomplish too much with her bazaar," biographer Heineman argues. "Americans saw her bazaar as a dangerous and subversive attempt to change the entrenched patterns of American life. Activities scheduled for the bazaar were designed to mingle men and women in social and economic life. Even [her] advertisements . . . seemed directed at bringing women out into the public. . . . It was this dangerous proselytizing attitude regarding the social habits of American womanhood that was most provocative to the Cincinnati audience she hoped to attract."

Shortly before the grand opening Mrs. Trollope fell ill with malaria. For three months she was bedridden and at times so ill that her family feared for her life. Upon her recovery, she learned to her dismay that her creditors had sold off all her goods, often

for as little as 25 cents on the dollar. In desperation she staged several musical reviews and dramatic productions in the ballroom;
but these were poorly attended. The final performance drew an
audience of just six curious gentlemen from a visiting steamboat.

Mrs. Trollope's hopes for a prosperous retirement were utterly
shattered. Her Cincinnati venture lay in ruins. Her bout with
malaria had left her "very much thinner and very much older."
Her funds were exhausted. Her husband's financial situation was
so precarious that he could send no money for the return trip.
Hervieu advanced her what she needed. In early March 1830 she
and her family boarded a steamboat and departed Cincinnati. Her
years in America had yielded only heartache and several note-
books in which she had recorded her impressions. Her prospects
could not have looked bleaker.

5

When Frances Trollope arrived in England, she discovered
that her husband had exchanged their spacious home near
Harrow for the cramped quarters of an uncomfortable farmhouse.
His response to their developing financial crisis was to undertake
a bizarre project, a comprehensive *Encyclopedia Ecclesiastical* in
which he planned to reduce the entire history of the Christian
church to a series of alphabetical entries. (By the time of his death
in October 1835, he had reached the letter D.)

The first winter back in England proved a terrible ordeal. Mr.
Trollope's creditors threatened foreclosure. One piece of furniture
after another was sold to raise money for food. Mrs. Trollope even
parted with their pillows. For almost six months they could not
afford to buy tea or butter. She staked all her hopes on a book-
length manuscript based upon her American experiences. (She
eliminated all references to her role at the Western Museum and
the ill-fated bazaar.) Her friend Hervieu provided the illustrations.
In the autumn of 1831 the publishing house of Whittaker and

Treacher bought her manuscript for publication. On March 19, 1832, nine days after her fifty-third birthday, *Domestic Manners of the Americans* finally appeared and was an instant success. Mrs. Trollope suddenly found herself a celebrity. "The Countess of Morley told me she was certain that if I drove through London proclaiming who I was, I should have the horses taken off and be drawn in triumph from one end of town to the other!" she gleefully wrote her son. "Lady Louisa Stewart told me that I had quite put English out of fashion and that everyone was talking Yankee talk. In short I was *overpowered*." Even more important than fame, the book brought money, more than £500, a considerable sum in those years. She went on a splurge. She bought clothes for herself and her family, filled their home with new furniture, paid six months' rent in advance, and hired servants. And even better, she signed a contract with Whittaker and Treacher for a novel on America. Mrs. Trollope suddenly found herself with a new career, one which promised to be very lucrative.

In *Domestic Manners* Mrs. Trollope revolutionized the writing of travel books. Earlier writers had broken the backs of their narratives by including as much "scientific information" as possible, favoring facts and figures rather than anecdotes. But Mrs. Trollope focused on the human side of her travels and wrote with the eye of a novelist, providing a strongly delineated narrator, a coherent plot, sharply defined characters, and lively dialogue. *Domestic Manners* changed forever the nature of the travel memoir.

In *Domestic Manners* Mrs. Trollope accurately noted the peculiarities of social structure in America but wrongly attributed them to a decay of British standards rather than to the growing pains of a new country freshly carved out of the frontier. Because of the residual hostility many English felt from the War of 1812, the public in 1832 was ready to find her tart, critical tone amusing. Her book appeared in the middle of the fierce debate over the Reform Bill, which radically extended the franchise. Its Tory opponents seized upon *Domestic Manners*, citing its portrayal of

Americans as a dreadful warning as to what would happen to England if "the mob" got the vote.

"Let us know the truth," Ralph Waldo Emerson had challenged the English. "Draw a straight line, hit whom and where it will." Mrs. Trollope had taken him at his word. As a result, *Domestic Manners* proved a fruitful source of international ill will for two generations. The young country was touchy to an extreme. And Mrs. Trollope had plucked numerous raw nerves. Although her generalizations were often wrong, her observations of the particulars were accurate. "She was merely telling the truth, and this indignant nation knew it," Mark Twain later admitted in a suppressed chapter to *Life on the Mississippi*. "She was merely painting a state of things which did not disappear at once. It lasted to well along in my youth, and I remember it."

(Mrs. Trollope would undoubtedly have been pleased to know that her *Domestic Manners* stimulated a boom in etiquette books among American publishers: 28 appeared in the following decade. Of course, they often reflected the values of Jacksonian America. "Always keep callers waiting," Fanny Fern advised her readers in *Rules for Ladies,* "till they have had time to notice the outlay of money in your parlours.")

Domestic Manners firmly established Mrs. Trollope in a writing career that ended in 1856 when she was 76. By then she had produced 114 volumes of novels and travel memoirs. "Her career offers great encouragement to those who have not begun early in life, but are still ambitious to do something before they depart hence," her son Anthony concluded in his *Autobiography*.

But there was another lesson her son might have drawn from his mother's experiences. "I do not like Americans," Mrs. Trollope had admitted at the end of *Domestic Manners*. And yet the experience in Cincinnati had established her in a career as a writer that was to bring her fame and fortune. Out of adversity she had created opportunity. And those qualities that later made her a success back in England—her determined self-reliance, aggressiveness, energy, and entrepreneurial spirit—were, ironically, all qualities of the American frontier she had absorbed in her 25 months in Cincinnati.

6

Mrs. Trollope's bazaar survived in Cincinnati until the end of the century, a grotesque monument to her earlier hopes and failures. "Trollope's Folly" refused to go away, however, and remained a constant source of irritation. In a way it became her revenge upon the city, for she had fashioned her temple so bizarrely that no one was ever able to put the building to profitable use. "For what the original inventor intended this structure, Heaven only knows," one frustrated proprietor exclaimed in later decades. "In my time it has undergone a dozen alterations, at least, to endeavor to make it fit for something. But its first plan was so curiously contrived that every effort Yankee ingenuity could suggest to make it useful has successively failed."

In later years Mrs. Trollope's bazaar passed through numerous transformations, becoming an inn, a dancing school, a Presbyterian church, and a military hospital. When her son Anthony visited Cincinnati in 1861, he discovered the bazaar housed a "Physico-medical Institute . . . under the dominion of a quack doctor on one side and a college of rights-of-women female medical professors on the other."

Hard luck followed the bazaar until its final days, almost as if a curse lay over the structure. As one disgusted owner lamented, "I believe, sir, that no man or woman ever made a dollar in that building; and as for rent I don't ever expect it." The bazaar was finally demolished in 1881. In its final years it had housed a brothel.

Chapter

§ 2 §

Fanny Kemble:
British Mistress of a Georgian Plantation

In 1873 the American novelist Henry James was vacationing in Rome, where he met the retired British actress, Fanny Kemble, then 64. "I went a couple of nights since to a little party," the youthful James wrote to a friend. "I met everyone, including the terrific Kemble herself, whose splendid handsomeness of eye, nostril, and mouth were the best things in the room." The legendary actress, "draped in lavender satin lavishly d´écolleté," quite over-awed James. But their acquaintance ripened over the years into intimacy, and the two remained fast friends until her death 20 years later. "My sublime Fanny—the first woman in London—one of the consolations of my life," James said later in appreciation.

Few women in London could boast of a life filled with a greater variety of incidents than James's beloved Fanny. He found her conversation rich in the social anecdotes that illuminated an earlier age. Born at a time when a triumphant Napoleon threatened England, she died in 1892 in the forty-fifth year of Queen Victoria's reign. She had moved among the elite of the day, having sat for a portrait by the celebrated eighteenth-century painter Sir Thomas Lawrence, dined with the Scottish novelist Sir Walter Scott, and visited President Andrew Jackson in the White House. She had seen enormous changes in society, remembering a youth in pre-industrial England in which transportation was tied to the horse at land and the sail at sea. "Even if Mrs. Kemble had been a less remarkable person she would still have owned a distinction to the far away past to which she gave continuity," James observed.

But Fanny Kemble had other distinctions. The most celebrated actress of her day, she was also distinguished as a poetess and dramatist. Her memoirs were bestsellers. In 1834, at the height of her success as an actress, she gave up wealth and glory to marry Pierce Butler, the absentee owner of two large plantations and 700 slaves on the Georgian coast. The marriage ended in disaster, and the experience turned her into a confirmed abolitionist. She became the most effective advocate for the cause in England. James praised her book, *Journal of a Residence on a Georgian Plantation in 1838–1839*, as "the most valuable account of impressions begotten of that old Southern life which we are apt to see today through a haze of Indian summer."

Frances Ann Kemble was born on November 27, 1809, into England's leading family of the stage. Fanny's aunt Sarah was the incomparable Mrs. Siddons, the foremost Shakespearean actress from 1782 until her retirement in 1812. Her uncle John Philip managed the Drury Lane and Covent Garden theaters for 30 years. Her father, Charles, enjoyed a reputation as one of England's leading Shakespearean actors.

When Fanny was 12, her parents sent her to an English school in Paris. She spent four years there, studying the great French playwrights Racine and Corneille, learning to read Dante in Italian, and developing a passion for dancing. "I was a very romantic girl with a most excitable imagination," she recalled later. When she finally returned home, her parents saw that their daughter had developed into a beautiful young woman, on the short side, with lovely, dark hair and an expressive face that revealed her every mood. About this time an attack of smallpox coarsened her features and gave her a sensitivity about her appearance she never lost.

In these late teenage years Fanny pondered her future. She wrote poetry in the Byronic style and began work on a play. Although popular with men, she had little desire for marriage. The stage beckoned as an alternative that might provide her with the financial independence she desired so she could pursue her literary ambitions. In the autumn of 1829 Fanny returned to her parents' home in London after a year with a cousin in Edinburgh and found them near despair. Their creditors were ready to foreclose on the Covent Garden Theater, now under her father's management. "Our property is to be sold," her tearful mother informed her. "The theater must be closed, and I know not how many hundred poor people will be turned adrift without employment." Fanny quickly volunteered to join the family on the stage if her parents wanted her help. Both thought the prospects of another Kemble doing Shakespeare might be just what was needed to turn around the family fortunes. They quickly cast her as Juliet. (Her mother returned after a 20-year break to play Lady Capulet, Juliet's mother, while her father took the part of Mercutio.) But Fanny had no formal training in acting and only three weeks to work up her part.

On the night of her debut a nervous Fanny sat in her dressing room, "the palms of my hands pressed convulsively together and the tears . . . brimming down over my rouged cheeks." Soon the dreaded moment arrived, and the terror-stricken girl stood in the shadows waiting for her cue. "Never mind 'em, Miss Kemble," one of the actors reassured her. "Don't think of 'em any more than if they were so many rows of cabbage!" Seconds later her cue came, and she was rudely pushed onstage. In *Records of a Childhood* she remembered what happened next:

> I ran straight across the stage, stunned by the tremendous shout that greeted me, my eyes covered with mist and the green baize flooring of the stage feeling as if it rose up against my feet. I . . . stood like a terrified creature at bay confronting the huge theatre full of gazing human beings. I do not think a word I uttered during this scene could have been audible. In the next, the ballroom, I began to forget myself. In the following one, the balcony scene, I had done so and, for aught I knew, I was Juliet—the passion I was uttering sending hot waves of blushes all over my neck and shoulders, while the poetry sounded like music to me as I spoke it, with no consciousness of anything before me, utterly transported into the imaginary existence of the play.

After the performance, Fanny stepped out from behind the curtain "amid a thunderous storm of applause." London audiences had been Kemble fans for several generations and were only too eager to see this latest addition to the family succeed. The reviews, too, were favorable. The critic for the *Times* of London raved, "Upon the whole we do not remember to have seen a more triumphant debut." Overnight Fanny became a celebrity, the toast of London society. The celebrated painter Sir Thomas Lawrence sketched her portrait; hundreds of copies quickly appeared in the London shops. Stories about her ran almost daily in the newspapers. Plates and saucers bearing her likeness also proved a popular item. Gentlemen wore neck scarves with her picture emblazoned on them.

Fanny quickly fell into the routine of her new life. She acted three times a week, dined in the middle of the day ("invariably on a mutton chop"), and did needlework while she waited in the wings for her cue to go on stage. Her father fixed her salary at 30 guineas a week, enough to provide her with a comfortable living. At 20 her life had changed as dramatically as if a fairy godmother had waved a magic wand over her. She wrote later:

> It would be difficult to imagine anything more radical than the change which three weeks had made in my life. From an insignificant schoolgirl, I had suddenly become an object of general public interest. I was a little lion in society and the town talk of the day. Approbation, admiration, adulation were showered upon me. . . . Instead of the twenty pounds a year which my father had squeezed out of his hard-earned income for my allowance, I now had an assured income of at least a thousand pounds a year. Instead of trudging long distances through the London streets, I had an elegant carriage. I was allowed to take riding lessons and before long had a charming horse of my own. The faded, threadbare, turned and dyed frocks were exchanged for fashionable dresses of fresh colours and fine textures. . . . Our door was besieged by visitors, our evenings bespoken by innumerable invitations, and

every night that I did not act I might . . . have passed in all the
gaiety of the fashionable world and the great London season.

For the next two years Fanny kept a careful balance between
the demands of her theatrical career and her social engagements.
For all her fame as an actress, she always maintained a distance
from her profession. Her success with a role varied widely from
one performance to another, a fact she correctly attributed to her
lack of formal training. One night her mother would embrace her
daughter as she came off the stage, saying, "Beautiful, my dear!"
But other times her mother would be sharply critical: "Your performance was not fit to be seen! You had better give the whole
thing up at once than go on doing it so disgracefully ill."

Another problem was that Fanny had always looked askance on
the theater. "The theatrical profession was, however, utterly dis-
tasteful to me, though *acting* itself was not," she admitted in her
memoirs. "Nor did custom ever render this aversion less; and liking
my work so little and being so devoid of enthusiasm, respect or love
for it, it is wonderful to me that I ever achieved any success in it at
all." She worried, too, about the erosion of her "real self" through
the impersonation of so many different roles. And she longed for a
literary career. She wrote a play, *Francis I*, which John Murray, Lord
Byron's friend and publisher, bought for £450. "Was there ever such
publishing munificence?" an excited Fanny wrote to a friend. "I am
so happy, so surprised and charmed to think that what gave me
nothing but pleasure in the doing has given me such a profit."

Fanny's success gave Charles Kemble only a brief respite from
his financial problems. His debts continued to accumulate.
Covent Garden Theatre now had six lawsuits against it. The
great political debate surrounding the passage of the Reform Bill
generated numerous riots throughout England, which cut heavily
into theatrical attendance. For a time it looked as though the
country stood on the edge of a civil war. Then a cholera epidemic broke out. The government closed the theaters. In desperation
Charles Kemble decided upon a two-year tour of America. The

larger cities there, such as New York and Boston, boasted vigorous theatrical districts. Fanny was dismayed at the idea when her father asked her to accompany him, chaperoned by her Aunt Adelaide ("Dall") De Camp. "Go to America?" she cried. "How terrible! That dreadful place!" But she never really had a choice in the matter. She and Charles Kemble were a team—father and daughter, leading man and leading lady. (However, she made a conscious decision not to read Frances Trollope's *Domestic Manners of the Americans*, which had appeared a few months before, not wanting to prejudice herself against the country that would be her home for the next two years.) On August 1, 1832, the Kembles and Aunt Adelaide boarded the S.S. *Pacific*. A month later, on September 4, they arrived in New York. As Fanny stepped ashore, Fanny had no idea of the momentous changes awaiting her.

2

The Kembles made their triumphant New York debut before a full house in Thomas Otway's 1682 play *Venice Preserved*. Their appearance marked something of an epoch in the American theater. "We have never seen her equal before on the American stage," Philip Hone, a former mayor of the city, enthusiastically remarked in his journal. And the critic for the *Mirror* praised "the charm and glory of this young girl's acting" and insisted that "her hate is sardonic . . . and almost intolerable; her love, deeply impassioned and tender, all bashful girlishness and full of exquisitely graceful touches. . . . This is indeed *acting*."

The Kembles had brought many letters of introduction and were soon deluged with social invitations. Everywhere Americans besieged them with questions about Mrs. Trollope's recent book. Fanny's own response to America was decidedly mixed. There was much about New York that pleased her. Like many other English visitors, she was impressed by the abundance of food ("an Aladdin's treasure") at the fish and fruit markets, which she saw as proof of "the wondrous bounteousness which has dowered this land." She found the people often better mannered than in London. One evening she and her father took a long walk down Broadway. "The street was very much thronged," she wrote in her journal. "And I thought the crowd a more civil and orderly one than an English crowd. The men did not jostle or push one another, or tread upon one's feet, or crush one's bonnet into one's face, or turn it round upon one's head, all of which I have seen done in London streets. . . . I observed that the young men tonight invariably made room for women to pass, and many of them, as they drew near us, took the cigar from their mouth, which I thought especially courteous."

But many American customs jolted Fanny's sensibilities. Overall she thought New York "ill-paved, ill-lighted, and indifferently supplied with a good many necessaries and luxuries of modern civilisation." The refusal of Americans to respect her privacy quickly put her into "a sulky fit." People entered her hotel suite without invitation or a warning knock. The hotel management sent up total strangers when they asked for her at the front desk. "It seems to be that the people of this country have an aversion to solitude, whether eating, sleeping, or under any other circumstances," she complained in her journal. Elsewhere she wrote: "As to privacy at any time or under any circumstances, 'tis a thing that enters not the imagination of an American. They live all the days of their lives in a throng, eat at ordinaries of two or three hundred, sleep five or six to a room, take pleasure in droves and travel by swarms."

Like many other English visitors, Fanny thought the service in American hotels and homes far below English standards. She deplored the lack of servility among hotel servants. And the cordial friendliness of the clerks in stores struck her as "insolent" after the obsequious London salesmen. "I have no idea of holding parley with clerks behind a counter, still less of their doing so with me," she insisted. The egalitarianism of American society grated heavily upon her, as it had upon Mrs. Trollope.

And like her fellow countrywoman, Fanny deplored the

American preoccupation with making a dollar to the neglect of the finer arts. "Where are the poets of this land?" she complained after a lengthy trip up the Hudson River. "Is there none to come here and worship among these hills and waters till the hymn of inspiration flows from his lips and rises to the sky? . . . How marvelously unpoetical these people! How swallowed up in life and its daily realities, wants, and cares! How full of toil and thrift and money-getting labour!"

(But even as she wrote, Fanny was helping an embryonic poet in a small way. One of her most devoted New York fans was an impressionable 13-year-old Walt Whitman. Again and again he took the ferry from Brooklyn to Manhattan to see her performances. Fifty years later he recalled in *Specimen Days* those youthful adventures, which "undoubtedly enter'd into the gestation of *Leaves of Grass*" and specifically acknowledged Fanny Kemble: "Nothing finer did ever stage exhibit—the veterans of all nations said so, and my boyish heart and head felt it in every minute cell.")

After a month's engagement in New York, the Kembles set out for Philadelphia, traveling by stagecoach, railway, and steamboat. (Fanny thought the large American paddle wheels looked like "castles on the main.") The 100-mile journey took ten hours. Philadelphia was caught up in the election fever of 1832. The streets were in an uproar all night, people shouting and bonfires burning. Henry Clay, the Whig candidate, was heavily favored in the city. "I saw a caricature of Jackson and Van Buren, his chief supporter, entitled, 'The King and his Minister,'" Fanny noted in her journal. "Van Buren held a crown in his hand, and the devil was approaching Jackson with a scepter." (Jackson was enormously popular, and the result of the campaign was never really in doubt. Old Hickory won 219 electoral votes to Clay's 49.)

Fanny's tour was a great success. This father-daughter partnership graced the American stage for almost two years and delighted audiences in Philadelphia, Baltimore, Washington, and Boston. "We are just now in the full flush of excitement about Fanny Kemble," Catherine Maria Sedgwick, America's foremost woman novelist, wrote enthusiastically in 1833. "She is a most captivating creature, steeped to the very lips in genius. . . . I have never seen any woman on the stage to be compared with her, nor ever an actor that delighted me so much."

The pace was exhausting. But most productions sold out, and the Kembles found themselves earning better money than they ever had in England. Often they performed with American companies whose members were little more than amateurs. In Baltimore Fanny had a hilarious evening when she played Juliet opposite an American Romeo who "looked like a magical figure growing out of a monstrous strange-coloured melon, beneath which descended his unfortunate legs thrust into a pair of red slippers." Tragedy almost became comedy in the final scene, which Fanny noted in her journal:

Romeo: Tear not our heart strings thus. They crack! They
    break!—Juliet! Juliet!
(*dies*)
Juliet (*whispers to corpse*): Am I smothering you?
Corpse (*to Juliet*): Not at all. Could you be so kind, do you think,
    to put my wig on again for me? It has fallen off.
Juliet (*to corpse*): I'm afraid I can't, but I'll throw my muslin veil
    over it. You've got broken the phial, haven't you?
(*Corpse nods*)
Juliet: Where's your dagger?
Corpse: 'Pon my soul, I don't know.

From Baltimore the Kembles traveled by stagecoach to Washington, still very much a city in the making. Fanny thought it "a rambling red brick image of futurity, where nothing *is*, but all things *are* to be." Even the White House shared this same half-finished look. She described it as "a comfortless, handsome looking building with a withered grass plot enclosed in wooden palings in front and a desolate reach of uncultivated ground down to the river behind." (Apparently no one informed her that British soldiers had torched the previous White House in their brief occupation of the American capital during the War of 1812.)

The Kembles played in *Macbeth* before an enthusiastic audience that included Dolly Madison and John Quincy Adams. Afterward they toured the city. Fanny looked with interest upon the original Declaration of Independence, visited Congress, and heard Daniel Webster speak in the Senate. Later she was presented to President Andrew Jackson and thought him "erect and dignified in his carriage—a good specimen of a fine old well-battered soldier."

In April 1833 the Kembles proceeded to Boston, where they spent five weeks. Fanny quickly fell in love with New England's most celebrated city. "I am fond of Boston," she wrote in her journal. "I prefer it to the rest of America that I have seen." There she enjoyed phenomenal success, greater than anything thus far on her tour. Some 60 years later, in an article in the *Atlantic Monthly*, Henry Lee remembered the excitement the English actress generated in Boston: "Every young girl who could sported Fanny Kemble curls—to be thought to look like her was their aspiration. I remember making a long pilgrimage on horseback to gaze upon a young lady whose attraction was a fancied resemblance to Fanny Kemble. As for us Harvard students, we all went mad. As long as our funds held out, there was a procession of us, hastening breathless over the road to Boston as the evening shade came on."

And the daughter of the president of Harvard University observed: "Miss Kemble looked remarkably handsome. There is something exceedingly striking in her face. It is one of those that haunts you, after you have seen it, like some Sibyl or enchantress."

From her hotel window Fanny watched in amusement as the crowds formed each morning outside the theater's box office across the street. Many of these included scalpers who bought up entire boxes to resell them for enormous profits in the evening. "They smear their clothes with molasses in order to prevent any person of more decent appearance from coming near the box office," she noted in her journal.

Boston was important for yet another reason. There Fanny

found herself falling in love with a dashing young Southern gentleman, Pierce Butler. He first appears in her journal in a brief entry for October 13, 1832, when she was in Philadelphia: "Came to tea and found a young gentleman sitting with my father; one Mr. Butler. He was a pretty spoken, genteel youth. He drank tea with us and offered to ride with me. He has, it seems, a great fortune." Fanny quickly seized upon Butler's offer. He found her an excellent horse well suited to her ability, and soon they were riding together almost every day.

Although Southern, the Butlers were a leading Philadelphia family. The city was geographically Northern; but it was also a gateway to the South and, as such, popular with wealthy absentee landlords of plantations who had come north in search of a more sophisticated and varied life than that offered in the South. The Butlers had lived in Philadelphia for three generations. Pierce's grandfather had originally arrived in 1787 as a delegate from South Carolina to the Constitutional Convention that met in Philadelphia. With the proceeds from his enormous cotton and rice plantations on the Georgian coast, he built a mansion in the city and invested additional thousands of dollars in vast tracts of real estate elsewhere in Pennsylvania.

The young Pierce Butler, Fanny's companion on her rides, had been educated as a lawyer. But he rarely practiced his profession, spending his days instead at social engagements and playing his flute in a local chamber orchestra. Wealthy, handsome, and charming, he was considered one of Philadelphia's most eligible bachelors. "Pierce Butler, a man of good family and fortune, became desperately enamored of the marvelous creature, who to the sorcery of the stage added rare charms of person, brilliant accomplishments, and high culture," a close friend remembered in later years. "Pierce Butler was envied, and almost detested, by a swarm of rivals for his victory over the Kembles."

The two spent so much time together that Fanny soon was asking herself, "I wonder what he'll do for an interest by and by, when we are gone." Butler's solution was simple. He simply added himself to their group and traveled with the Kembles back to New York and then on to Boston. Because of his skills as a flutist, he often managed to get a place in the orchestra to be near Fanny when she acted.

By the spring of 1833 Fanny found herself growing quite fond of Butler. And as she fell in love, her attitude toward America and Americans changed. "This is a brave new world in more ways than one," she wrote home to her closest friend. "We are in every way bound to like it, for our labour has been amply rewarded in its most important result, money. And the universal kindness which has everywhere met us since we first came to this country ought to repay us even for the pain and sorrow of leaving England."

That summer Fanny made a fateful trip up the Hudson and Mohawk rivers to Niagara Falls. She was accompanied by her father, Aunt Dall, Pierce Butler, and a new companion, Edward Trelawny. Trelawny was an extraordinary Englishman—an explorer, adventurer, and close friend of both Byron and Shelley. He had been with Shelley at Leghorn, Italy, when the poet drowned, and had supervised the cremation of his body on the beach. (He had pulled Shelley's charred heart from the flames.) "What a savage he is," Fanny observed in her journal. "His face is as dark as a Moor's—with a wild, strange look about the eyes and a mark like a scar upon his cheek. His whole appearance gives one an idea of toil, hardship, peril, and wild adventure."

The party stretched the expedition over two weeks. While in Buffalo, Butler proposed and Fanny accepted. Together they explored the mighty spectacle of Niagara Falls. For once Fanny was at a loss for words. "I can't describe it," she wrote in her journal of the falls. "I only know it was extremely beautiful and came pouring down like a great rolling heap of amber." She sat on the edge, her feet dangling over the dark caldron of boiling water far below, just opposite a brilliant rainbow, until she grew dizzy and Butler had to help her back to the hotel. Then, in the early morning of July 16, disaster overtook them when their coach suddenly overturned. Fanny, her father, and Butler all escaped injury. Trelawny was badly shaken. But Aunt Dall suffered a severe head wound. She appeared to recover, but during the winter she grew weaker; she died in Boston in the spring of 1834. Dall had been closer to Fanny than her own mother, and the death devastated her. Five weeks later she married Pierce Butler in Philadelphia.

3

At the time of her marriage Fanny was at the pinnacle of her success, the most popular actress in the English-speaking world. She had gained a degree of financial independence uncommon among the women of her day. And yet she had no regrets about giving up her stage career. Indeed she looked forward to marriage for the opportunity it afforded for "rest, quiet, leisure to study, to think, and to work, and legitimate channels for the affections of my nature." She had long harbored literary ambitions and longed to do extensive writing. As matters quickly developed, it was this ambition that provoked the first serious quarrel with Butler. A few months before her marriage, Fanny had contracted with her publisher in London and another in Philadelphia for a book on America based on the detailed journal she had kept throughout her tour. She gave Butler leave to read her manuscript and he found much that he thought offensive and inappropriate. He demanded numerous and fundamental changes. Outraged and embarrassed over the prospects of his wife going public with her thoughts, Butler visited her American publishers and offered them a substantial sum to break their contract for the book.

As Fanny's biographer Constance Wright observes, the dispute quickly escalated to "embrace the whole question of matrimony and the duty that a wife owed her husband." Butler insisted upon the conventional interpretation of the marriage vow and demanded obedience and submission from his wife. Never expecting resistance, he was baffled and angry when his wife refused to comply with his wishes.

Fanny, for her part, argued that marriage should be a partnership in which both husband and wife had equal rights. She absolutely rejected Butler's right to control her actions. "Is it because you are better than myself?" she asked him. "I am sure you would not say so, whatever I may think. Is it because you are more enlightened, more intellectual? You know that isn't so!"

The quarrel reached a climax in November when Fanny packed a bag and fled her in-laws's house, in which the couple had been living. She returned that evening but only because she could not find a hotel.

Butler thought the crisis a result of her pregnancy and hoped she would return to normal after the birth of their child. But Fanny understood that fundamental differences of philosophy, character, and values stood between them. She also realized too late that marriage, as defined in the nineteenth century, ran contrary to her nature. In 1828 she had confided her feelings in a letter to a close friend. She wrote:

> You know that independence of mind and body seems to me the great desideratum of life. I am not patient of restraint or submission to authority, and my heart and head are engrossed with the idea of exercising and developing the literary talent which I think I possess. This is meat, drink, and sleep to me. . . . I do not think I am fit to marry, to make an obedient wife or affectionate mother. My imagination is paramount with me and would disqualify me, I think, for the everyday matter of fact cares and duties of a mistress of a household and the head of a family. I think I should be unhappy and the cause of unhappiness to others if I were to marry. I cannot swear I shall never fall in love. But if I do I will fall out of it again, for I do not think I shall ever so far lose sight of my best interest and happiness as to enter into a relation for which I feel so unfitted.

Fanny at 24 had ignored the excellent advice she had given herself at 19. And she had learned another terrible truth of the cost of marriage: "I lose everything by my marrying and gain nothing in a worldly point of view." As a celebrated actress, she had enjoyed independence, wealth, freedom, fame, and social excitement. Marriage stripped her of all those advantages. She became only Mrs. Pierce Butler and highly vulnerable in a way she had never known before. Like Mrs. Trollope before her, Fanny was about to experience a rude awakening to the realities of the place of women in Jacksonian America.

Fanny's dream of a marriage in which husband and wife came together as equal partners, neither making any attempt to control, was hopelessly idealistic in an age in which women were conspicuously lacking in both rights and opportunities. Most authorities and the vast majority of women rejected such ideas as dangerously subversive of a woman's proper role in society. The plight of women at this time has been neatly summarized by social historian Carroll Smith Rosenberg:

> Women in Jacksonian America had few rights and little power. Their role in society was passive and sharply limited. Women were, in general, denied formal education above the minimum required by a literate early industrial society. The female brain and nervous system, male physicians agreed, were inadequate to sustained intellectual effort. They were denied the vote in a society which placed a high value upon political participation; political activity might corrupt their pure feminine nature. . . . Most economic alternatives to marriage . . . were closed to women. Their property rights were still restricted and females were generally considered to be the legal wards either of the state or of their nearest male relative. In the event of divorce, the mother lost custody of her children—even when the husband was conceded to be the erring party. Women's universe was bounded by their homes and the career of father or husband; within the home it was the woman's duty to be submissive and patient.

In the context of the age, a woman expressed her duty to her husband through a submission to his will. Virtually all the women's magazines and conduct books stressed this virtue over all others. *The Young Lady's Books* in 1830 voiced the popular wisdom of the day when they urged upon its female readers the necessity of passivity: "It is, however, certain that in whatever situation of life a woman is placed from cradle to her grave, a spirit of obedience and submission, pliability of temper, and humility of mind are required from her." It went without saying that business was men's business. According to the wisdom of the day, women should never intrude into the professional affairs of their husbands, but concern themselves strictly with the domestic supervision of their homes and families. As late as 1850, wife beating "with a reasonable instrument" was legal in all states. New York courts upheld the right of a Methodist minister to beat his wife with a horsewhip once a month to ensure proper obedience.

(Fanny's problem was never the result of any unique or peculiar status accorded women by American law and custom. In virtually every area there was agreement between American and British law when it came to the rights of women.)

The Butlers' first crisis passed uneasily with none of the fundamental differences resolved. In January 1835 they moved into a refurbished house on 300 acres far outside Philadelphia. Fanny's days were given over to the domestic business of engaging servants, ordering china and furniture, and selecting appropriate carpets, curtains, and linens. At Butler's Place, or "The Farm" as she called it, they had six servants, an extensive vegetable garden, and their own dairy and poultry operations. The domestic help left much to be desired. "Managing republican servants is a task quite enough to make a Quaker kick his grandmother," a frustrated Fanny complained to a friend back in England. She continued to prepare her journal for publication, although the joy of literary creation had disappeared since the bitter quarrel with her husband. Her book appeared later that same year to strong disapproval, exactly as Pierce Butler had predicted. She had written frankly and often critically about numerous social engagements and people she had encountered in her first two years in America. The critics accused her of poor taste, ingratitude, and rudeness.

On May 28 Fanny gave birth to a daughter she named Sarah. Married life on The Farm proved a disappointment. The house was too remote from Philadelphia for the Butlers to maintain an active social life. Occasionally they went into the city for the theater or a dinner party, but Fanny had no close friends. Even worse than the social isolation was the intellectual stagnation. "No one that I belong to takes the slightest interest in literary pursuits," she complained in a letter to an English friend. "I feel most seriously how desirable it is that I should study because I positively languish for intellectual activity. And yet what would under other circumstances be a natural pleasure is apt to become an effort when those with whom one lives do not sympathize with one's pursuits."

Some six months after their marriage Fanny made a shattering discovery: her husband's income derived entirely from two large plantations on the Georgian coast run by some 700 slaves. A confirmed abolitionist, she was horrified to learn that her husband belonged to one of the South's largest slave-owning families. (The census of 1860 showed that only 11 planters in the entire South owned more than 500 slaves.) "When I married Mr. Butler," Fanny wrote in 1839, "I knew nothing of these dreadful possessions of his." Her ignorance of such a critical matter is mute testimony to the degree to which husbands in Jacksonian America routinely kept all business affairs from their wives. The Butler plantations then belonged to an aged aunt, Frances Butler. But Fanny was still appalled, calling slavery "a grievous sin against humanity." She wrote a friend that she would rather return to "the toilsome earning of my daily bread in the theatre" than live off money gained through slave labor.

The American institution of slavery had shocked Fanny from her first day in New York. Shortly after the Kembles arrived in America, a black steward from their ship had called at the Kembles' hotel to request a ticket for the performance. "It must be for the gallery, if you please, for people of colour are not allowed to go to the pit or any other part of the house," he advised them. "I believe I must have turned black myself, I was so indignant," an outraged Fanny wrote later that day in her journal. "The prejudice against these unfortunate people is incomprehensible to us."

In Boston Fanny met Dr. William Channing, who won her over to his newly formed Unitarian Church and aroused her abolitionist fervor. His 1835 book *Slavery* profoundly shaped her ideas on the subject. Apparently Pierce Butler's own discovery of his wife's abolitionist sympathies did not come until he read the journal she had prepared for publication. He was shocked and demanded she censor from the text all references to slavery. Fanny did, but only after several fierce quarrels and then only with great reluctance. "I have just finished writing a long and vehement treatise against Negro slavery," she complained in a letter of June 1835, "which I wanted to publish with my journal, but was obliged to refrain from doing so lest our fellow citizens should tear our house down and make a bonfire of our furniture—a favourite mode of remonstrance in the past with those who advocate the rights of unhappy blacks."

Fanny's commitment to the abolitionist movement quickly developed a missionary zeal. She took as her personal cause the salvation of Pierce Butler from the dreadful sin of slave ownership. She was utterly indifferent to "the amazement and dismay, the terror and disgust" with which the Butler family reacted to her views. "Religious conviction and boredom combined to make Fanny peculiarly vulnerable to the call of a cause," her biographer Dorothy Marshall argues.

But there was yet another factor. In Fanny's mind the issue of slavery was closely entwined with that of the rights of women. Except for the fact that they could not be arbitrarily sold, women were not much better off than slaves under the law. For many reformers of the period the connection between the two causes was obvious. (In 1866 militant women's rights groups refused to endorse the Fourteenth Amendment to the Constitution, defining the civil rights of male Negroes, because it did not also legislate for women.)

In the decade of the 1830s the reform movements for abolition and women's rights developed side by side, the one often drawing upon the other for volunteers and inspiration. Fanny's progress from a concern with the proper role of women in marriage to the more heated cause of the abolition of black slavery thus reflected the larger progress of many of her contemporaries in that decade. The female advocates of abolition were among the first American women to challenge the completely submissive, domestic role society had thrust upon them.

In late 1836 Miss Frances Butler, the guardian of the Georgian plantations and the aunt of Pierce Butler, died. Her death brought dramatic changes to Fanny's situation. Possession and hence the actual responsibility for the operation of the two plantations passed to Butler. Having denounced slavery in the abstract, she was now eager to see its actual workings. She had accepted Channing's position in *Slavery* that abolitionists should patiently plead the cause of the slave with his owner, making him understand the nature of his sin and thus bringing him to repentance. "The personal character and influence of a few Christian men and women living daily among [the planters will] put an end to slavery more speedily and effectually than any other means whatsoever," Fanny wrote confidently in an essay on slavery. Having already defined her role as Butler's Christian conscience, she longed for the opportunity to put her ideas to a test in the field.

Butler, for his part, was eager for his wife to observe slavery firsthand, convinced that she would then be persuaded by the evidence of her own eyes that slavery was not the great horror the abolitionists made it out to be. Fanny, in turn, agreed to go to Georgia with an open mind. "Assuredly I am going prejudiced against slavery," she wrote to an abolitionist friend in Boston, "for I am an Englishwoman, in whom the absence of such a prejudice would be disgraceful. Nevertheless, I go prepared to find many mitigations in practice to the general injustice and cruelty of the system—much kindness on the part of the masters and much content on that of the slaves."

Events conspired to postpone the Butlers's departure to the Georgian coast for almost two years. In that interval Fanny gave birth to a second child and made two trips back to London. Finally, in December 1838, the Butlers departed Philadelphia for Georgia. Fanny looked forward to the experience with enormous expectations. Such a visit would provide numerous opportunities for a close study of the actual workings of a large slave plantation. Fanny, too, had heard many stories of the grand mansions and luxurious lifestyles of the Southern planters. And after the long boredom of her existence outside Philadelphia, the promise of fresh adventures captured her imagination. "Who knows," she wrote a friend, "but I might die of fever, be shot from behind a tree for abolitionism, or be swallowed by an alligator."

4

August 25, 1845. On a field some distance from Richmond, Virginia, a large crowd of well-dressed planters and their families gathered beneath a hot summer sun. They pressed against a wooden fence 300 yards in length that encompassed an arena. At either end brightly costumed heralds and trumpeters stood beside closed gates. Suddenly a trumpet sounded. Slowly a calvacade of knights and attendants rode into view. In spite of the oppressive humidity the knights all wore full suits of medieval armor. Shields with heraldic devices hung from their left arms. Their right hands tightly gripped long wooden lances. A trumpeter sounded a call for silence. A herald then announced the names of the competing knights, Sir Brian de Bois-Guilbert and Wilfred of Ivanhoe.

The two knights saluted the grandstand and then slowly rode to opposite ends of the arena to await the signal announcing the formal start of the tournament. Wilfred of Ivanhoe, on his Kentucky thoroughbred, was the favorite. A reporter from the Richmond *Enquirer* observed what followed next:

At the Tournament today the most exciting interest prevailed throughout. While the tilting was in progress, the sound of a horn was heard. All eyes turned to the wood—a herald was sent to ascertain who it was that thus interrupted the contest of the knights. The returning herald announced the approach of the renowned Knight of *La Mancha*, who had heard of this conflict and desired permission to shiver a lance among them.

Dressed in armor, with his faithful squire on a mule, with a crown of a hat about three feet high, the Don, in stately dignity, approached the Lady Judges. The assembled hills were convulsed with laughter, and after Sancho refreshed the Don with the contents of his wallet, the latter distinguished himself by the singular success of his lance.

Taking it all in all, it was the richest scene I ever saw enacted on any theatre. It far surpassed any Tournament we ever had.

Between 1813 and 1823 alone five million copies of Sir Walter Scott's historical romances were sold in the United States. The most popular with Southern readers was *Ivanhoe,* his romance of Saxon and Norman conflict at the time of Richard the Lion-Hearted. The sales of Charles Dickens's novels languished south of the Mason-Dixon Line while Southern men and women turned to Scott's novels as models of life and good breeding. The Old South regarded itself as the guardian of the chivalric ideal with its emphasis on the cults of manners and woman, the ideal of the gallant knight, and the loyalty to caste. Much later, in *Life on the Mississippi,* Mark Twain lashed out against "the Sir Walter Scott disease," insisting in gross exaggeration that the English novelist did "measureless harm, more real and lasting harm than any other individual that ever wrote. . . . Sir Walter Scott had so large a hand in making Southern character, as it existed before the War, that he is a great measure responsible for the War."

Scott's Waverley novels made the Southern planter feel like a chivalrous lord of the manor. As historian Rollin G. Osterweis observes in *Romanticism and Nationalism in the Old South*:

> The plantation of the pre-Civil War South was the coun-
> terpart of the medieval manor. The planter was the repository
> of social dignity, of judicial power, of political leadership for
> his neighborhood, in quite the same fashion as the eighteenth-
> century English squire whom he strove to emulate. Both were
> survivals of the feudal tradition. The presence of the Negro
> slaves, however, gave an added intensity to feudal feeling in
> the South. Here was a factor far closer to the serf of the
> Middle Ages than anything in Georgian England. . . . The
> Southern planter stood at the top of a stratified society, cher-
> ishing the country-gentleman ideal—his lordly sense of
> leadership fed by the presence of slaves. His code demanded
> courtesy, deference to women, hospitality to strangers,
> defense of his honor, consideration for social inferiors.

Even before the Civil War Americans began to idealize the Southern plantation and view it through a romantic haze. At the center of the fantasy stands a great mansion of tall columns where courtly gentlemen and exquisitely gowned ladies converse against a backdrop of rose gardens and dueling grounds. Around the big house, neatly cultivated cotton fields reach to the horizon. The slaves are too numerous to count, and the social life is a thing of Old World splendor from a distant past. The stage is peopled with certain stock types—the colonel, the belle, the black mammy. In this century the fantasy has appealed powerfully to an innate mod-ern American love of feudalism on the part of many Americans. Both the Tara Plantation of Margaret Mitchell's *Gone with the Wind* and the Kennedy compound at Hyannis Port with its associ-ations of Camelot satisfy this romantic hunger in a certain segment of our population for some allegory of aristocracy.

The antebellum reality, however, was something very different. "The South was no more thick-set with elegant mansions than

Elizabethan England was crowded with Kenilworth Castles," historian Francis Gaines observed in the 1920s. A true Southern aristocracy flourished only in scattered pockets, largely around urban centers such as Richmond, Natchez, Charleston, and Mobile. Contrary to our popular temptation to define the antebellum South largely in terms of the planter class, the 1860 census counted only 46,274 planters out of a population of some eight million. Of these, fewer than 3,000 owned more than 100 slaves. Those planters with a lifestyle approximating the legend numbered fewer than 500. The vast majority of Southern families lived on small farms rather than plantations.

The fact is that much of the South in 1860 was still frontier, or at most one generation removed. The log cabin, not the great mansion, was a much more common building on Southern "plantations." When Frederick Law Olmsted traveled through Alabama in 1853, he observed that the majority of the planters lived in double log cabins with a breezeway between the two rooms. Such homes often lacked windows. The front door was sometimes removed at mealtimes and used as a table. Many of the men who shouted the Rebel yell as they charged the Northern positions at Gettysburg and Shiloh had fought Cherokee or Creek war parties in their youth.

The Southern frontier, of course, differed sharply from the other frontiers in American history. Against the egalitarianism of the West, Southern ideology sanctioned a quasi-aristocratic, hierarchical social structure in which heredity and "breeding" counted at least as much as talent. Even so, Southern society still offered opportunity for poor men to rise to the top. President Andrew Jackson, a frontier aristocrat and wealthy cotton planter, had his roots in the Carolina backwoods. But the range of opportunities there was drastically limited in contrast to the frontiers of the Midwest. The plantation perpetuated frontier conditions even up to the Civil War: a sparse population in a vast area. A handful of planters controlled large tracts of the best land and effectively blocked immigration. In 1860, 85 percent of all immigrants lived north of the Mason-Dixon Line. The reasons were clear: good, cheap farmland and the opportunity to rise in the world were much more limited in the South than in the expanding West.

Thus, after 1830 the South was largely a static society walled off by a dike of laws and customs intended to preserve this static character. The North's energy and enterprise had yielded a widespread prosperity. But in the decade before the Civil War many Southern slaveholding families had a standard of living that had changed little since their grandparents' time. Frederick Law Olmsted observed after his 1853 tour through the South: "From the banks of the Mississippi to the banks of the James, I did not . . . see, except perhaps in one or two towns, a thermometer, nor a book of Shakespeare, nor a pianoforte or sheet of music. . . . I am not speaking of what are commonly called 'poor whites.' A large majority of all these houses were the residences of slaveholders, a considerable proportion cotton-planters."

Fanny Kemble had two years in which to prepare herself for the transition to the Butler plantations on the Georgian coast. Little did she expect she would exchange the comforts of her Philadelphia life for a undeveloped frontier that had changed little in fifty years.

5

On the Friday morning of December 21, 1838, the Butlers departed Philadelphia for Georgia. The trip took nine days by rail, steamboat, and stagecoach. Once they arrived in the South, travel conditions turned primitive. Much of Southern society was primitive, still reminiscent of the frontier. Railroads often ended abruptly in the middle of a dense forest. Crudely constructed inns offered only the roughest sort of accommodations. "Here [we are] in this wilderness in a house which seemed just cut out of the trees, where a tin pan was brought to me for a basin and where the only kitchen . . . was an open shed, not fit to stable a well-kept horse in," she complained.

Everywhere Fanny saw unpainted houses, filth, impassable roads, dilapidated railroads, and inertia. The poverty in North Carolina particularly depressed her. "The few detached houses on the road were mean and beggarly in their appearance," she wrote to a Boston friend. "In the meantime the coaches were surrounded by a troop of gazing boors. . . . A more forlorn, fierce, poor, and wild-looking set of people, short of absolute savages, I never saw. They wandered round and round us, with a stupid kind of dismayed wonder." She was shocked to discover the women chewed tobacco.

In comparison to the bustling Northern cities, even the famed Charleston seemed no better than a second-rate town on the banks of the Hudson. Fanny thought the city "highly picturesque" but found it "pervaded with an air of decay . . . [like] a distressed elderly gentlewoman." She was shocked to discover that a 9:00 P.M. curfew for all blacks was in effect, reflecting the Southern fear of an armed slave uprising. "No doubt these daily and nightly precautions are but trifling drawbacks upon the manifold blessings of slavery," Fanny wrote caustically to a friend. "Still, I should prefer going to sleep without the apprehension of my servants' cutting my throat in my bed."

From Charleston Fanny's group traveled by small coastal craft to Savannah and then to the tiny town of Darian on the mainland opposite Butler's plantations. "As we grazed the wharf, it seemed to me as if we had touched the outer bounds of civilized creation," she noted forlornly. Nearby were waiting two small boats with black crews, slaves from the Butler plantation. "Oh, massa!" they shouted enthusiastically. "How do you do, massa? Oh, missis! Oh! li'l missis! Me too glad to see you!" Within a few minutes the boats were loaded, and Fanny found herself traveling down the broad Altamaha River through forbidding-looking swamp lands. Soon they left the river and entered a canal between two high dikes enclosing rice fields. Suddenly she saw several buildings ahead. The steersman lifted a huge conch shell to his lips and "in the barbaric fashion of early times in the Highlands, sounded out our approach." Scores of slaves excitedly crowded the little dock, jumping, dancing, shouting, and clapping their hands as the two boats pulled up at Butler's Island. Fanny stepped ashore. Dozens of slaves seized her hands, kissed her dress, and shouted their joy.

One tall, gaunt woman broke through the throng to embrace her in her arms. Fanny could understand their joy at seeing her husband. But why, she asked herself, all these extravagant demonstrations of delight over her and her children? It was several weeks before she learned the answer. No Butler had lived on the island for 19 years. For many years the family had discussed the possibility of selling their plantations and all the slaves. To Butler's slaves, Fanny and her children meant continuity and an end to worries that their families would be separated on the auction block.

Fanny's journey through the Southern countryside with its air of decay and inertia must surely have prepared her for Butler's Island, a low swampy area of some 1,800 acres. The Great House, once a splendid structure, was now a ruin. (In 1804 Colonel Aaron Burr had stayed in the guest house for several weeks, seeking a low profile after killing Alexander Hamilton in a duel.) The Butler family moved into the dilapidated cottage of the white overseer.

The two Butler plantations—one rice, the other sea-island cotton—dated back to the 1790s. For 50 years a small group of wealthy and powerful families had owned vast estates in the enormously fertile Altamaha River region. Some, like the Butlers, lived on isolated barrier islands where they ruled liked petty despots, far beyond the restraints that life in a city would necessarily have imposed. ("It's not law here, it's all power," one Georgian planter was heard to say.)

In 1838 the Georgian coast was in a state of general decline. Virgin lands in the Southwest sucked population away from the older coastal areas where much of the farmland was sadly exhausted. Scores of mansions and entire towns sat abandoned. Land values had fallen precipitously. The plunge in the price of cotton from 17 ½ cents a pound to 13 ½ cents had brought on a depression. But the price of rice had risen dramatically. This, not cotton, now formed the basis of the Butler family prosperity.

The Butler plantation was a completely self-sufficient frontier operation with its own blacksmiths, coopers, bricklayers, and carpenters. Pierce Butler's grandfather had built an elaborate system of dikes, floodgates, and drainage ditches to flood and drain the rice fields with the tides. The fields ranged in size from 12 to 22 acres. The seeds were sown in the spring. After the rice plants had sprouted, slaves periodically hoed and irrigated the fields. They harvested in late summer. On most plantations the rice was threshed by hand, but the Butler Plantation boasted three threshing mills. The task system was in effect. All slaves, including the women, were given specific tasks at the start of each day. If they worked quickly and finished early, then the rest of the afternoon was theirs to do with as they pleased. Because of their extreme isolation, the slaves rarely came into contact with outsiders and thus spoke Gullah, an odd mixture of seventeenth-century English and African dialect. (Joel Chandler Harris wrote his Uncle Remus tales in a modified form of Gullah.)

"[Butler's Island] is one of the wildest corners of creation," Fanny wrote to a friend shortly after her arrival. "It is a sort of hasty pudding of amphibious elements, composed of a huge rolling river, thick and turbid with mud, and stretches of mud banks scarcely reclaimed from the water. . . . A duck, an eel, or a frog might find life here as in paradise."

Island life was as primitive as it was isolated. The Butlers lived in a dilapidated six-room cottage with bare, unpainted walls, sagging doors and window frames, and a dirt floor in the kitchen. The largest room measured 15 by 16 feet and served as both sitting and dining room. Enormous centipedes darted over the walls and tables. "We live here in a very strange manner," she noted in her journal. "The house we inhabit is inferior to the poorest farm house in any part of England. The little furniture is of the coarsest and roughest description, and the household services are performed by Negroes who run in and out, generally barefooted and always filthy. This unlimited supply of trained savages (for that is what they really are) is anything but a luxury for me. Their ignorance, dirt, and stupidity seem to me as intolerable as the unjust laws which condemn them to be ignorant, filthy, and stupid."

Fanny quickly discovered a basic fact about life on a frontier plantation—the utter absence of any privacy. She found it almost impossible to escape the "savage curiosity" of the slaves. When she went walking, they followed behind or spied on her from the bushes. Nor did she find privacy in the confines of her home as she sat in the evening writing in her journal. "One after another, men and women come trooping silently in, their naked feet falling all but inaudibly on the bare boards as they betake themselves to the hearth where they squat down on their hams in a circle, the bright blaze from the huge pine logs, which is the only light of this half of the room, shining on their sooty limbs and faces and making them look like a ring of ebony idols surrounding my domestic hearth," she noted. "I have had as many as fourteen at a time squatting silently there for nearly half an hour, watching me writing at the other end of the room. . . . You cannot imagine anything stranger than the effect of all these glassy whites of eyes and grinning white teeth turned toward me and shining in the flickering light. I very often take no notice of them at all, and they seem perfectly absorbed in contemplating me."

Fanny's house staff consisted of a cook, dairymaid, laundress, maid, and two butlers. Slaves, she quickly discovered, made poor servants. They all exhibited an appalling lack of any personal hygiene. No one in her service washed with any frequency. Their clothes were filthy, and their bodies encrusted with dirt. Mary, her maid, smelled so foully that Fanny could not bear to be in the same room with her. "How I have wished for a decent, tidy English servant of all work, instead of these begrimed, ignorant, incapable poor creatures who stumble about round us in zealous hindrance of each other, which they intend for help for us," she wrote in despair to a Boston friend. She learned to take nothing for granted. Once, after she was served a salad full of dirt, she demanded the butler "wash" the vegetables and later discovered him in the kitchen using a brush and soap on the lettuce.

On Fanny's first exploration of her husband's plantation she visited the threshing mills, blacksmith's shop, and cooper's shop, all under the supervision of competent blacks. Then she inspected the cluster of slave cabins. Each was a crude one-room structure, measuring 12 by 15 feet, pinned to a enormous stone chimney. The only furniture was a rude bedstead, on which a pile of dried Spanish moss served as the mattress, and perhaps a rough table. Sewage disposal was handled by a ditch in the rear which the tide flushed daily. Two families shared each cabin. "Such of these cabins as I visited today were filthy and wretched in the extreme and exhibited the most deplorable consequence of ignorance and . . . the inability of the inhabitants to secure and improve even such pitiful comfort as yet might be achieved by them," a dejected Fanny wrote later that day in her journal. "Instead of the order, neatness, and ingenuity, which might convert even these miserable hovels into tolerable residences, there was a careless, reckless, filthy indolence, which even the brutes do not exhibit in their lairs and nests." Later she would learn that the squalid conditions of the cabins were a direct consequence of long hours of exhausting fieldwork, which left the slaves with no stamina for improvements of their cabins.

Next Fanny visited the infirmary, a large two-story, whitewashed building with four rooms. Nothing she had seen thus far in America shocked her as much as this infirmary, a hospital in name only. "How shall I describe to you the spectacle which was presented to me on entering the first of these [rooms]?" she asked rhetorically in a letter to a friend in Boston. In the darkness—the windows were all shuttered—she found dirt, noise, and stench. Chickens and ducks wandered in and out. There was no fire to ward off the winter chill. The infirmary did not have a single bedstead or mattress. The patients, mostly women, lay huddled on the dirt floor under piles of tattered and filthy blankets. Many were in the final stages of pregnancy. Others suffered from the pains of miscarriage, rheumatism, and fevers. One young girl had leprosy; her hands and feet were literally rotting away. Rose, an aging black midwife, provided the sole medical attention. "Now pray take notice that this is the hospital of an estate where the owners are supposed to be humane, the overseer efficient and kind, and the Negroes remarkably well cared for and comfortable," she wrote in despair to her friend.

"How can I improve the lot of these slaves?" Fanny asked herself later that day. Granting them their freedom was obviously beyond her power. Her goals would have to be more modest. "Yet it cannot be but from my words and actions some revelations should reach these poor people," she wrote in her journal that evening. "By going in and out among them perpetually, I shall teach, and they learn involuntarily a thousand things of deepest import. They must learn . . . that there are beings in the world, even with skins of a different color from their own, who have sympathy for their misfortunes, love for their virtues, and respect for their common nature."

The next day Fanny returned to the infirmary. Under her supervision several slaves flung open the shutters, swept up the piles of trash, washed the walls, and built a fire. Rose, the old midwife, followed at her heels, shaking her head and muttering, "Let be." Fanny lectured the mothers on the importance of cleanliness to the good health of their babies. They told her they wrapped their babies in red flannel diapers and never changed or washed them. A disgusted Fanny ordered Rose to bring her a large tub of warm water and washed two babies, much to the dismay of their mothers standing nearby. "Anything much more helpless and inefficient than these poor ignorant creatures you cannot conceive," Fanny observed. "They actually seemed incapable of drying or dressing their own babies, and I had to finish their toilet myself." She got her most dramatic results when she announced she would pay one penny for each child scrubbed clean. To others she handed out new clothes, extra rations of food, and blankets.

Some were beyond her help. An old slave named Friday died in her arms. She found him lying on a pile of straw, with several sticks for a pillow. Flies swarmed around his open mouth. A tattered shirt and a pair of trousers barely covered his body. "There he lay—the worn-out slave, whose life had been spent in unrequited labor for me and mine, without one physical alleviation, one Christian solace, one human sympathy, to cheer him in his extremity—panting out the last breath of his wretched existence like some forsaken, overworked, wearied-out beast of burden, rotting where it falls!" an anguished Fanny wrote in her journal. As she watched, his eyelids quivered, his lower jaw relaxed, and then he was dead. "How I rejoiced for him . . . freed by death from bitter, bitter bondage," she cried.

Fanny filled her journal with revealing anecdotes. An old slave came to her kitchen to beg some sugar and saw her watch on the table. "Ah! I need not look at this," she said sadly. "I have almost done with time!" Another ancient slave, bedridden with an ulcerated leg, clenched Fanny's hand tightly and with tears streaming down her cheeks pleaded: "I have worked every day through dew and damp, and sand and heat, and done good work. But oh, missis, me old and broken now. No tongue can tell how much I suffer."

Fanny's guide around Butler's Island was Jack, a precocious black youngster whom the overseer judged too frail for hard physical labor. He had an intense curiosity about life beyond the island. One day Jack asked her for special permission to keep a pig. Fanny cut him short and suddenly asked her own question: did Jack wish to be free? The question took the boy completely by surprise. His face lighted up. He stammered, hesitated, and then became terribly confused, fearful of offending by uttering the forbidden wish. "Free, missis!" he blurted out. "What for me wish to be free? Oh no, missis, me no wish to be free, if massa only let we keep pig!" Fanny repeated her question. The frightened youngster refused to consider the option. "No, missus, me no want to be free," he cried out in anguish, "me work till me die for missis and massa."

Fanny learned how quickly the blacks picked up their master's contempt for their race, according certain slaves a higher status simply because they possessed some white blood. "Twenty-six black girls do not make mulatto yellow girl," her boatmen sang as they rowed her along the Altamaha River.

Fanny noted, too, the exaggerated pride in the white ruling class, together with an instinctive habit of command from early childhood, that slavery cultivated among the Southern whites. She saw the start of corruption in her own four-year-old daughter Sarah, as she lorded it over a troop of servile playmates who addressed her as "Little Missis." She had only to express a desire for a swing and within minutes one was rigged from a nearby tree limb and a dozen pushers stood at attention to send her flying through the air.

Fanny was particularly interested in the impact of slavery upon black women. It grotesquely distorted black motherhood. Black children represented potential cash value and were valued as such by both their mothers and white owners. The system had enormous incentives to encourage pregnancy. Lighter workloads, extra clothing allowances, and increased rations of food were the rewards that accrued to pregnant women. The Butler slaves all had a keen sense of their value as property. Black women took pride in the number of children they had brought into the world, hoping this would translate out into claims upon their master's good will. "Look, missis!" one black women called excitedly to Fanny, as she pushed a large brood of nearly naked children toward her. "Little niggers for you and massa; plenty of little niggers for you and little missis!"

But Fanny quickly learned that slavery encouraged only the breeding of children, not their parenting. The white overseer on the Butler Plantation discouraged slave marriages. Few black males were ready and willing to assume parental duties. "The father, having neither authority, power, responsibility, or charge in his children is, of course, as among the brutes the least attached to his offspring," she observed. One-parent families were the rule on the Butler Plantation. Thus, black women were deprived of even the minimal securities enjoyed by other American women, the comforts and protection of fathers and husbands. Furthermore, they were sent back into the fields within three weeks of their delivery, while their infants were left in the care of children too young for work. In the late afternoon the women returned to their cabins too exhausted after their labor for either parenting or housekeeping. Infant mortality was high. Over one-third of all children on the Butler Plantation died before their fifth birthday.

Rape was so commonplace that black women accepted it as a fact of life. With no husbands to protect them, they were at the mercy of any man who wanted them. Fanny was appalled. "Did nobody ever tell or teach any of you that it is a sin to live with men who are not your husband?" she naively asked one woman who had once been raped by a black field supervisor. The slave suddenly seized her white mistress's wrist and with a look of abject misery told her: "Oh yes, missis, we know—we know all about dat well enough. But we do anything to get our poor flesh some rest from de whip. When he made me follow him into de bush, what use me tell him no? He have strength to make me."

(Fanny also saw numerous mulattos, the offspring of the previous overseers. Miscegenation was widely practiced in the antebellum South. In 1835 a planter's wife bitterly informed the English visitor Harriet Martineau that she was but "the chief slave in the harem.")

Fanny had come face to face with the fundamental fact of slavery: it rested on force. In the system the black man or woman was nothing but another, more valuable domestic animal without a will of his or her own. Violence or the threat of violence always lurked in the background. The overseer and his assistants carried whips. Lashings were a common occurrence on the Butler Plantation. In her journal Fanny recorded the dismal tale of Die, an older black woman whose grief-filled life brought tears to her mistress's eyes. Of her 16 children, 14 were dead. She had suffered four miscarriages. One had happened after a fall when she had been forced to carry a heavy load on her head. Another had come during a lashing for some minor offense. Fanny demanded the details. Die told her. The overseer bound Die's hands together at the wrists and then tied her arms high up on a post. He stripped her clothes off her back and lashed her repeatedly with a cowhide whip. She aborted her child soon afterward. With other planters the punishments for more serious offenses were often sadistic and vicious. Fanny heard about a slave from a nearby plantation who had attempted to escape the island. Captured, he was stripped naked and bound to a tree in the swamp, a prey to the torture inflicted by the venomous mosquito swarms. He died three days later.

Fanny had traveled to Georgia with an open mind, hoping to find slavery less burdensome than the abolitionists made out. She was profoundly disappointed. On the Butler Plantation she discovered few examples of the kindness of masters and the contentment of slaves. Instead, slavery had demoralized both blacks and whites alike. Everywhere she looked Fanny saw a pattern of unrelieved misery and brutality. And all this occurred on a plantation where the treatment of the slaves was considered more humane and enlightened than generally found elsewhere.

Fanny learned, too, important truths about her husband. She had underestimated the hold which Southern traditions held over Pierce Butler. He was much too Southern ever to shed or modify his regional values. When she found she could not sway him away from slavery, she redefined her goals and pleaded with him on behalf of individual cases of hardship. She sought, for example, to extend from three weeks to four the time women had off from heavy labor after giving birth. Butler quickly lost patience with her. "Why do you believe such trash?" he demanded. "Don't you know the niggers are all damned liars?" Whereas Fanny's concern was the morality of slavery, Butler's was the preservation of his home against actions he saw as deeply disturbing and subversive. By agitating on the part of his slaves, she had in his eyes stepped out of the woman's proper domestic sphere and intruded herself into his business. And her actions threatened to undermine the discipline necessary for the smooth operation of a large plantation.

On February 26 Butler informed Fanny he would no longer hear any petition on behalf of a slave. The blacks, he insisted, were simply taking advantage of her ignorance and gullibility to tell her lies. He demanded obedience and submission. "I must return to the North," a heart-stricken Fanny wrote in her journal that evening, "for my condition would be almost worse than theirs—condemned to hear and see so much wretchedness, not only without the means of alleviating it but without permission even to represent it for alleviation. This is no place for me since I was not born among slaves and cannot bear to live among them."

("Nothing is more difficult than to judge the abuses of past ages in their contemporary framework," Fanny's British biographer Dorothy Marshall argues. "The conditions which [Fanny] found intolerable on her husband's plantations were no worse than those which English society, apart from a small band of social reformers, was prepared to countenance for their own working people." Within memory English female vagrants had been stripped and cruelly whipped. Butler exempted all children under 12 from labor. But in England the Factory Act of 1833 merely prohibited the employment in factories of children under nine and limited those between nine and 13 to a 48-hour week. Until 1844 young children and pregnant women labored deep underground in coal mines under conditions far more appalling than any on the Butler Plantation.)

Fanny learned something, too, of the isolation common to the Southern plantations. Butler Plantation was an independent social unit, a self-contained and largely self-sufficient little world all its own, free from any dependence upon its neighbors. She had no guests except occasional visits from nearby planters. Her only contact with the outside was an infrequent shopping expedition to the little town of Darien on the mainland where Yankee shopkeepers charged double and triple prices for inferior goods.

On February 16 Butler moved his family to Hampton Point, his second plantation on St. Simons Island. The slaves piled all the household furniture, kitchen utensils, bedding, clothing, and livestock into a large boat and slowly rowed them the 15 miles to Hampton Point. Once again the conch shell was sounded to announce their arrival. By evening they were all settled into a dilapidated structure in the midst of unkempt grounds. "The smallest Yankee farmer has a tidier estate, a tidier house, and a tidier wife than this member of the proud Southern chivalry, who, however, inasmuch as he has slaves, is undoubtedly a much greater personage in his own estimation than those capital fellows . . . who walk in glory and in joy behind their plows upon your mountain sides," Fanny wrote soon afterward to a Boston friend.

The chief crop at the Hampton Point Plantation was sea-island or long-staple cotton. This was of a much finer quality than the more common upland cotton and generally brought twice the price.

Fanny found much about Hampton Point to depress her. The slave accommodations were more wretched than at Butler Island. In one ten-foot-square cabin she found three adults and eight children living. Once again she announced she would give a penny for every child washed clean and every cabin tidied up. The result was a sudden improvement in the living conditions. She quickly learned that hordes of rattlesnakes infested the island's thickets. In the intense summer heat they often climbed trees and coiled around branches in an attempt to cool off.

But Fanny also found many new pleasures. The physical beauty of the barrier island with its thick forests of weirdly contorted live oaks, their spreading limbs laced with woody vines and dripping Spanish moss, fascinated her. Armadillos rooted around in the fan-shaped leaves of the palmetto palms. She loved the miles of hard-packed sandy beaches that stretched uncluttered and empty to the horizon. Ghost crabs scurried over the fine quartz sand, while fiddler crabs patrolled the mud flats. Overhead, gulls and terns screamed in the wind. Fanny choked down her fear of rattlesnakes and went on long walks, often in the evening. "The scene just beyond the house was beautiful," she wrote in her journal. "The moonlight slept on the broad river, which is here almost the sea and on the mass of foliage of the great Southern oaks. The golden stars . . . shown in the purple curtains of the night. And the measured rush of the Atlantic unfurling its huge skirts upon the white sands of the beach . . . resounded through the silent air."

On St. Simons Island Fanny once again could indulge her passion for riding. No matter how depressed and distraught she might find herself, a hard horseback ride along the sand beaches always lifted her spirits. (She confided in her journal her choice for the kind of death she wanted—"to break my neck off the back of my horse at full gallop.") On some days she rode to nearby plantations to pay social visits, something she never could do on the more isolated Butler Island. Her closest neighbor was an expatriate Scotsman, John Couper, then 80 years old, who lived in a handsome mansion and passed his days cultivating an exquisite garden. On these visits she was also able to judge firsthand the condition of slaves on the other plantations; in almost all cases they were worse off than those on the Butler Plantations.

From these visits she also gained a better appreciation of Southern aristocracy. She recognized their popularity with many of her countrymen and insisted this reflected certain narrow prejudices. "Good manners have an undue value for Englishmen," she wrote later. "The Southerners are infinitely better bred men, according to English notions, than the men of the Northern states." Of the many English travelers to visit the South, only Fanny Kemble refused to succumb to the fabled charm of the Southern aristocracy. With "their furious feuds and slaughterous combats, their stabbings, and pistolings, their gross sensuality, brutal ignorance, and despotic cruelty, [they] resemble the chivalry of France before the horrors of the *Jacquerie* admonished them that there was a limit even to the endurance of slaves."

The readiness with which Southern gentlemen resorted to duels to resolve their differences particularly disturbed Fanny. The stylized ceremony of a proper Southern duel between two gentlemen, replete with a detailed set of regulations, set it off sharply from the common brawl or "shooting scape" of the Far Western frontier in the latter part of the century. Only gentlemen fought duels, and then only in defense of their honor. Legal action in court was never a viable option because the law provided no remedy for insulting innuendoes. During Fanny's stay on St. Simons Island two of her neighbors fought a duel over a boundary dispute. One man was killed. The terms of the challenge included the stipulation that the winner had "the privilege of cutting off [his opponent's] head and sticking it up on a pole on the piece of land which was the origin of the debate."

Fanny's days at Hampton Point swiftly drew to a close. Her estrangement from Pierce Butler was complete. No longer concerned about his opinion, she acted with increasing recklessness. She gave reading lessons to one precocious black boy even though such an action was punishable by imprisonment and a fine of $500. Convinced that Southern slavery's greatest evil was its denial of the opportunity for blacks to develop their capabilities fully, she initiated a policy of payment in an effort to introduce her slaves to the concept of wages and monetary incentives. Finally, Fanny went on a hunger strike, refusing to eat any food produced by slave labor. She cried out a prayer for the destruction of St. Simons Island: "Beat, beat the crumbling banks and sliding shores, wild waves of the Atlantic and the Altamaha! Sweep down and carry hence this evil earth and these homes of tyranny and roll above the soil of slavery and wash my soul and the souls of those I love clean from the blood of our kind!"

On April 19, 1839, the Butler family departed Hampton Point. Their stay had lasted just 15 weeks. Back in Philadelphia the tensions increased until Fanny demanded a separation. "You can never repair the injury which you have done in marrying me," she wrote Butler. "I will not remain here to be your housekeeper, your children's nurse, or what yet you make of me that is still more degrading and revolting." But she did not leave. The two continued to live uneasily together. In December 1841 the entire family sailed for London. Butler may have hoped that a complete change of scene would reduce the domestic tensions. They remained in England for almost a year. It was a tempestuous time—they separated, came together again, and then separated once more. Now their positions had reversed and it was Butler who wanted a divorce. "Our position is so perilous," an agitated Fanny, fearful of losing her children, wrote her husband. "For God's sake and for your children's sake, Pierce, my husband, oh, still most tenderly loved, let us be wise before it is too late." Butler's demands for a reconciliation included Fanny's acceptance of the principle of a wife's absolute obedience to her husband in all disagreements. This she refused, saying, "I consider it my duty not to submit my conduct to any other human being."

Fanny returned to the stage, reading Shakespeare in a one-woman show. In the early spring of 1849 she was back in America, once more on tour. "Mrs. Butler, the veritable Fanny Kemble, has taken the city by storm," Philip Hone wrote in his journal on March 13 after her first appearance in New York. "Delicate women, grave gentlemen, belles, beaux, and critics flock to the doors of the entrance and rush into such places as they can find two or three hours before the lady's arrival. . . . She makes two or three thousand dollars a week, and never was money so easily made."

Butler filed for divorce. Fanny agreed not to contest it in exchange for a promise of $1,500 a year and the right to have her children visit for two months each summer. In September the divorce was granted on grounds of "willful" desertion. Butler won custody of their two daughters, but he failed to live up to his end of the bargain. Clearly, he blamed the collapse of their marriage on her stubborn refusal to put wifely duty ahead of her principles. He decided to put an end to Fanny's influence over their daughters.

Fanny spent the 1850s giving her readings from Shakespeare, which continued popular. Even in middle age she cut an imposing figure. The poet Elizabeth Barrett Browning met Fanny in Rome in 1853 and remembered her later: "Fanny is looking magnificent with her black hair and radiant smile. A very noble creature indeed. Somewhat inelastic, unpliant to the eye, attached to the old modes of thought and convention, but noble in quality and defects. I like her much."

On the other hand, Butler's fortunes had suffered a sharp

decline during the 1850s. He became heavily addicted to gambling and ran up an enormous mountain of gambling debts. In 1859 his creditors forced him to sell 436 of his slaves at auction in Savannah, Georgia. This represented half the slave force on his two plantations. The sale lasted two days. One black family brought $6,000, while an older man and woman without off-spring sold for a mere $250 apiece. As each slave was sold off and led away, Butler handed the man, woman, or child four new quarters as a token of his appreciation. The auction earned him a total of $303,850.

When the Civil War broke out Fanny was in the United States, now her second home. Like so many Americans, she was firmly convinced the conflict would be short-lived and within a few months the Southern resistance would crumble. She understood such a scenario depended upon other countries, especially England, adopting policies of non-intervention. She was wrong on both counts. By 1862 it was clear to all observers that the war would be long and bloody. And to Fanny's distress, English sentiment ran strongly in favor of the South. Prime Minister Henry J.T. Palmerston urged a policy of both recognition and aid to the Confederacy. In light of the Northern blockade of the Southern coast such a policy would quickly have led to another British–American war.

In June 1862 Fanny returned to England, arriving at a time when the Anglo-American relationship was at its stormiest. The North had suffered stunning reversals. Robert E. Lee, the newly appointed general of the Confederate Army, had just routed the Union forces under the command of General George McClellan and was marching confidently toward Maryland and Pennsylvania. The *Times* of London predicted a quick victory: "The North has tried the great experiment of coercion and failed; the South has tried the great experiment of independence and made good its position." On September 17, 1862, the Northern forces finally checked Lee's advance at the Battle of Antietam. Five days later President Abraham Lincoln issued his first Emancipation Proclamation, announcing his intention to free all slave on January 1, 1863.

Against this background of political and military turmoil, Fanny decided to publish the lengthy journal she had kept during her stay on the two Georgian plantations of Pierce Butler. "She felt she would thereby illuminate the nature of the Union's newly declared war aim, convince her English friends of its justness and necessity, and strike a blow at the pro-slavery apologetics of the government and of the London press," her editor and biographer John A. Scott argues. "In addition she hoped to contribute to a true understanding in England of the American struggle, help rally English opinion to the side of the North, and hence minimize the danger of British intervention on behalf of the Confederacy."

In May 1863 Fanny published her *Journal of a Residence on a Georgian Plantation in 1838–1839.* Three months later Harper and Brothers brought out an American edition. Contemporary reviews were largely favorable. *Harper's New Monthly Magazine* hailed it as "the most powerful anti-slavery book yet written." And the reviewer for the *New York Evening Post* argued what he thought was the book's importance: "Her sex brought her specially in contact with slave women. A man, unless he had been a physician, would have known nothing of most of the sorrows and sufferings which were confided to her without scruple."

Certainly no other English observer wrote with greater insight and sensitivity about slavery. Nor did Fanny ever allow her passion to cloud her judgment. The task system of the Butler Plantations was by no means representative of the South, where small slaveholdings were the rule. Nonetheless, Fanny's *Journal* skillfully brings to life a slave community and remains the finest insider's account of the actual conditions of slavery. The 1863 assessment of a reviewer for the *Atlantic Monthly* is just as true today: "A sadder book the human hand never wrote."

Museum of Fine Art, Boston

Chapter

§ 3 ❧

Charles Dickens:
The Great Quarrel with America

I can give you no conception of my welcome here," Charles Dickens wrote to a friend on January 31, 1842, shortly after his arrival in America. "There never was a king or emperor upon the earth so cheered and followed by crowds, and entertained in public at splendid balls and dinners, and waited on by public bodies and deputations of all kinds. I have had one from the Far West: a journey of 2,000 miles! If I go out in a carriage, the crowd surrounds it and escorts me home. If I go to the theatre, the whole house (crowded to the roof) rises as one man, and the timbers ring again. You cannot imagine what it is. I have 5 Great Public Dinners on hand at this moment, and invitations from every town, and village, and city in the States."

No foreign visitor has ever received such an enthusiastic and triumphant welcome as the Americans accorded the celebrated English novelist Charles Dickens on his 18-week tour. Not even the Beatles's reception on their first American tour matched the depth and intensity of feeling that Dickens generated across the entire spectrum of American society over a century earlier. And yet within weeks of his arrival he had embarked on what G.K. Chesterton called "his great quarrel with America." That quarrel, like his reception, was also of epic proportions, dwarfing even that of Mrs. Trollope.

One of a handful of writers who can be compared without embarrassment to Shakespeare, Dickens was the most beloved literary figure of his century. His books were bestsellers in every major European country from France to Russia. In England perhaps one in ten literate adults regularly read his novels. "It would be difficult to name any novelist of our own time who has so commanded the respect of serious criticism and at the same time reached anything like so widespread an audience," his modern biographer Edgar Johnson has written. More than any other English writer of his time, Dickens was the conscience of his age, employing his novels to attack a broad range of social abuses, injustices, and cruelties.

Novelist, dramatist, editor, journalist, actor, husband, father, and long-distance hiker—few writers in history have displayed such an incredible energy. "I write because I can't help it," Dickens admitted once to John Forster, his biographer and closest friend. His literary output alone totals 14 novels in 30 years (eight of them running almost 900 pages in modern reprints); five novelettes and 18 stories published for the Christmas season, of which *A Christmas Carol* is the best known; a half-dozen plays; two travel memoirs; a history of England; and scores of short stories, sketches, articles, and miscellaneous writings. He was also a voluminous letter-writer. The *Pilgrim Edition* reprints 13,452 of his letters in five thick volumes. "I hold my inventive capacity on the stern condition that it must master my whole life, often have complete possession of me, make it own demands upon me, and sometimes for months together put everything else away from me," he insisted.

No other artist was so ardent for public appearances and performances. In great demand as a public speaker, Dickens gave 115 speeches in his lifetime. In December 1853 he embarked upon the first of a series of public readings from his works; an 1861 tour included 47 appearances throughout England. In addition, Dickens mounted numerous dramatic productions with himself in leading parts and often took them on tour. "He was the stage-director, very often stage-carpenter, scene-arranger, property-man, prompter, and bandmaster," his friend Forster recalled in his biography. "Without offending any one he kept every one in order. . . . He adjusted scenes, assisted carpenters, invented costumes, devised playbills, wrote out calls, and enforced as well as exhibited in his proper person everything of which he urged the necessity on others. . . . He was the life and soul of the entire affair."

In spite of all these obligations, including that of being a father to ten children, Dickens still found the energy and time to edit one newspaper and three magazines. At his death he was busily at work on his fifteenth novel while editing *All the Year Round,* a weekly magazine with a circulation of 300,000.

Success came early to Dickens. In 1836 he began publishing serially his first novel, *The Pickwick Papers.* Almost overnight it became a bestseller and was soon selling 40,000 copies of each monthly number. Pickwick mania swept England. Pickwick hats, Pickwick cigars, Pickwick canes, and Pickwick coats appeared everywhere. Dramatic adaptations filled the London theaters. Booksellers hawked Pickwick sequels, parodies, and plagiarisms. "It is doubtful if any single work of letters before or since has ever aroused such wild and widespread enthusiasm in the entire history of literature," biographer Edgar Johnson insists. "Barely past the age of twenty-five, Charles Dickens had already become a world-famous figure beaten upon by a fierce limelight which never left him for the remainder of his life."

On the heels of his success, Dickens's responsibilities rapidly multiplied. He married Catherine (Kate) Hogarth on April 2, 1836. His first son was born on January 6, 1837. In November he accepted the editorship of a monthly magazine, *Bentley's Miscellany,* and a few months later began writing for monthly serialization his second novel, *Oliver Twist,* a sulfurous melodrama suffused with angry pathos. His popularity increased with each monthly installment. In April 1838 *Nicholas Nickleby* started its monthly serialization, and the first part sold an astounding 50,000 copies. The circulation passed the 100,000 mark for the final parts of *The Old Curiosity Shop* in late 1841. Dickens's melodramatic tale of the pathetic wanderings of the delicate child Little Nell and her senile grandfather, with a maniacal dwarf in pursuit, tugged at the public's heartstrings. No sooner had he completed that novel than he launched another, *Barnaby Rudge,* a historical romance set during the Gordon Riots of 1775. By then Dickens had emerged as the supreme example of the Victorian success story, whose life demonstrated to the fullest the Victorian virtue of self-reliance.

As 1841 drew to a close, Dickens had been writing without interruption for five years. Now he needed a sabbatical. He proposed to his publishers Chapman and Hall that he make a trip to America to gather material for a travel book. Anticipating yet another golden bestseller, they eagerly endorsed Dickens's plans. "I am . . . haunted by visions of America, day and night," he told Forster. "Washington Irving writes me that if I went, it would be such a triumph from one end of the States to the other, as was never known in any Nation."

Dickens looked forward to America with feverish enthusiasm, a pilgrim about to embark for the Promised Land. Always the reformer, he had long been optimistic about the American experiment. He firmly believed that in America under a republican system of government the daily practices of life would reflect the highest principles, whether in business, politics, or religion. There he hoped to find a freedom from the corruptions of feudal privilege, social injustice, and discredited snobbery that characterized English society. America would be a signpost pointing the way for England to follow. All his life Dickens had sympathized with the underdog. Hence, he was quick to defend the young, vigorous egalitarian republic against the charges of his countrymen. On his return, he expected to challenge the bestselling books of Frances Trollope and the other Tory travelers. Unlike them, he would travel with an open and receptive mind, resolving that "in going to a New World . . . [I will] utterly forget and put out of sight the Old [World] and bring none of its customs or observances into the comparison."

The Americans, for their part, looked upon Dickens as one of their own, a self-made man who aroused all their democratic feelings. They celebrated him as a young messiah of democracy and an embodiment of the American protest against English institutions, especially those of rank and class. A writer in the *Boston Evening*

Gazette insisted: "We are principally struck in Mr. Dickens's novels with his singular freedom from aristocratic feeling and influence. . . . He has dared to select as his heroes and his heroines . . . those who crouching at the base of the social structure had been looked upon as too low and contemptible, for any literary purpose, save that of the grossest ridicule. . . . This we think constitutes the true democratic feeling." Many Americans were certain that Dickens's pen would correct the aristocratic distortions of Mrs. Trollope.

"I cannot describe to you the glow into which I rise," Dickens on the eve of his departure wrote to Gaylord Clark, the editor of the American *Knickerbocker Magazine,* "when I think of the wonders that await us, and all the interest I am sure I shall have in your mighty land."

2

Dickens and his wife, Kate, sailed for Boston on January 4, 1842, on the Cunard steamer *Britannia.* The ship sported both sails and two huge steam-driven, side paddle wheels. The mixture greatly increased the risk of fire. A transatlantic crossing was hazardous and exhausting at any time, but especially so in midwinter. The ordinary British tourists who fanned out from England across Europe rarely ventured to America until much later when the speed, comfort, and safety of ships had undergone major improvements. Before 1850, travel to the States was largely limited to those with high motivation, unusual courage, ample time, and substantial income.

The small size of the *Britannia*'s cabins dismayed Dickens. "There are two horse-hair seats in it, fixed to the wall—one opposite the other," he wrote to a friend. "Either would serve for a kettle holder. The beds (one above the other, of course) might be both sent to you per post, with one additional stamp. The pillows are no thicker than crumpets." The dining saloon catered to 86 passengers and was little better. He thought it like "a gigantic hearse with windows in the sides" with a "melancholy stove at the end." But Dickens's happiness at the upcoming adventure to America was so great that he refused to lose his sense of humor over his accommodations, writing a friend that he "laughed so much at its ludicrous proportions that you might have heard me all over the ship."

The passage across the Atlantic was one of the stormiest in memory. Dickens was sick and terror-stricken for much of the trip. The ship's bright red smokestack had to be lashed down to keep it from toppling over in the gale-force winds and setting fire to the wooden planking with its red-hot sparks. "The agitation of a steam-vessel is, on a bad winter's night in the wild Atlantic, . . . impossible for the most vivid imagination to conceive," he recalled in *American Notes.* "She is flung down on her side in the waves, with her masts dipping into them, and . . . springing up again, she rolls over on the other side, until a heavy sea strikes her with the noise of a hundred great guns and hurls her back—she stops and staggers and shivers, as though stunned, and then with a violent throbbing at her heart darts onward like a monster goaded into madness, to be beaten down and battered and crushed and leaped on by the angry sea."

On the afternoon of January 22 the *Britannia* drew alongside the Cunard dock in Boston harbor, and Dickens had his first indication of the frenzied welcome awaiting him in America. "No sooner was it known that the steamer with Dickens on board was in sight, than the Town was pouring itself out upon the wharf!" noted one local observer. Even before the *Britannia* was securely tied down, a dozen men leaped on board with great bundles of newspapers under their arms. "'Aha!' says I, 'this is like our London Bridge': believing, of course, that these visitors were news-boys," an astounded Dickens wrote Forster. "But what do you think of their being EDITORS? And what do you think of their tearing violently up to me and beginning to shake hands like madmen?"

Dickens and Kate checked into the Tremont Hotel, one of

Boston's finest. ("It has more galleries, colonnades, piazzas, and passages than I can remember.") The next morning the Englishman donned his great fur-skin coat (described by the *Wooster Aegis* as "a shaggy coat of bear or buffalo skin that would excite the admiration of a Kentucky huntsman") and eagerly set out to explore the sights. Everything appeared new and fresh. "When I got into the streets upon this Sunday morning," he recalled later in *American Notes,* "the air was so clear, the houses were so bright and gay; the signboards were painted in such gaudy colours; the gilded letters were so very golden; the bricks were so very red, the stone was so very white, the blinds and area railings were so very green, the knobs and plates upon the street doors so marvelously bright and twinkling . . . that every thoroughfare in the city looked exactly like a scene in a pantomime."

Boston in 1842 was a prosperous city of 125,000 people, largely of English descent, with shade trees lining the well-paved streets. The Back Bay district had not yet been developed and was still a swamp. The city boasted 28 banks, six newspapers, two theaters, and eight railroad stations. Most British visitors thought its atmosphere more English and less foreign than other American cities. Boston was widely recognized as the intellectual center of the country.

On Tuesday morning Dickens visited the studio of Boston artist Francis Alexander to have his portrait painted. The Boston newspapers had announced the time of his first appointment. Long before that hour crowds of people thronged the sidewalk outside the Tremont House and silently and respectfully accompanied Dickens to Alexander's studio, several blocks away. They waited patiently for him to emerge two hours later and then escorted him back to his hotel. This was repeated each morning when he went to the studio. "The tone of society in Boston is one of perfect politeness, courtesy, and good breeding," he wrote later. He was dumbfounded at the number of people he met who were able to recite from memory long pages of text from his novels.

A reporter for a Wooster paper left behind a detailed word sketch of the 30-year-old Dickens: "We found a middle-sized person in a brown frock coat, a red figured vest, somewhat on the flash order, and a fancy cravat that concealed the collar and was fastened to the bosom in rather voluptuous folds with a double pin and chain. His proportions were well rounded and he filled the dress suit he wore. His hair was long and dark, grew low upon the brow, and had a wavy kink."

Armed with numerous letters of introduction, Dickens and Kate quickly plunged into a social whirl. On January 26 they attended a welcoming ball at Boston's elegant Papanti's Hall. There he met Richard Henry Dana, Jr., the author of *Two Years Before the Mast*; W. H. Prescott, at work on his monumental history of Mexico; and George Bancroft, another eminent historian. Dickens's brilliant crimson waistcoat, further ornamented by a profusion of gold watch chains, stood out conspicuously in the crowd of black satin waistcoats, then the national costume for gentlemen in America. "When my eye first fell upon him, I was disappointed," Dana recalled later. "But the instant his face turned towards me, there was a change. He has the finest of eyes; and his whole countenance speaks *life* and *action*—the face seems to flicker with the heart's and mind's activity. You cannot tell how dead the faces near him seemed."

Boston's lionization of Dickens quickly threatened to get out of hand. "How can I give you the faintest notion of my reception here," he wrote to his friend Forster, "of the crowds that pour in and out the whole day; of the people that line the streets when I go out; of the cheering when I went to the theatre; of the copies of verses, letters of congratulations, welcomes of all kinds, balls, dinners, assemblies without end?" William Story, the sculptor and poet, wrote his father on February 3: "People *eat* him here! Never was there such a revolution. Lafayette was nothing to it."

The initial excitement quickly wore away to frustration and then exhaustion. One evening Dickens met the energetic young mayor of Boston, Jonathon Chapman.

"Mr. Dickens, will you dine with me?" the mayor requested.

"I'm sorry," the Englishman replied. "I am engaged."

"Will you sup with me?" Chapman persisted.

"I am engaged."

"Will you lunch with me?"

"I am engaged."

"Will you breakfast with me?"

"I am engaged."

"Well, will you sleep with me?"

"Thank you, with the greatest pleasure," Dickens answered. "Nothing would gratify me more than to accept an invitation to sleep."

Whereas Frances Trollope had assessed American manners, Dickens was far more interested in the country's institutions. He quickly took advantage of every opportunity to visit factories, prisons, orphanages, churches, and asylums to determine "the social and political life of Americans." One of his first stops was the celebrated Perkins Institute for the Blind. He noticed immediately that, unlike in British institutions, the children were not forced to wear uniforms and thus kept their individuality. Dickens thought that very American. There he met Laura Bridgman, the Helen Keller of 1842. A cheerful 13-year-old girl, Laura was blind, deaf, and mute, without the ability to taste and smell. In spite of her handicaps Dr. Samuel Howe, the Institute's chief teacher, had broken through the barriers and taught her to read, write, feed and dress herself, and communicate with others by sign language. "Her face was radiant with intelligence and pleasure," Dickens noted. "Her hair, braided by her own hands, was bound about a head whose intellectual capacity and development were beautifully expressed. . . . The work she had knitted lay beside her. Her writing book was on the desk she leaned upon. From the mournful ruin of such bereavement there had slowly risen up this gentle, tender, guileless, grateful-hearted being."

There were additional visits to the State Hospital for the Insane ("admirably conducted on those enlightened principles of conciliation and kindness"); an orphanage for very young children where all the stairways and furniture were "of Lilliputian measurement;"

and a House of Reformation for Juvenile Offenders that embodied the philosophy of reclaiming "the youthful criminal by firm but kind and judicious treatment." Dickens toured Harvard University and came away full of praise. Unlike their British counterparts, he insisted, American universities "disseminate no prejudices; rear no bigots; dig up the buried ashes of no superstitions; . . . exclude no man because of his religious opinions; above all, in their whole course of study and instruction, recognize a world, and a broad one, lying beyond the college walls."

Dickens was most delighted with the famous woolen and cotton mills of Lowell, the best-known manufacturing city in the United States. Situated at the junction of the Merrimac and Concord rivers, the town possessed an abundance of water power that made it an ideal place for factories. When Dickens visited there, the mills employed more than 8,000 people, mostly women and young girls. From Lowell in an average year flowed over 40,000,000 yards of cotton goods. Francis C. Lowell, the inventor of the first American power loom, was a man of social vision who operated his mills without degrading labor. He paid high wages to daughters of New England farmers ($3 plus room and board for a 70-hour week) and provided strictly chaperoned dormitories. Many of these young women sought work in the factories because they had too much pride to enter domestic service. For a generation the Lowell factory girls with their neat dresses, correct deportment, and literary pursuits were one of the wonders of America. Their lot stood in sharp contrast to the wretched mill towns of England where tens of thousands of workers crowded together in miserable squalor in damp cellars.

Dickens found Lowell a model city—clean, fresh, neat. He visited woolen, carpet, and cotton mills. He learned that the women workers remained at their jobs for several years, saved some money for a dowry or paid off family debts, and then left to marry. After working 12-hour days, they often spent their evenings attending lectures and classes. He was amazed at their fine clothing, healthy complexions, and tidy bedrooms.

Immorality among the mill girls was virtually unknown. Three discoveries in particular stunned Dickens: the boardinghouses provided pianos; most of the women subscribed to a local library; and finally the women wrote, edited, and published a thick magazine of short fiction and poetry called *The Lowell Offering*. In *American Notes* he headed off British complaints that such activities were "above their station" by arguing: "Are we quite sure that we in England have not formed our ideas of the 'station' of working people, from accustoming ourselves to the contemplation of that class as they are and not as they might be?"

Dickens was enormously pleased with America during his first several weeks. "There is a great deal afloat here in the way of subjects for description," he wrote home on January 31. "I keep my eyes open pretty wide, and hope to have done so to some purpose by the time I come home." He was particularly impressed with the institutions he had visited in the Boston area, taking them as models against which he judged both those back in England and others he would visit elsewhere in America. "Boston is what I would like the whole United States to be," he stated as his stay there drew to a close.

Dickens left Boston on February 5 for Wooster and then traveled on to Hartford. He toured a local institution for the deaf and dumb, an insane asylum, and a prison. On February 8 he and some 70 guests attended a lavish banquet where the bill of fare listed more than 70 dishes. The evening marked a turning point in his relations with America and Americans. Dickens had long brooded over the issue of international copyright. Each day brought constant reminders of his enormous popularity in America. His books had sold hundreds of thousands of copies. Yet America had refused to sanction the international copyright. Publishers routinely pirated the works of English writers. To date Dickens had received just £50 from the American editions of his novels. He resolved to speak forcefully out on the issue, to use each and every appropriate occasion to demand that America become a signatory to the copyright agreement. He argued privately that such protection was equally important to Americans if they wished to have a strong and vigorous national literature. Yet popular opinion ran strongly against him on the issue. He was appalled to discover that many American writers were fearful to speak out. Others, such as James Fenimore Cooper and George Bancroft, took the position that literary creations were above the law and belonged to all mankind.

When the time came for Dickens to address the banquet in Hartford, he had worked himself into a combative mood on the issue of copyright. He advised his audience that he had "made a kind of compact" with himself to speak out on the subject. "I would beg leave to whisper in your ear two words, International Copyright," he told his listeners. He pointed out the great injustice suffered by the British novelist Sir Walter Scott who died "crushed in body and mind" by financial difficulties. With more than five million copies of his books sold in America, a copyright law would have saved him from these sufferings. "From the land in which his own language was spoken," Dickens lamented, not "one grateful dollar-piece . . . [came forth] to buy a garland for his grave."

The response to Dickens's speech was sharp and immediate. He was charged with conduct unbecoming a gentleman and abusing the hospitality of the United States by criticizing his hosts for mere monetary gain. "It happens that we want no advice upon this subject," the *Hartford Daily News* commented, "and it will be better for Mr. Dickens if he refrains from introducing the matter hereafter." The *New World* followed on February 12 with a more vigorous attack: "The time, place, and occasion taken into consideration—to us they seem to have been made in the worst taste possible." The same writer insisted that Dickens's popularity in America was a direct result of the absence of such a law, which allowed cheap, pirated editions of his work to reach the largest number of readers. And furthermore, the paper trumpeted, while fewer than 4,000 of the original monthly parts to a Dickens novel sold in America, the *New World* reprints of those same parts on its pages insured that more than 20,000 copies "were disseminated every week throughout the entire land."

Dickens was stunned, infuriated, and perplexed by the savage attacks on his stand, which suddenly appeared in many American newspapers after his Hartford speech. He had clearly misjudged the situation. Back in England he had successfully used his soaring popularity to negotiate more favorable terms from his publishers. He expected the same tactics to work on American publishers. But he was dead wrong.

"A stranger who injures American vanity, no matter how justly, must make up his mind to be a martyr," Alexis de Tocqueville had warned in *Democracy in America*. Dickens was about to discover that truth himself. Like a submerged rock shattering the hull of a speeding ship, the issue of international copyright would wreak havoc on his tour and good feelings toward Americans.

3

America in 1842 was in the final stage of a disastrous depression that had ravaged the country for almost five years. The crash was precipitated by a plunge in the price of cotton, the failure of the wheat crop of 1836, and the collapse of three English banking houses in early 1837. The mountain of debt and bad currency that had accumulated under the Jackson administration quickly collapsed. The situation soon became grave. Banks and mercantile houses failed, and riots broke out in New York over the high cost of flour. By 1841 some 400,000 bankruptcies had occurred. Several states defaulted on their bonds. Most of the capital for these public works bonds had been raised in England. On the international exchange the British pound sold at a premium while the American dollar was almost worthless.

The depression was especially hard on the American publishing industry. Prices for books plunged—from an average of $2 in the 1820s to around 50 cents in 1838. Major book publishers either folded or survived by the thinnest margins. In 1837 the leading American publisher Harper & Bros. of New York found itself unable to pay its English creditors. Publishers cut the annual number of new titles by two-thirds.

A mania for cheapness swept over the trade. Cheap newspapers and magazines suddenly proliferated, radically changing the nature of American publishing. They dominated the book trade and came to symbolize the worst in American journalism. The first of these was the weekly *Brother Jonathon,* which announced it would be "the largest folio sheet in the world." For a price of just six cents, readers could have the latest monthly installment of Dickens's newest novel, *Nicholas Nickleby. Brother Jonathon* was soon followed by the *New World* and a host of other imitators. By 1841 these leviathans had grown to absurd proportions, measuring almost six feet by four feet in size and boasting a surface area of 104 square feet of reading matter in 48 columns of tiny print. Most employed agents in London to buy the latest English books and magazines and rush them back to America. They often pirated an entire novel in a single issue. The big publications took the country by storm and quickly developed national markets. The speed with which the editors of these "mammoth" newspapers worked and the income which they diverted from the book publishers, to say nothing of English authors, is suggested by the following announcement in the November 12, 1842, issue of the *New World*:

> DICKENS'S AMERICAN NOTES was received by us at eight o'clock on Sunday evening. They make two octavo volumes in the English edition of six hundred pages. We printed them complete in a double extra number of the *New World* and issued them at one o'clock on Monday—being precisely seventeen hours from the time "the copy was put in hand."

The *New World*'s first printing of Dickens's book was for 24,000 copies. So heavy was the demand for the issue that within a month the newspaper had run off an additional 75,000 copies. The cost per copy was just 12 ½ cents.

Such practices outraged Dickens. "Is it not a horrible thing that scoundrel-booksellers should grow rich here [in America] from publishing books, the authors of which do not reap one farthing from their issue, by the scores of thousands?" he angrily wrote home to his brother-in-law. "And that every vile, blackguard, and detestable newspaper—so filthy and so bestial that no honest man would admit one into his house for a water-closet doormat—should be able to publish those same writings, side by side, cheek by jowl, with the coarsest and obscene companions . . . ? I vow before High Heaven that my blood so boils at these enormities that when I speak about them I seem to grow twenty feet high and to swell out in proportion. 'Robbers that ye are'—I think to myself, when I get upon my legs—'Here goes!'"

In 1842 the concept of an international copyright was still quite new. Parliament had passed legislation enabling England to become a party to such agreements only four years before. (Until then English publishers had routinely pirated the work of American authors.) Most European countries had not yet become signatories. French publishers pirated every bit as voraciously as did their American counterparts and even went one step further, counterfeiting first editions of English books and then smuggling vast quantities of these into the country where unscrupulous booksellers offered them illegally to customers at one-fourth the cost of the legitimate articles.

The English novelist had little knowledge of the American publishing and literary scene and woefully underestimated his opposition. No matter how much morality might suggest that literary piracy was simple robbery, Americans were deeply suspicious about international copyright and fearful that it would lead to the domination of their book trade by the larger British publishing houses. Furthermore, America was deep in a terrible depression (a fact that Dickens never appears to have realized), and few politicians were prepared to alienate the 200,000 Americans employed in the various branches of the publishing trade.

As a country, America at this time was akin to a modern underdeveloped nation, which recognizes its dependence on those more commercially and technologically advanced and desires the fruits of civilization in the cheapest and most convenient ways. Reprinting English literature seemed easy and inexpensive, and so America stole voraciously.

There were other, less obvious reasons why Dickens's efforts were doomed to failure. His 1842 trip occurred during a backdrop of unsettled Anglo-American controversies in which American feelings of Anglophobia ran high. A dispute over the boundary between Maine and New Brunswick, Canada, threatened to erupt into war between the two countries. When six Western states repudiated their bonds, British investors were outraged. "Americans have bubbled our citizens of about forty millions sterling," the *National Intelligence* bellowed. Such massive defaults struck indiscriminately at all classes, from pensioners to bankers. The London *Morning Chronicle* called the default "a fraud as enormous as ever disgraced the worst king of the most degraded nation of Europe." On the other hand, American passions were inflamed by a British insistence on the right to stop and search all ships flying the stars and stripes to search for slaves. The practice infuriated American nationalists. But equally inflammatory to British opinion was the American refusal to abolish slavery. By 1842 the situation between the two countries had degenerated to the point where the influential *Westminster Review* was moved to describe Anglo-American relations as "nothing but a state of unarmed hostility."

It was against this background that Dickens raised the issue of international copyright. Much as he was loved for his novels, many Americans started to suspect him of traveling as an agent for British publishers and authors.

4

On February 12 Dickens and Kate arrived in New York, then a city of some 300,000 people, and settled into a suite of rooms at the Carlton House. There he met for the first time the American author Washington Irving, who became his constant companion for the three weeks Dickens remained in New York. A highlight of his stay occurred two days after his arrival—the Boz Ball, a grand affair of lavish splendor held at the Park Theater. More than 3,000 people in evening dress attended, while another 5,000 had to be turned away. The theater's interior was decorated with festoons of bunting and draperies of white muslin, while 20 medallions representing scenes from Dickens's works hung on the walls. After the mayor received the couple, the three of them headed up a parade of dignitaries that circled the ballroom. Between the quadrilles and waltzes there were *tableaux vivants* of scenes from *The Pickwick Papers*, *Oliver Twist*, and his other novels. The crush of the crowd was overwhelming. "It was like dancing in a canebrake," one spectator observed, "the poor girls clinging to their partners to avoid being swept beyond their power to protect them." The reception so overpowered Dickens and Kate that they retired early to their hotel. The New York *Herald* published a special issue devoted to the event. "If he does not get his head turned by all this, I shall wonder at it," wrote Philip Hone, one of the organizers.

Hard on the heels of the Boz Ball came the great Dickens Dinner on February 18, presided over by a very nervous Washington Irving. Distressed over the controversy Dickens had stirred up after his Hartford remarks on the issue of international copyright, the organizing committee pleaded with him not to pursue the subject. But Dickens refused to give in. "I answered that . . . nothing would deter me," he wrote Forster. "The shame was theirs, not mine; and as long as I would not spare them when I got home, I would not be silenced here."

Dickens's reception in New York dwarfed even that in Boston. "Boz-mania" swept the city. "Imagine Kate and I—a kind of Queen and Albert—holding a Levee every day (proclaimed and placarded in the newspapers) and receiving all who choose to come," an astonished Dickens wrote home. He refused to have his hair cut for the first three months of his tour, joking that he feared "the barber (bribed by admirers) should clip it all off for presents." His concern was not farfetched. His fine fur coat had taken on a scraggly appearance because dozens of eager fans had plucked out tufts of hair for souvenirs of his visit.

Dickens still found time to explore New York City. He noted the streets jammed with a confusion of omnibuses, hackney cabs, gigs, phaetons, and private carriages. The city's splendidly attired women especially impressed him. "Heaven save these ladies, how they dress!" he exclaimed. "We have seen more colours in these ten minutes than we should have seen elsewhere in as many days. What various parasols! What rainbow silks and satins! What pinking of thin stockings and pinching of thin shoes and fluttering of ribbons and silk tassels and display of rich cloaks with gaudy hoods and linings!"

Dickens visited Wall Street and the Stock Exchange, then headed up Broadway toward the Bowery. Like Mrs. Trollope, he observed with consternation the hundreds of scavenger pigs with their scruffy brown backs, "like the lids of old horsehair trunks"; long, gaunt legs; and peaked snouts. "Here is a solitary swine lounging homeward by himself," he noted. "He has only one ear, having parted with the other to vagrant dogs in the course of his city rambles. . . . He is in every respect a republican pig, going wherever he pleases and mingling with the best society, on an equal if not superior footing, for every one makes way when he appears and the haughtiest give him the wall, if he prefer it."

Dickens saw no beggars on the streets. But because of his strong interest in the plight of the poor, he insisted upon a tour of the New York slums and found there poverty and wretchedness enough. One evening he climbed a flight of rickety stairs to the attic of a dilapidated tenement. He struck a match in the darkness. "The match flickers for a moment and shows great mounds of dusty rags upon the ground," he recalled later. "Then the mounds of rags are seen to be astir and rise slowly up; and the floor is covered with heaps of Negro women, waking from their sleep. . . . They have a charcoal fire within; there is a smell of singeing clothes or flesh, so close they gather round the brazier. And vapours issue forth that blind and suffocate. . . . Where dogs would howl to lie, women and men and boys slink off to sleep, forcing the dislodged rats to move away in quest of better lodgings." He walked through the Irish slums, where filth stood four feet deep in the streets, and found the conditions there no better. (By 1850, 133,000 Irish emigrants had crowded into an area between Broadway and the Bowery, America's worst slum. But most British visitors admitted they had seen much worse in London and Dublin.)

Dickens's initial enthusiasm for America had by now soured considerably. The cultural shock he had experienced upon arriving in America had been compounded by the unusual stresses of his trip. His status as a celebrity proved an increasingly heavy burden, costing him both his privacy and peace of mind. "I can do nothing that I want to do, go nowhere where I want to go, and see nothing that I want to see," he complained bitterly in a letter to Forster. "If I turn into the street, I am followed by a multitude. If I stay at home, the house becomes, with callers, like a fair." The constant overheating of American rooms further wore him out. "The effect upon an Englishman is very easily told," he insisted. "He is always very sick and very faint; and has an intolerable headache morning, noon, and night." And his wife, Kate, was miserably homesick.

Dickens's greatest disillusionment came during three days when illness confined him to his hotel rooms. Then for the first time he had the leisure to read at length the reports in the newspapers about his remarks on the issue of international copyright. He found himself attacked and insulted viciously by the very periodicals that most profited from the unscrupulous pirating of his novels. "I vow to Heaven that the scorn and indignation I have felt under this unmanly and ungenerous treatment has been to me an amount of agony such I never experienced since my birth," he insisted in a letter to Jonathon Chapman, the mayor of Boston. And to a friend in England, Dickens wrote in near despair: "I believe there is no country, on the face of the earth, where there is less freedom of opinion on any subject in reference to which there is a broad difference of opinion, than in this."

The dispute over international copyright quickly cost Dickens his sense of perspective, balance, and objectivity. Afterward his outrage over the piracy of his works colored his reaction to everything and everyone American. "This is not the Republic I came to see," he wrote to actor William C. Macready back in London. "This is not the Republic of my imagination. I infinitely prefer a liberal Monarchy . . . to such a Government as this. In every respect but that of National Education, the Country disappoints me. . . . In everything of which it has made a boast—excepting its education of the people and its care for poor children—it sinks immeasurably below the level I had placed it upon. And England, even England, bad and faulty as the old land is and miserable as millions of her people are, rises in comparison."

For Dickens, the great villains subverting American ideals were the newspapers, for which he developed an extreme hatred. In *American Notes* he insisted that until the press was elevated from "its present abject state, high moral improvement in that country is hopeless." He never lost an opportunity to savage them. In his novel *Martin Chuzzlewit*, when his hero arrives in America, the first sounds he hears are the cries of the newsboys hawking their papers:

>"Here's this morning's *New York Sewer!*" cried one. "Here's this morning's *New York Stabber!* Here's the *New York Family Spy!* Here's the *New York Private Listener!* Here's the *New York Peeper!* Here's the *New York Plunderer!* Here's full particulars of the patriotic loco-foco movement

yesterday, in which the Whigs was so chawed up; and the last
Alabama gouging case; and the interesting Arkansas duel
with Bowie knives."

Like most foreign visitors of the time, Dickens was astonished
at the unrestrained liberty of the American press and the amount
of personal abuse of public figures that the papers constantly
exhibited. His criticisms did not sit well with most Americans,
who were quick to point proudly to their press as a cornerstone of
their ideal of democratic equality.

His next stop after New York was Philadelphia. "It is a handsome city but distractingly regular," Dickens recalled. "After
walking about it for an hour or two, I felt that I would have given
the world for a crooked street." He visited the Eastern
Penitentiary, an experience that affected him profoundly. Crime
had fascinated him for years. As a young reporter, he had interviewed condemned prisoners in London's infamous Newgate
Prison. In the summer of 1840 he attended the execution of a
notorious murderer. In both *Oliver Twist* and *Barnaby Rudge* he
had explored at length the criminal mentality. Perhaps the most
celebrated American prison of its day, the Eastern Penitentiary
with its facade of a vast medieval fortress was opened in 1830.
Prison reform was a major issue in Jacksonian America, a time
when many believed that the moral rehabilitation of criminals was
an attainable ideal and should be made the chief object of the
prison system. As a consequence, American prisons introduced the
most advanced reforms in the world. The Eastern State
Penitentiary embodied the concept that the moral and mental
rehabilitation of the criminals, rather than simple punishment,
should be the goal of the penal system. This was to be achieved
through hard work and daily Bible readings in solitary confinement, which, it was hoped, would bring the prisoners to
repentance for their past deeds.

The Eastern State Penitentiary was designed as an octagonal
central tower from which extended seven long, one-storied corri-

dors, lined on both sides with cells, each designed for a single inmate. A massive wall surrounded the prison. Each cell had its own toilet, a private courtyard, and furniture. (Such features were virtually unknown in the world's prisons in the 1830s.) The prisoner was isolated in his cell for the length of his sentence, allowed no visits by family or friends, and forced to work with tools on tasks assigned him by the prison officials. The Bible was his only reading material.

Dickens thought the practice of solitary confinement cruel and wrong. "I believe that very few men are capable of estimating the immense amount of torture and agony which this dreadful punishment, prolonged for years, inflicts upon the sufferers," he observed angrily. "There is a depth of terrible endurance in it which none but the sufferers themselves can fathom and which no man has a right to inflict upon his fellow-creatures." He was particularly appalled at the reception prisoners received upon entering the prison. The prisoner was always brought there at night, then bathed and dressed in prison garb. A heavy black hood was then slipped over his head, and guards marched him to his cell, out of which he did not stir until his sentence had been completed. He was allowed no news whatsoever of his family or the outside world. The guards knew him only by a number.

Dickens spent an entire day in the prison and interviewed numerous inmates. "I looked at some of them with the same awe as I should have looked at men who had been buried alive and dug up again," he wrote later. One man, a former sailor, had spent 11 years in his solitary confinement and was due for release in several months. Dickens congratulated him on his impending return to the outside world. "It is his humour to say that he does not look forward to going out," he noted, "that he is not glad the time is drawing near; that he did look forward to it once, but that was very long ago; that he has lost all care for everything. It is his humour to be a helpless, crushed, and broken man."

From Philadelphia Dickens traveled to Washington, "the headquarters of tobacco-tinctured saliva." No other American habit so revolted him. "I can bear anything but filth," he complained to a friend. "I would be content even to live in an atmosphere of spit, if they would but *spit clean*. But when every man ejects from his mouth that odious, most disgusting compound of saliva and tobacco, I vow my stomach revolts, and I cannot endure it. The marble stairs and passage of every handsome public building are polluted with these abominable stains. They are squirted about the base of every column that supports the roof. And they make the floors brown. . . . It is the most sickening, beastly, and abominable custom that ever civilization saw."

If Dickens disliked Americans as a group, he responded warmly to certain Americans as individuals. He admitted an admiration of American courtesy ("travellers have grossly exaggerated American rudeness"), frankness, hospitality, and generosity. "When an American gentleman is polished, he *is* a perfect gentleman," he insisted in a letter of early March. "I have not travelled anywhere yet without making upon the road a pleasant acquaintance who has gone out of his way to serve and assist me. I have never met with any common man who would not have been hurt and offended if I offered him money for any trifling service he has been able to render me. Gallantry and deference to females are universal. . . . I have never once been asked a rude question, except by an Englishman—and when an Englishman has been settled here for ten or twelve years, he is worse than the Devil." But for Dickens America's faults always outweighed its virtues.

In Washington Dickens and Kate visited Congress. Familiar with conditions in the British Parliament from his days as a reporter, he noted with approval that the public's right to attend and have an interest in the proceedings was fully recognized. "There are no grim door-keepers to dole out their tardy civility by the six pennyworth," he added. There he met such distinguished men as John Quincy Adams, John Calhoun, and Henry Clay. The latter had been working unsuccessfully for five years to gain an American recognition of the international copyright. Dickens presented Clay with a petition to Congress from two dozen prominent American writers and editors urging immediate acceptance. He met, too, some "noble specimens" from the American West: "Splendid men to look at, hard to deceive, prompt to act, lions in energy . . . Indians in quickness of eye and gesture, Americans in affectionate and generous impulse."

Dickens had a short private meeting in the White House with President John Tyler, or "His Accidency," as many called to him. He had been elected Vice President in 1840 on a ticket with the aging General William Henry Harrison, whose inauguration day was the coldest on record. Harrison refused a coat and took more than 90 minutes to deliver his speech. He fell ill almost immediately with a dreadful cold that quickly developed complications. A month later he earned the distinction of being the first President to die in office. There was some question as to Tyler's new status. Was he the Vice President acting as President or had he become the actual President? Tyler insisted upon the latter interpretation, thus setting a precedent that has endured to the present day.

Dickens thought Tyler looked "worn and anxious." Their meeting was awkward. "Is *this* Mr. Dickens?" he asked when the Englishman was ushered into his office. "Sir," said Dickens, "it is." "I am astonished to see so young a man," the President replied. They shook hands and then sat down to stare in silence at each other for several minutes until Dickens excused himself. He and Kate returned on the evening of March 15 for a levee. The institution of the levee, or reception at which the President met all who wished to be present, was always a great novelty to British visitors. Most thought the informality and equality of these functions typically American. The crowds were often enormous. Some 2,000 people were present at the levee Dickens attended, and most were much more interested in shaking hands with him than with the President. "Wherever he moved, it was like throwing corn among hungry chickens," a reporter for the New York *Express* observed.

Each experience seemed to widen the gap between Dickens and his American hosts. After Washington, he made an excursion to Richmond where he had his first close look at slavery. A confirmed abolitionist, he had recoiled earlier in Washington and Baltimore from having to accept the services of slaves. His three days in Virginia proved an ordeal. On the train down he visited the black car and discovered a woman and her children weeping because they had been sold away from their husband and father. On a Richmond bridge he observed a notice against fast driving that read in part: "Penalty—for whites, five dollars; for slaves, fifteen stripes." He visited a plantation and walked through the slave quarters, "crazy, wretched cabins near to which groups of half-naked children basked in the sun or wallowed on the dusty ground." When a Southerner insisted that self-interest kept owners from abusing their slaves, an outraged Dickens answered angrily: "It is not in a man's interest to get drunk, or to steal, or to game, or to indulge in any other vice, but he did indulge in it for all that." He was greatly relieved when he finally left the South. "My heart is lightened as if a great load had been taken from it," he wrote Forster. "I really don't think I could have borne it any longer."

From Virginia the Dickenses headed toward Pittsburgh, traveling largely through undeveloped wilderness. He longed to see Indians camped among the trees. The Indians had long since fled the area, but Dickens was deeply moved by the beauty of much of the scenery. He wrote Forster: "The prettiest sight I have seen was yesterday when we—on the heights of the mountain and in a keen wind—looked down into a valley full of light and softness: catching glimpses of scattered cabins; children running to the doors; dogs bursting out to bark; pigs scampering home, like so many prodigal sons; families sitting in their gardens; cows gazing upward, with a stupid indifference; men in their shirt-sleeves looking on at their unfinished houses and planning work for tomorrow. And the train riding on, high above them. But I know this is beautiful—very—very beautiful."

Dickens and Kate traveled from Harrisburg to Pittsburgh by slow-moving canal boat in the company of 30 passengers jammed into a dirty, foul-smelling cabin hardly tall enough to allow a man room to stand erect. He quickly discovered the absence of amenities on the American frontier. At night a red curtain divided the cabin into halves. The women slept on one side, the men on the other, on three tiers of 16-inch-wide shelves. "You can never conceive what the hawking and spitting is, the whole night through," Dickens complained. "Upon my honour and word I was obliged this morning to lay my fur coat on the deck and wipe the half dried flakes of spittle with my handkerchief. And the only surprise seemed to be that I should consider it necessary to do so. When I turned in last night, I put it on a stool beside me. And there it lay, under a cross fire from five men." The next morning he found that the washing facilities for all the passengers consisted of two dirty towels, three small wooden basins, a mirror, two pieces of soap, a comb, and a brush.

At Pittsburgh Dickens boarded the river steamer *Messenger* for the trip to Cincinnati. The Ohio River suddenly brought home to Dickens for the first time the enormous size of America. "Think of what rivers are in this country!" he wrote in a letter back to England. "The Ohio is nine hundred miles long, virtually as broad as the Thames at Greenwich—and very often much wider."

The American steamboats fascinated him. "These Western vessels are foreign to all the ideas we are accustomed to entertain of boats," he wrote later. "I hardly know what to liken them to or how to describe them. They have no mast, cordage, tackle, rigging or other such boat-like gear; nor have they anything in their shape at all calculated to remind one of a boat's head, stern, sides or keel. Except that they are in the water, and display a couple of paddle-boxes, they might be intended . . . to perform some unknown service, high and dry, upon a mountain top." Because he had heard many horror stories of exploding boilers and frequent fires, he fitted his little group with life preservers and insisted they be worn the entire time they were on the river.

Dickens quickly found the curiosity of western Americans most annoying. No sooner had he boarded the *Messenger* than he was fastened upon by a stranger who first fired a fusillade of questions about his fur coat—where he bought it, how much it cost, what kind of fur it was—and then moved on to his watch "and asked what *that* cost and whether it was a French watch and where I got it and how I got it and whether I bought it or had it given me and how it went and where the keyhole was and when I wound it, every night or every morning, and whether I ever forgot to wind it at all, and if I did, what then?"

Like Mrs. Trollope before him, Dickens was appalled at the dining-room manners of his fellow passengers. They bolted their food, stuck enormous knives into their mouths, drank water rather than wine with their evening meals, and sat in such stony silence that "you might suppose the whole male portion of the company to be the melancholy ghosts of departed bookkeepers who had fallen dead at their desks."

(Five years later when George Ruxton traveled by steamboat to St. Louis on his way home from the Far West, he noticed a distinct improvement in the manners of Americans and attributed it to the widely publicized criticisms of Mrs. Trollope and Charles Dickens:

> I must say that since a former visit to the States, made three years ago, I perceived a decided improvement, thanks to the Trollope and Boz castigations, in the manners and con-duct of steamboat travellers and in the accommodations of the boats themselves. With the exception of the expectorating nuisance, which still flourishes in all its disgusting monstros-ity, a stranger's sense of decency and decorum is not more shocked than it would be travelling down the Thames in a Gravesend or Herne Bay steamer. There is even quite an arbi-trary censorship established on the subject of dress and dirty linen, which is, since it is submitted to by the citizens, an unmistakable sign of the times. As a proof of this, one evening as I sat outside the cabin reading, a young man, slightly "corned" or overtaken in his drink, accosted me abruptly:
>
> "Stranger, you haven't a clean shirt to part with, have you? The darned—(hiccup)—Capen says I must go ashore bekase my 'tarnal shirt ain't clean."
>
> And this I found to be the fact, for the man was actually ejected from the saloon at dinnertime, on his attempting to

take his seat at the table in a shirt which bore the stains of
julep and cocktail.)

Dickens arrived in Cincinnati just a dozen years after Mrs.
Trollope's departure. In that time the city had established itself as
the largest inland port in the nation, the supreme pork producer
in the world, the leading beer and liquor producer in the nation,
and the chief soap, furniture, shoe, and boat manufacturer in the
West. Pittsburgh washed itself clean with Cincinnati soap. New
Orleans ate Cincinnati ham. And every youngster studied
Cincinnati *McGuffey's Eclectic Readers.*

"Cincinnati is a beautiful city—cheerful, thriving, and animat-
ed," Dickens wrote later. "I have not often seen a place that
commends itself so favourably and pleasantly to a stranger at the
first glance as this does with its clean houses of red and white, its
well-paved roads, and foot-ways of bright tile. . . . The streets are
broad and airy, the shops extremely good, the private residences
remarkable for their elegance and neatness."

Dickens's party remained one night in Cincinnati. In the
evening they attended a large dinner party given by one of the
city's leading families, where he was introduced to "at least one
hundred and fifty first-rate bores." The occasion seemed to last
an eternity. "I really think my face has acquired a fixed expression of sadness from the constant and unmitigated boring I
endure," a weary Dickens wrote Forster. He took advantage of
the stay to visit one of the city's celebrated public schools. A class
of young girls—even in their elementary schools Americans separated the sexes—demonstrated their reading abilities while he
quizzed them to his satisfaction on world history. He was
impressed. The American school system was the envy of most foreign visitors. Dickens admitted admiration for the popular,
nonsectarian system of public schooling that extended into even
the wildest frontier settlements. The American commitment to
popular education at all levels of government contrasted sharply
with that of Parliament, which in 1842 voted only £30,000 for

education but £70,000 for the construction of the Royal Stables and Royal Dog Kennels at Windsor.

Dickens and his party departed Cincinnati on April 5 and traveled by steamboat to St. Louis. The river scenery generally bored him, but the Mississippi River impressed him by its wildness: "choked and obstructed everywhere by huge logs and whole forest trees, now twining themselves together in great rafts . . . , now rolling past like monstrous bodies, their tangled roots showing like matted hair, now glancing singly by like giant leeches, and now writhing round and round in the vortex of some small whirlpool like wounded snakes."

(While Dickens was making his way up the Mississippi River toward St. Louis, the American artist John Banvard was busy depicting the entire length of the river on canvas in his studio in Louisville, Kentucky. Two years earlier he had made his way alone in a small skiff along its entire length sketching the scenery with a goal of creating "the largest picture in the world." When he finished, Banvard's *Geographical Panorama of the Mississippi and Missouri Rivers* covered three miles of a canvas specially woven at Lowell, Massachusetts. Mounted on two enormous rollers, the great painting slowly unwound, presenting viewers with a continuous perspective of the river's length. Numerous steamboat captains and pilots testified to its accuracy. Dickens saw the panorama in London when it went on display at the Egyptian Hall in December 1848. "To see this painting is, in a word, to have a thorough understanding of what the great American river is," he observed. Banvard later painted a similar panorama of the Nile River.)

Dickens and his party arrived in St. Louis and checked into the Planter's House, the city's finest, where George Ruxton would stay several years later. By now Dickens was so bored that his traveling had degenerated to little more than a habit as he counted the days until he returned to England. His hosts arranged an overnight excursion to view the prairie. After a 12-hour journey, they arrived on the edge at sunset. Ahead to the horizon stretched a vast expanse of grassland. Beyond lay the West. Like America as a whole, it failed to live up to his expectations. "The widely famed

Far West is not to be compared with even the tamest portions of Scotland or Wales," a disappointed Dickens wrote to Forster. "The excessive flatness of the scene makes it dreary but tame. Grandeur is certainly not its characteristic." They sat in the grass, ate a picnic supper of ham, cheese, buffalo's tongue, roast fowls, and champagne, and watched the sun set in a burst of brilliant colors.

If Dickens was unimpressed with the West, the West in turn was not particularly impressed by Dickens. A local reporter took one look at his pretty looks, flowing locks, brightly colored vests, and outlandish clothes and dismissed him as "foppish," much to the Englishman's distress. But the judgment was accurate. Dickens was traveling much too quickly and superficially to appreciate, even remotely, the dynamics at work in the countryside around him. He was totally encapsulated in his egotism, unable to see America with the eyes of an immigrant, settler, or visionary. He rarely broke out of his own British provincialism. Like Mrs. Trollope before him, he had no appreciation of America as a vigorously expanding nation. He saw most Americans as crude, boastful, utilitarian, and wasteful, without ever understanding that these qualities suggested the temporary phase of an immature society, uncertain of its values and often retreating into arrogance to conceal its own uncertainties. He dismissed the rough settlements carved out of the wilderness and had only pity for the tough pioneers who lived there. To him a log cabin was a crude hut, not a transitory item of a pioneer society. The clearings and tree stumps were aesthetic blemishes, not new land ready for productive use. The earth was a mixture of decay and corruption, not rich organic material fertile and yet to be plundered.

On April 14 Dickens and his party gratefully turned toward home—by steamboat back to Cincinnati, by stagecoach to Sandusky, and by steamboat again across Lake Erie to Niagara Falls. The roughest part was the coach ride from Columbus to Sandusky over a corduroy road made by pressing tree trunks into the mud. "If you had only felt one of the least of the jolts with which the coach falls from log to log!" Dickens wrote to home. "It is like nothing but going up a steep flight of stairs in an omnibus."

When Dickens arrived at Niagara Falls, the sheer spectacle of the sight momentarily made all the hardships of his travel seem inconsequential. He stood at the foot of the mighty cascade "stunned and unable to comprehend the vastness of the scene." The experience provoked in him a religious communion with God. He felt "Peace of Mind, tranquillity, calm recollections of the Dead, great thoughts of Eternal Rest and Happiness."

After Niagara, Dickens made a brief excursion northward to the Canadian cities of Toronto, Montreal, and Quebec before heading south once again toward New York City. His last major stop was New Lebanon, New York, the headquarters of the Shaker church. The Shaker communities were one of the American wonders, visited by numerous foreign travelers. In 1842 they numbered perhaps 6,000 members living in prosperous contentment in 18 communities from Maine to Kentucky. The Shaker insistence upon absolute equality between men and women was revolutionary; many women embraced the faith as a refuge from marriage or the need to marry for economic and social security. The most distinctive feature of their worship was the group dance in which men and women, always apart, shuffled to a common and sometimes quite frenzied rhythm. They practiced both celibacy and communal living and devoted their lives to work. From out of the Shaker communities flowed a constant stream of inventions: the common clothespin, the flat broom, the circular saw, the apple parer, water-repellent cloth, and the pea sheller.

Dickens's party lingered in New Lebanon only a few hours. From a distance he observed the men at work in the fields with their "broadest of all broad-brimmed hats" but thought them "wooden." He stopped at the church and demanded to see a Shaker church service. To his dismay an elder denied him permission, explaining that all their religious meetings were closed to the general public. Later Dickens took his revenge on the Shakers in *American Notes* in his description of his brief visit to New Lebanon: "We walked into a grim room, where several grim hats were hanging on grim pegs, and the time was grimly told by a grim clock which uttered every tick with a kind of struggle, as if it broke the grim silence reluctantly and under protest."

As Dickens prepared to depart for England, he may have reflected on the extent to which his journey through America had been one of self-discovery. The man who boarded the sail packet *George Washington* on June 7 was very different from the eager writer who briskly stepped ashore at Boston four months earlier. He was a changed man, having been forced by his travels to reconsider both his politics and the nature of his allegiance to England. "I tremble for a Radical coming here, unless he is a Radical on principle, by reason and reflection," he wrote earlier, describing in effect his own political conversion. "I fear that if he were anything else, he would return home a Tory." And to Forster he wrote: "Apart from my natural desire to be among my friends and to be at home again, I have a yearning after our English customs and English manners, such as you cannot conceive."

5

"Charles Dickens has just come home in a state of violent dislike of the Americans and means to devour them in his next work," the novelist Mary Shelley wrote to a friend in 1842. His American experiences stayed with him like a festering abscess that refused to heal. "I very often dream I am in America again," he confided to a friend in 1843. "I am always endeavouring to get home again in disguise and have a dreary sense of the distance."

Dickens began work almost immediately on a travel book about his American experiences. "I have spoken very honestly and fairly," he insisted in a letter to Henry Wadsworth Longfellow on September 28, "and I know that those in America for whom I care will like me better for the book." He completed the manuscript in early October. Within two weeks his publishers had the book out under the title, *American Notes for General Circulation.* Dickens omitted all mention of his controversy over the matter of international copyright while criticizing America for faults that were not exclusively American. The result was a narrative that was both bland and misleading. When the *Edinburgh Review* asked the great historian William Macaulay to review it, he refused, pronouncing the book "at once frivolous and dull." Most critics agreed. *American Notes* met with almost universal condemnation from the British reviewers. *Blackwood's* dismissed the work as "a very flimsy performance" and worried that it would exacerbate belligerent nationalistic feelings: "We utterly . . . despise all those who would seek to set us against [Uncle Sam], by dwelling . . . with irresolute ill-nature on the weak parts of his character—needlessly wounding his vanity and irritating national feelings."

However, the impact of *American Notes* on the other side of the Atlantic was an altogether different matter. Thomas Carlyle later registered his surprise at "all Yankee-doodle-dom blazing up like one universal soda-water bottle" because of Dickens's book. No sooner had the first pirated copies hit the streets than an angry clamor went up. The critic for the *New York Herald* pronounced Dickens's mind "coarse, vulgar, impudent, and superficial" and his book "the essence of balderdash, reduced to the last drop of silliness and inanity." The fallout eventually did immense damage to Dickens's reputation in America.

Those passions were further inflamed the following year when Dickens began the monthly serialization of his next novel, *Martin Chuzzlewit,* a tale of the American dream gone sour. In the fifth installment he abruptly dispatched his title hero to America to make his fortune. From an unscrupulous speculator he buys land in a town called Eden, in distant Illinois, which proves to be a malaria-infested frontier settlement. He falls dangerously ill and almost dies. The satire is savage. At the end of his American stay, Martin redesigns the American eagle: "like a Bat, for its short-sightedness; like a Bantam, for its bragging; like a Magpie, for its honesty; like a Peacock, for its vanity; like an Ostrich, for its putting its head in the mud and thinking no body sees it."

Dickens's portrayal of America in *Martin Chuzzlewit* is entirely negative. He eliminated from his portrait all the good he saw during his 1842 visit, which he had acknowledged in *American Notes*. He concentrated instead upon the most unpleasant traits, isolated them into complete characters, and made them the central features of American personality and life to the exclusion of the positive attributes. He reduced America to a madhouse of sleazy business ethics, rampant lawlessness and violence, ravenous feeding, crass materialism, and insufferable bores. Typical of the heavy-handed satire is Dickens's portrait of a "typical" American patriot, Hannibal Chollop:

> He was much esteemed for his devotion to rational Liberty; for the better propagation whereof he usually carried a brace of revolving pistols in his coat pocket, with seven barrels a-piece. He also carried, among other trinkets, a swordstick, which he called his "Tickler" and a great knife, which (for he was a man of a pleasant turn of humour) he called "Ripper," in allusion to its usefulness as a means of ventilating the stomach of any adversary in a close contest. He had used these weapons with distinguished effect in several instances, all duly chronicled in the newspapers and was greatly beloved for the gallant manner in which he had "jobbed out" the eye of one gentleman, as he was in the act of knocking at his own street-door.

Most American reviewers and readers of *Martin Chuzzlewit* thought it an obscene libel on the people and nation. The depth of their passions against Dickens became apparent when his close friend William Macready, the greatest actor of his age, traveled to America in 1848 for a lengthy theatrical tour. Anti-British sentiment ran high. In May 1849, while he was playing in a production of *Macbeth* at the Astor Place Theater in New York, riots broke out. The first involved perhaps 500 persons in the theater and quickly resulted in Macready being driven from the stage. The editor of the *New York Herald* the next day charged Macready with provoking the riot by being "one of the Dickens' clique." More than 500 policemen and soldiers were on hand for Macready's next appearance. The streets outside the Astor Place Theater quickly filled with an angry mob variously estimated at 10,000 to 20,000. They stormed the theater, flinging flagstones and threatening to torch the building. The soldiers fired several volleys and charged the crowd. Thirty-one people died. Macready abandoned the stage in the final act and fled the theater wearing a disguise. He immediately cancelled his tour and returned to England, happy to be home "under the scrutiny of law and order and free from the brutal and beastly savages who sought my life in the United States."

6

Ironically, throughout the time that Dickens was denounced in America, his books continued to enjoy enormous popularity. (His death in 1870 brought forth something like a period of national mourning.) Twenty-five years after his first American tour he returned for a second time. For 15 years his public readings from his works had taken England by storm; and once more America beckoned. His backers there promised him a financial windfall. Dickens finally agreed to a tour of 76 readings. He was optimistic about his reception. "Since I was there before, a vast and entirely new generation has arisen in the United States," he told a group of well-wishers at a farewell banquet on the eve of his departure. "I am inspired by a natural desire to see for myself the astonishing change and progress of a quarter of a century over there." Dickens himself had gone through substantial changes. The Crusader had mellowed into the Elder Statesman, more tactful, better able to see both sides of an issue, and more willing to make allowances.

Dickens arrived in America on November 19, 1867. Seven thousand people gathered at the dock in Boston to greet him. He also learned that the ticket sales had exceeded all expectations. The line at the box office had started forming the night before and by early morning stretched more than half a mile. He was flabbergasted to learn that $14,000 had been taken in. "Mr. Dickens comes as a simple writer—to fill his pocketbooks," one paper trumpeted, "and, like a generous people, we are disposed to see that his wants are supplied. . . . If we succeed in propitiating the mighty genius, the title of his next volume will not be *American Notes* but *Greenbacks*." After the first reading (*A Christmas Carol* and the trial scene from *The Pickwick Papers*) an excited Dickens wrote home to his son: "Success last night quite beyond description or exaggeration. The whole city is quite fanatic about it today, and it is impossible that prospects could be more brilliant."

Dickens's welcome in New York City was even more tumultuous. After the readings sold out, scalpers started demanding and getting $100 a ticket. "An immense chord of feeling has been touched and sounded by Charles Dickens," a reviewer for the *New York Tribune* wrote after the first reading. "Something of this affectionate feeling was heartily expressed by his audience last night; not in all that great throng was there a single mind unconscious of the privilege it enjoyed in being able, even so partially, to thank Charles Dickens for all the happiness he has given to the world."

Dickens's "Second Coming," as the newspapers took to calling it, lasted until April 1868. He restricted himself to the eastern United States, traveling no farther south than Washington and west than Buffalo. Everywhere he observed vast changes in the America he had once known: "changes moral, changes physical, changes in the amount of land subdued and peopled, changes in the rise of vast new cities, changes in the growth of older cities almost out of recognition, changes in the graces and amenities of life, changes in the Press."

Two days before Dickens's departure, the *New York Times* editorialized: "At all previous times there had been a good deal of harsh language used about him for his American delineations. But his presence in the country put . . . a total stop to this. The American people acknowledge him a man of such noble genius, of such a large nature, of such fine humanity, of such beneficent life and works, that it is impossible not to entertain for him the admiration which these qualities instinctively call forth."

By the time Dickens sailed for England on April 22, his seventy-six readings had grossed $228,000, for a nightly average of $3,000. After expenses this equaled £20,000. (The most money one of his English reading tours had generated was £13,000.) Dickens had finally realized his American Dream.

Perhaps the best summary of Dickens's relationship with America was that by Britisher Michael Slater, a modern Dickens scholar with the University of London. He writes:

> The truth is, I think, that Dickens was a natural American and therefore had just the same love/hate relationship with America as he had with the country of his birth. In his touchy pride, his ruthless energy, his unwavering belief in the rewards of industry, his rejection of the past, and his faith in the future Dickens was very much an American. Had he not been so American in his idealism in 1842, moreover, he would never have been so bitterly bewildered and disappointed by the imperfections he found obtruding themselves on him as he travelled around the country. With a much deeper truth than the late President Kennedy claiming to be a Berliner, Dickens might have said, "I am an American."

Part

2

The Far West

The possible destiny of the United States of America—as a nation of a hundred millions of freemen—stretching from the Atlantic to the Pacific, living under the laws of Alfred and speaking the language of Shakespeare and Milton, is an august conception," the great British Romantic poet Samuel Taylor Coleridge enthused in the April 10, 1833, number of his popular "Table Talk" column. "Why should we not wish to see it realized? America would then be England viewed through a solar microscope; Great Britain in a glorious state of magnification."

Americans thought so, too. They proclaimed in the 1840s that they had a "Manifest Destiny" to expand and occupy the vast undeveloped regions of the southern and western portions of their continent, and extend their country's territory all the way to the Pacific Ocean. This doctrine was cited as a powerful reason for the declaration of war against Mexico in 1846 and the earlier annexation of Texas. Eventually, the doctrine would lead to the American purchase from Russia of the Alaska territory in 1867 and the annexation of the Hawaiian Islands in 1900.

"Democratic nations care little for what has been, but they are haunted by visions of what will be," de Tocqueville observed in *Democracy in America* in 1835. " In this direction their unbounded imagination grows and dilates beyond all measure. Their eyes are fixed upon their own march across these wilds, draining swamps, turning the course of rivers, peopling solitudes, and subduing nature. This magnificent image of themselves does not meet the gaze of Americans at intervals only; it may be said to haunt every one of them in his least as well as his most important actions and to be always flitting before his mind."

The specific trigger for the great westward push was, of course, the discovery of gold by James Marshall on January 24, 1848, at Sutter's Mill on the American River in northern California. This brought about the greatest stampede in U.S. history. The Eastern newspapers whipped the gold fever to a frenzy with exaggerated reports of the riches of the California strike. "Lumps of gold have been picked up," one account insisted, "each large enough to make a crown." Favorite tales, frequently rerun as gospel by irresponsible editors, included the one about the housewife who collected $25,000 in gold dust when she shook out her husband's clothes at the end of the day after he had returned from working his claim. Within two years the population of the California territory had swelled from 14,000 to more than 90,000. Congress voted California statehood in 1850. The millions of ounces of gold that the miners wrestled out of the streams and hillsides of the Mother Lode country altered the economy of the entire world. (As a footnote, the California Gold Rush also created a tremendous demand for the improved models of the popular Colt revolvers. They were shipped westward by the tens of thousands.)

The discovery of gold in California and the available of good, cheap land there and in Oregon were the two magnets that produced an irresistible wave of migration that nothing could have stopped. If Indians got in the way, then the Americans rushing westward had just one Indian policy—stand aside or be killed. Within ten years the trickle of emigrants had swelled to a river. Prior to 1845, fewer than 20,000 Americans lived west of the mighty Mississippi River, about the time that an untamed spirit of Manifest Destiny swept across the country. By 1860, the burgeoning Western states claimed a population of about 500,000 emigrants who had surged out of the eastern states. By then, the frontier had been squeezed inward. However, the Great Plains and Rocky Mountains remained a wilderness long after the crowds of settlers in their covered wagons had crossed the continent and even after the telegraph and railroad had connected the two coasts.

Most of the settlers got their start in St. Joseph, Missouri. In 1850 W. S. McBride noted in his diary that "St. Joseph resembled in some respects a vast besieged city. . . . All the principal roads leading to the town were thickly beset with white tents. . . . Auctioneers were selling mules & horses and all kinds of merchandise all through the streets. Music of every variety could be heard from the groceries and gambling houses. Intelligent looking men, ignorant men, dandies, clownish & old gray head men & negligently clothed men, beardless boys, Negroes, Indians, and all sorts of men could be seen crowding along together. . . . Minstrel girls promenaded the streets singing, 'Oh California, that is the land for me,' with great crowds of men and boys following them."

Many of the settlers traveled heavily armed. "We were well equipped, each man carrying in his belt a revolver, a sword, and a bowie knife; the mounted men having besides a pair of holster-pistols and a rifle slung from the horn of their saddles, over and above which there were several shotguns and rifles suspended in loops where they could be easily accessible," William Kelly recalled after his trip across the country to the California gold fields.

But the actual risk of violent death or injury at the hands of the Indians was wildly exaggerated during these early years before the Civil War. Disease was always a much greater threat. Historian Bil [sic] Gilbert observed, "Between 1840 and 1850 an estimated 5,000 of the 90,000 men, women, and children who made the overland crossing died en route. Only 115 people were killed by Indians, usually in retaliation for unprovoked assaults committed by nervous, trigger-happy emigrants or racial fanatics. Travelers' memoirs suggest that more people drowned or were killed or maimed in firearms accidents. Many emigrants said that, in retrospect, they had felt more threatened by careless gunplay in their own companies than by hostile natives."

The most amazing aspect of the Western settlers' whole achievement was the incredible speed with which they transformed a wilderness into a civilized, populous, and prosperous commonwealth. This had been true of the settlement of the Eastern frontier in the second half of the eighteenth century, and it was equally true of the Western frontier. Between 1855 and 1873 the development of the Great Plains and the Far Western frontiers became increasingly dominated by large capital concerns (particularly the railroads and mining interests) rather than by the individualistic settlement patterns of the agrarian frontier. By 1880 the increased levels and importance of trade and capital accumulation, which had come to dominate the American economy in the eastern half of the United States, were also profoundly changing the character of the Western states, as Oscar Wilde was to learn on his 1882 tour.

As the West matured, the level of violence there decreased dramatically. The "shootists," or gunfighters as they are called today, lie at the heart of the mythology of the American West. They were spawned by the conditions of the time when a man's best friend was his gun and vast areas of the West lacked any organized law. For some years in certain parts of the Western frontier the line between the lawman and the outlaw was often poorly defined and varied from circumstance to circumstance and place to place.

"Westerners were people used to making on-the-spot decisions who were contemptuous of the Easterners' obsession with legal formalities, an attitude that in some areas still survives," historian Joseph G. Rosa observed in *Age of the Gunfighter*. "The Westerners held similar views on law and order. What suited the Easterner, used to the courts and due process, meant little to a man in the wilds of Wyoming or the Great Plains who had stock rustled. . . . Where no law existed, or it was too extended to rely upon, people tended to take care of their own problems."

Or, as a common expression of the time asserted, "There is more law in a Colt six-gun than in all the law books."

Each of the Western states progressed, often quite rapidly,

through an initial period of lawlessness that was soon followed by the growth of vigilante movements designed to bring law and order to the disputed territory. Most became reasonably civilized within a decade after gaining statehood.

But even at its most violent the West was never as violent as popular mythology and Hollywood would have us believe. Historian W. Eugene Hollon once interviewed dozens of elderly people who had helped settle the Oklahoma Territory in the late 1880s and early 1890s about what they remembered most from those years. He found that the extreme loneliness and almost total lack of excitement in their lives were the most significant traits of frontier life in those final years of the nineteenth century. He also investigated through public records and local newspapers the history of homicide in several of the most notorious towns where, according to legend, shootings and killings were an almost-nightly occurrence. In actual fact, killings were uncommon, rarely exceeding five a year, even in the most dangerous towns.

"Deadwood, South Dakota, has long been a favorite example of one of the most violent frontier mining towns that ever existed," Hollon argued in *Frontier Violence: Another Look*. "It was here, in 1876, that [Wild Bill] Hickok was shot in the back while playing poker in a local saloon. Yet only three other killings took place in Deadwood that year. . . . Other crimes were committed, but the lawless aspect of the community's early history has been greatly over-emphasized to the exclusion of other factors which made significant contributions to the town's stability and permanence."

In fact, the East boasted a much higher incidence of violence for much of the nineteenth century than did the West. George Armstrong Custer and some 250 of his soldiers died at the battle of the Little Big Horn on June 25, 1876, but more than 1,500 civilians perished in the Anti-Draft Riots that occurred in New York City in 1863. Violent crime and death were rampant in many of America's largest Eastern cities throughout the second half of the century. And, finally, hundreds of thousands of American soldiers died in the bloody conflicts of the Civil War, most of which were fought on Eastern, not Western, soil.

Still, the myth of the American West continues to loom large in our collective imagination. "Our basic myth is that of the frontier," Garry Wills wrote near the end of his fine book *John Wayne's America*. "Our hero is the frontiersman. To become urban is to break the spirit of man. Freedom is out on the plains, under the endless sky."

In the next two chapters we shall see that the English visitors, George Ruxton and Captain Richard Burton, explored the West during two very different stages of its development. When Ruxton visited the remote fastness of the Colorado Territory during the winter of 1846–1847, he found himself in a pristine wilderness where only a handful of whites had ever penetrated. When Burton rode his stagecoach from St. Joseph to Salt Lake City in 1860, the westward tide of migration and development had totally transformed the Great Plains and reduced its once vast buffalo herds to just a handful of stragglers.

Chapter

§ 4 ◊

Ruxton of the Rockies

In the spring of 1847 at Fort Leavenworth, on the Indian frontier, a group of U.S. Army soldiers stood staring at a remarkable figure clad in fringed buckskin that was decorated with porcupine quills and stained with buffalo grease. A crimson turban shaded a clean-shaven face tanned to a deep mahogany. His long, unwashed hair hung in Indian fashion over his shoulders. Across one arm he cradled a double-barreled rifle of English manufacture. The troopers quickly fell into an argument over the Indian's tribe.

"That's a Pottawatomie," said one. "You can tell by his red turban."

"How long have you been in the West," cried another, "not to know a Kickapoo when you see him?"

"Pshaw!" exclaimed a third. "That's a white trapper from the mountains. A regular mountain boy that, I'll bet a dollar."

One skeptical soldier squinted closely into the face of the mysterious man, then turned to his comrades and said, "Well, boys, I'll just bet you a dollar all round that Injun's no other than a British officer. Wagh! And what's more, I can tell you his name."

As the perceptive soldier recognized, the Indianized white man was George Augustus Frederick Ruxton—a British subject, a veteran of a Spanish civil war, a former officer in the 89th Foot Regiment, and a traveler with remarkable powers of survival and endurance. Few men have crowded so much adventure into so few years. He had just completed an extraordinary 2,000-mile trek through Mexico and the Rocky Mountains. Perhaps no other nineteenth-century British traveler to America faced such difficulties, both human and natural, as Ruxton on his journey of discovery. Yet few visitors achieved such a sympathy for the West as this Englishman did for his beloved Rocky Mountains. Later he would write:

> Although liable to an accusation of barbarism, I must confess that the very happiest moments of my life have been spent in the wilderness of the Far West; and I never recall but with pleasure the remembrance of my solitary camp in the Bayou Salado, with no friend near me more faithful than my rifle, and no companions more sociable than my good horse and mules, or the attendant coyote which nightly serenaded us.

Ruxton also achieved an intense bond with the legendary mountain men, the trappers who roamed the Rocky Mountains in pursuit of beaver. He shared their lodges, listened to their stories, mastered their dialect and lore, and fought with them against Indian war parties. His travel book, *Adventures in Mexico and the Rocky Mountains,* and a novel, *Life in the Far West,* together present the most authentic, colorful, and complete portrait of the mountain man and his time that has ever been written. Had he not died at 27, Ruxton might have gone on to greatness as both an explorer and novelist.

George Ruxton was born on July 24, 1821, on a country estate in Oxfordshire, the third of six sons. His Irish father was John Ruxton, a surgeon with the 24th Dragoons, and his Scottish mother the daughter of an officer with the East India Company. Both families boasted long lines of soldiers and adventurers. His parents filled Ruxton's youthful mind with tales of ancestral derring-do. In later years he recalled his early enthusiasm for adventure: "My memory carries me back to the fourth year of my age. Even then I was a vagabond in all my propensities, for there was not a dark closet or interdicted staircase or corner under taboo of nursemaid that I had not explored ready to battle with the bogy who, the nursery legends affirmed, inhabited it and devoured the naughty children who were rash enough to enter his retreat."

Ruxton's father died when he was eight, and he grew up under the indulgent control of his mother. His studies were desultory at best, little more than a succession of scrapes and mischief. Later he confessed: "Everything like restraint, and consequently all application to studies, were irksome to me." When he was 13 his mother enrolled him in the Sandhurst Royal Military Academy where he "learnt to drink and smoke, to say nothing of the art of wiring hares and rabbits, and other accomplishments too numerous to mention."

Ruxton found the regimen at Sandhurst stultifying. Matters were hardly helped by his discovery of James Fenimore Cooper's popular novels that make up "The Leather-Stocking Tales." The impressionable youth eagerly read of Natty Bumppo's adventures on the American frontier in the company of his Mohican sidekick. "I was now a strong, active boy of fifteen, with a mind filled to the overflow with a love of adventure and excitement," he recalled later. "Everything quiet and commonplace I detested, and my spirit chafed within me to see the world and participate in scenes of novelty and danger."

Ruxton's contempt for the military academy, coupled with a disregard for its rules, led to his expulsion after two years. He was 16 years old, handsome, powerfully built, and utterly unrepentant. Eager for adventure and military action, he turned his eyes south to Spain where a civil war raged in which the forces of the Pretender, Don Carlos, sought to unseat the nine-year-old Queen Isabella II. The English youth sought adventure rather than a cause—but Isabella's plight appealed to his romantic nature, and he determined to join the British legion fighting there on behalf of the Spanish queen. Ruxton quickly sailed from England to Le Havre and made his way through France, arriving at the Spanish frontier on a snowy December day in 1837. After showing his passport, he crossed into Spain. He recalled the moment later: "With a cry of delight I threw my cap into the air and hurrahed for Spain—Spain, land of love and war, of romance and robbery, of murder and miracles, of curiosities and contrarieties."

In Navarre, Ruxton was commissioned as a Cornet of Lancers in the British Auxiliary Legion attached to the regular Spanish division commanded by General Diego Leon, where he served with distinction for 18 months. For his part in the assault on the fortified town of Belascoain he was made a knight of the first class of the Order of San Fernando. He fought in the bloody battle at Tafalla on December 2, 1838, where he and his squadron of 100 cavalry soldiers suddenly found themselves surrounded by 800 Carlists. The British fought like fiends. "Cut and stab was the order of the day," Ruxton wrote later. "After showing fight for some time, the [Carlists] fairly turned tail and ran for it, leaving three hundred on the field. No quarter was given or expected, and a scene of butchery commenced which defies description."

Ruxton returned to England, a decorated military veteran at the age of 17. (His side had won the civil war for the Spanish queen.) Almost immediately he was granted a commission as a lieutenant in the 89th Foot Regiment. The youth who just two years before had been expelled in disgrace from Sandhurst now found himself a distinguished officer of the prestigious Royal Irish Fusiliers. In the summer of 1841 he was ordered to the Canadian frontier along the Detroit River. He was beside himself with excitement. The station promised excellent hunting, Indians, and the adventure of a true wilderness.

In Canada, Ruxton quickly befriended several Indian hunters and spent long days in the woods with them, learning their ways. He developed a real affection for his Indian mentors. "People at home are much mistaken in thinking that the North American Indian is now rarely if ever met with in anything like his original character," he wrote later. "In some parts . . . they maintain their old customs and live as primitively as in the days when the Leatherstocking and the Mohican chief followed the Mingo Trail in the woods of the Susquehanna."

In the spring of 1844 Ruxton returned to England. He was soon bored, but then an event happened that changed his life. On May 13, 1846, the American Congress, at the insistence of President James Polk, declared war on Mexico. Ruxton was no longer a soldier. But wars provided plenty of opportunity for the kind of adventure for which he hungered. He decided upon a lengthy overland journey through Mexico into the remote frontier of New Mexico. The authorities issued him credentials stating that he represented British commercial and diplomatic interests. One of his duties apparently was to check on the British share of the lucrative overland trade from the United States into Mexico by way of the Santa Fe Trail. It was a good cover. But Ruxton had ideas of his own. His official responsibilities would end upon his arrival in Santa Fe, but northward lay the Rocky Mountains, an enormous region populated only by Indians and a handful of mountain men. It was as remote, exotic, and unknown to most Englishmen as the unexplored regions of Africa. Ruxton determined to go there. On July 2 he sailed from Southampton for Mexico. Ahead loomed the greatest adventure of his life.

2

Manifest Destiny.

That two-word phrase more than any other sums up the major forces at work in the America of the 1840s. The editor John O'Sullivan sounded a trumpet call for the entire country when he proclaimed in his newspaper, "Our manifest destiny . . . [is] to overspread the continent allotted by Providence for the free development of our yearly multiplying millions." The term "Manifest Destiny" quickly became the rallying cry of the Democratic Party and the theme of numerous orations, editorials, and political speeches. It implied the inevitability of the continued territorial expansion of the United States into the undeveloped continental areas to the west and south.

The lodestone of the West tugged deeply at the American heart. "Eastward I go only by force, but westward I go free," Henry David Thoreau insisted. "I should not lay so much stress on this fact if I did not believe that something like this is the prevailing tendency of my countrymen. I must walk toward Oregon and not toward Europe." A popular joke of the times insisted that the first question asked of St. Peter by Americans arriving at the Pearly Gates was, "Which way is west?" The pioneers who packed their belongings and families into the big canvas-topped wagons and headed West toward Oregon and California in 1846 would have endorsed Alexis de Tocqueville's observation in *Democracy in America* that the continual westward thrust exhibited a "providential solemnity." The hand of God seemed to push them forward.

In the spring of 1846 some 2,500 Americans gathered at places like St. Louis, Fort Leavenworth, and Independence, awaiting the springtime growth of the prairie grass before starting across the Great American Desert toward the Pacific coast. Ahead lay the American Eden, where fertile lands waited only the magic touch of man to produce wealth. Many carried copies of Lansford W. Hastings's *The Emigrants' Guide to Oregon and California*; he recommended per-person rations of 200 pounds of flour or corn meal, 20 pounds of sugar, and ten of salt, plus a supply of beads, tobacco, knives, and fishhooks for trade with the Indians. The trip was costly, $1,000 or more for a family. The expense alone largely kept out the riffraff and poor, at least until news of the California gold strike splashed across the front pages of the country's newspapers. "The majority [of our fellow travelers] were plain, honest, substantial, intelligent, enterprising, and virtuous," observed the Virginian Jessy Thornton, who set out that year for Oregon. ("The notion that the free lands on the frontier served as a 'cushion' to our cyclical depressions is textbook economics," historian Bernard DeVoto has argued. "Only a small fraction of the dispossessed ever 'went west' at any time—they simply could not afford to—and the fraction grew smaller as the frontier got farther from the industrial districts.")

The hundreds of westward-bound emigrants in 1846 included two groups destined to imprint themselves upon the American imagination. On March 1 a large number of Mormons pointed their wagons across Iowa toward the "Garden of Eden" their leader Brigham Young had promised them awaited in the remote valley of the Great Salt Lake. And on the morning of April 16 in Springfield, Illinois, the families of George Donner and James Reed yoked their oxen to nine wagons and headed West. Eventually the Donner-Reed party would swell to 87 people. Far ahead lay the high passes of the Sierra Nevada Mountains, where in late October they would find their way blocked by early winter snows. Trapped in a long ordeal of fierce cold and starvation, some of the few survivors of the Donner party would survive into 1847 only by resorting to cannibalism.

In 1846 James K. Polk was President of the United States. Hard, dour, with little imagination, he was not the man to inspire or rouse the people. He had served as the Speaker of the U.S. House of Representatives and the governor of Tennessee when, at the Democratic national convention in 1844, he was trotted out as the first dark horse in a presidential race. His opponent was the celebrated Whig Henry Clay. Polk won the election largely on the basis of his unequivocal stand in favor of Manifest Destiny, which perfectly suited the country's expansionist mood.

If Polk had looked at a map of the United States on January 1, 1846, he would have seen a very different country from the one we know today. The Pacific Northwest, comprising the present states of Washington, Oregon, and Idaho, was known simply as "Oregon" and was occupied jointly by the United States and Great Britain. Only three days before, the state of Texas had joined the union. Mexico refused to recognize the legitimacy of Texas statehood and threatened war. All the land beyond Texas to Oregon, including the present states of New Mexico, Arizona, California, Nevada, Utah, and much of Colorado and Wyoming, was marked on Polk's map as Mexican Territory and consisted of two large provinces called "New Mexico" and "California."

California, in particular, was only weakly held. Far removed from its parent government in Mexico City, it lacked authority, finances, and an effective army. By 1846 some 800 American farmers and trappers had moved there, most to the Sacramento Valley, Napa Valley, and San Francisco Bay area. They settled comfortably into the pastoral society of the Mexican Californians, a happy people who raised great herds of cattle in a land of eternal spring. One of these was William L. Todd, a nephew to Mary Todd (Mrs. Abraham) Lincoln, whose husband was the gangling Congressman from the Seventh District of Illinois. In a letter to his aunt dated April 17, William Todd stated prophetically: "The Mexicans talk every spring and fall of driving the foreigners out of the country. They must do it this year or they can never do it. There will be a revolution before long and probably the country will be annexed to the United States."

Soon after his election, Polk set about aggressively to secure his primary objectives of Oregon, California, and New Mexico. The first of these to be realized was Oregon, home to 7,000 Americans, most of whom had emigrated there in the previous four summers to settle in the Willamette and Columbia valleys. In 1818 the United States and Great Britain had agreed to a joint occupation of the disputed territory. In 1846 each country claimed the region by right of exploration and settlement. Imbued with a sense of Manifest Destiny, Americans demanded an end to the British interest in the region. Tempers ran high on both sides. For a time it looked as though the dispute might provoke a war. In June Polk settled the thorny Northwest boundary controversy, and the United States gained title to the Oregon country south of the 49th Parallel.

Polk was equally determined to have both California and the vast territory of New Mexico, by purchase if possible, by war if necessary. When negotiations collapsed, the President ordered American troops into the disputed area between the Nueces and Rio Grande rivers and provoked a skirmish with Mexican troops. On May 13 Congress passed a declaration of war. Soon afterward an army under the command of Zachary Taylor invaded Mexico. Stephen Watts Kearny, a veteran of the War of 1812, led a second force down the Santa Fe Trail, which ran from Independence, Missouri, to the New Mexican capital. On August 18 Santa Fe fell to the Americans without a shot being fired. Kearny divided his army and hurried toward California while Colonel Alexander W. Doniphan, a frontier lawyer, led his 900 Missouri volunteers deeper into Mexico toward Chihuahua.

The Mexican War was American expansionism in action, justified by an idealistic commitment to Manifest Destiny. "The *untransacted* destiny of the American people is to subdue the continent—to rush over this vast field to the Pacific Ocean—to animate the many hundreds of millions of its people, to cheer them upward . . . to confirm the destiny of the human race—to carry the career of mankind to its culminating point," William Gilpin, a major with Doniphan's Missouri volunteers, wrote home from the heat, thirst, and sickness of New Mexico.

3

On July 2, 1846, just two days before John C. Fremont proclaimed California the independent Bear Flag Republic, George Ruxton sailed from Southampton for Mexico, arriving in Vera Cruz in early August. He found the city "dreary and desolate beyond description," its former prosperity drained away by a corrupt military despotism. On July 16 he watched as a steamer from Cuba brought home General Antonio Lopez de Santa Anna, the man who had slaughtered the Texans at the Alamo, to assume the reins of the Mexican government. Ruxton described him as "a hale-looking man between fifty and sixty, with an Old Bailey countenance and a very well built wooden leg." With Santa Anna was his bride, a pretty girl of 17. Ruxton attended a reception for the general and was distinctly unimpressed. "His countenance completely betrays his character," he wrote later. "Oily duplicity, treachery, avarice, and sensuality are depicted in every feature, and his well-known character bears out the truth of the impress his vices have stamped on his face." In a speech, Santa Anna proclaimed his intention to win the war against the United States and his willingness to sacrifice his life and fortune in the defense of Mexico.

Armed with a double-barrel rifle, a carbine, two pistols, and a blunderbuss, Ruxton made his way by coach toward Mexico City. He quickly learned, to his disgust, that bandits roamed the countryside with impunity, plundering and murdering travelers without fear of retribution. "In a country where justice is not to be had—where injustice is to be bought—where the law exists but in name and is despicable and powerless, it is not to be wondered at that such outrages are quietly submitted to by a demoralized people," he complained.

Ruxton arrived safely in Mexico City. The regularity of the streets and the chaste architecture of its buildings impressed him. But he found the hotels wretched and the streets filled with beggars, lepers, and cripples. It seemed to him to be a city of dirt. "The streets are dirty, the houses are dirty, the men are dirty, and the women dirtier, and everything you eat and drink is dirty," he griped.

The city lacked any sort of police force to protect either inhabitants or visitors. At night entire neighborhoods became combat zones. Ruxton advised all visitors against nighttime travel in Mexico City. "One must depend upon his own nerve and bowie knife, his presence of mind and Colt's revolver," he wrote. "But armed even with all these precautions, it is a dangerous experiment and much better to be left alone." One evening he disregarded his own advice, dressed as a Mexican, and went (in the company of a guide) on a nighttime tour through the haunts of "pickpockets, murderers, burglars, and highwaymen." He saw one man stabbed to death and another seriously injured in knife fights.

In Mexico City Ruxton made his preparations for the long and dangerous journey to the north. He bought two horses, several mules, and his supplies. He experienced real difficulty finding a servant willing to accompany him, "New Mexico being here quite a *terra incognita* and associated with ideas of wild beasts and wilder Indians and horrors of all sorts." On the morning of September 14, just as a salvo of artillery announced the entrance of General Santa Anna into Mexico City, Ruxton and his small caravan departed the city through the north gate. The days passed uneventfully as he traveled through a ruggedly beautiful countryside, briefly stopping at Queretaro, Silao, Aguas Calientes, and Durango. He increasingly became an object of curiosity, often the first Englishman many of these Mexicans had ever seen. They examined him in detail and admired his arsenal of pistols, rifles, and carbines.

Ruxton looked upon most of the Mexicans he met with a jaundiced eye. "If the Mexican possesses one single virtue, as I hope he does, he must keep it so closely hidden in some secret fold of his serape as to have escaped my humble sight," he observed contemptuously. "They are a treacherous, cunning, indolent [people], without energy and cowardly by nature."

The Mexico through which Ruxton traveled was a land of "miserable anarchy." Since the country had won its independence from Spain in 1821, it had experienced, by Ruxton's count, 237 revolutions. Abortive, discordant movements of revolution or counterrevolution followed one another in meaningless succession, and each one ran down in chaos from which no governing class ever arose, or even a political party, but only some gangs.

Everywhere, Ruxton found a pervasive random violence plaguing the towns and roads. On October 22 he almost lost his life in "a little affair at Leon," a notorious stronghold for bandits. That evening the Englishman had strolled through the plaza, smoking a cigar, browsing at the stalls of sidewalk merchants, and mixing with the crowd of local peasants in their picturesque regional garb. As he made his way back to his inn, a group of knife-carrying local thugs jumped him, shouting, "Kill him, kill him." Armed only with his bowie knife, Ruxton ran down a dark alley and made his stand. One of the Mexicans, knife in hand, lunged at him. Ruxton nimbly sidestepped the thrust and buried his own bowie knife in the man's stomach. The Mexican slumped to his knees, shouted "¡Dios! Me ha matado— he has killed me," and fell forward, dead. With that, the others lost heart. Ruxton slowly backed away and returned to his inn without further incident.

Later, Ruxton's own servant turned against him. As they rode toward Chihuahua, the Englishman suddenly heard the sound of a pistol shot and the whine of a bullet near his ear. He quickly turned to confront his servant, who with a pistol in his hand looked very guilty and foolish. "Amigo," Ruxton said to him, "do you call this being skilled in the use of arms, to miss my head at fifteen yards?" He quickly disarmed the mozo of his weapons and methodically beat him with a heavy belt.

Ruxton rode north through a countryside that became increasingly grim, a scorched, unattractive land destitute of trees. At Zacatecas, a mining town of 30,000 inhabitants, all the talk was of Indians. Groups of 200 to 500 Comanches regularly raided southward from their strongholds in New Mexico, depopulating vast areas. Perhaps no Indian tribe was as dangerous as the Comanches, professional marauders and murderers who wreaked havoc over a wide area. ("No one has ever exaggerated the Comanche tortures," the historian DeVoto once asserted. "They had great skill in pain and cruelty was their catharsis.")

The Comanches were the principal fact of life on the northern Mexican frontier. The scattered haciendas were built as forts, with thick walls fitted with firing holes and high towers in which sentries kept a constant watch for raiding parties. Ruxton saw signs of the Comanches everywhere. Sometimes it was the still-warm scalped and mutilated body of a Mexican farmer, a Comanche arrow buried deep in his face. One evening Ruxton camped in the ruined village of Jarral Grande, its people wiped out in an Indian attack the preceding year. In one empty building he found evidence of a recent Indian campfire, an arrow, and a human scalp. "The sun set beauteously on this lonely scene," he wrote later. "In the distance the ragged outline of the sierra was golden with its declining rays, which shed a soft light on the ruins of the village; and everything looked so calm and beautiful, that it was difficult to call to mind that this was once the scene of horrid barbarities."

In the city of Chihuahua Ruxton met the American James Kirker, whom the city officials had hired as a bounty hunter to kill Apaches and Comanches. Kirker's band of professional Indian-killers included retired mountain men and dispossessed Delaware Indians. They collected $50 for each man's scalp, $25 for women's and children's. Ruxton saw their latest trophies, the scalps of 170 Apache men, women, and children dangling in front of the cathedral. A chief had approached Kirker with an offer of peace. To show his own good faith, the bounty hunter sent several kegs of cheap whiskey to the Indian village. After the Apaches became drunk, Kirker's people quickly moved in and butchered the unarmed Indians.

Ruxton rode north, always bearing in mind the American frontier maxim, "Keep your primin' dry, and your eye skinned." He never once stopped or made a detour on account of the Indians. He pushed ahead. And, as if under divine protection, he rode unscathed through the Comanche and Apache country while all around him Indian war parties ravaged the land.

One morning Ruxton went alone to hunt for antelope, his rifle in his hand, a double-barrel carbine slung across his back, and two pistols in his belt. As he cautiously stalked a herd of the animals, he suddenly saw, riding single-file directly toward him, 11 Comanches, naked to the waist, painted and armed for war. "Each had a lance and a bow and arrows, and the chief, who was in the advance, had a rifle in a gaily ornamented case of buckskin, hanging at his side," Ruxton wrote later. He quickly decided upon an ambush, confident of the outcome. "Although the odds were great, I certainly had the advantage, being in an excellent position and having six shots in readiness," he recalled. The Englishman rested his rifle in the fork of a bush that which hid him completely and set his gun sight on the Comanche chief riding toward him, noting his muscular chest shiny with oil. At the last possible second, the war party suddenly veered away from Ruxton's position. He held his fire and let them pass. Almost immediately he regretted not firing. He had thrown away a good fight. "It would not have been a rash act," he insisted later. "In my position and armed as I was, I was more than a match for the whole party."

Ruxton's spirits quickened as he approached the present boundaries of the United States. He had replaced his treacherous servant with a short Irishman who had spent so many years in Mexico that he had almost forgotten how to speak English. The man yearned to see the northern frontier, insisting that "the Indian isn't born who will take my scalp." In the small village of Mapimi thieves stole Ruxton's guns, baggage, and $3,000 in gold coins. The local prefect was outraged. The Englishman, after all, traveled with impressive credentials. Two suspects were rounded up. The official brought out a device resembling a torture rack. The thieves were quickly fastened in place. A large screw was then tightened until the men's bodies were in a state of painful tension and their bones almost dislocated. They confessed, and Ruxton recovered all his goods.

On November 10 Ruxton left Chihuahua and a week later arrived in El Paso, where he saw his first American prisoners of war. He left the next day. Local authorities forced upon him 15 Mexican troops so pathetic in their arms, horses, and uniforms that Ruxton thought the mere sight of them "would have broken the heart of Sir John Falstaff." He knew they would be no value whatsoever in the event of an Indian attack. Several days later they reached the dreaded desert called Jornada del Muerto, or "Journey of the Dead Man." To Ruxton's relief the Mexican troopers turned back. He obtained the use of a local guide and, traveling mostly at night, crossed the 90 miles of desert in just 20 hours. The small party rested in the empty ruins of Valverde, which marked the northern limit of Mexican authority. The next day, in a cold rain, Ruxton rode into the encampment of the First Missouri Mounted Volunteers, under the command of Colonel Alexander Doniphan, and for the first time looked into the face of Manifest Destiny.

Ruxton pitched his camp next to that of Lieutenant James W. Abert of the Topographical Engineers, whom the War Department had sent out in the summer of 1846 with orders to explore northwestern Texas and northeastern New Mexico. The American officers were keenly interested in the handsome Englishman with his splendid mustache and arsenal of fine British guns.

Ruxton, in turn, reviewed with a sharp eye the American encampment. The one thing most striking to him was the utter absence of any military discipline. "The men, unwashed and unshaven, were ragged and dirty, without uniforms and dressed as, and how, they pleased," he noted. "They wandered about, listless and sickly looking, or were sitting in groups playing at cards and swearing and cursing, even at the officers if they interfered to stop it." No sentinels were posted, even though they camped inside enemy territory. One night three Navajo Indians killed two soldiers and ran off 800 sheep. But the Americans were formidable fighters. "These very men, however, were full of fight as game cocks, and shortly after defeated four times their numbers of Mexicans at Sacramento, near Chihuahua," Ruxton admitted. "The Mexicans lost some 300 killed, about the same number wounded, and forty were taken prisoner. Colonel Doniphan had one man killed and eight wounded."

Ruxton presented his documents. One from the British government asked all American army officers to "extend every facility to English traders on their route to Chihuahua" through American territory. And what Ruxton encountered here would change his life: a strange breed of frontiersman the likes of which he had never known before. He spent several days hunting with a French Canadian and an American, "both trappers and old mountain men." Ruxton decided then and there upon a winter journey into the Rocky Mountains to experience for himself the life of the mountain man. That journey was to change him forever.

4

In the second decade of the nineteenth century Blackfeet Indians captured John Colter and a companion named Potts while the two were trapping beaver in present-day North Dakota. Both white men understood they faced certain death by slow torture. In desperation Potts broke free of his captors and tried to escape, but was quickly killed in a shower of arrows. The Indians then stripped Colter in preparation for the torture ceremony. But the Blackfeet decided instead to give him a sporting chance. They allowed the naked mountain man a running start of 300 yards before a pack of several hundred Indian warriors set out in pursuit. The chase lasted for hours, as Colter pushed himself on until blood gushed from his nostrils. He finally eluded the Indians by plunging into a river and hiding for several hours beneath a raft of dead timbers. "However, his situation was still dreadful," the first contemporary account of his escape noted. "He was completely naked, under a burning sun; the soles of his feet were entirely filled with thorns of the prickly pear; he was hungry, had no means of killing game although he saw abundance around him, and was at least seven days' journey from Lisa's Fort." Yet one week later a nude Colter reached the security of the fort, having survived the entire time on Indian turnips.

The mountain man was our first Western hero, the first American to make the wilderness truly his own. He was unique to his time and place and has no twentieth-century counterpart. He mastered survival skills to a degree probably unmatched in human history before or since. The Indian had his tribe and reaped all the benefits of a complex social fabric. But the mountain man had no such backup systems. He was utterly on his own. He relied entire-

ly on his own wilderness skills and physical prowess. If he erred
or his reflexes failed him, then he was dead and his hair was lifted.
As a result, the mountain man surpassed the Indian in such skills
as hunting, tracking, fighting, reading the minute signs of the
wilderness, enduring the heat and cold of nature, and surviving
the psychological trauma of prolonged periods of isolation. He
was the first American to feel comfortable in the vast land distances that European visitors have always remarked upon as one
of our most striking national attributes. (In nine years the great
mountain man Jedediah Smith traveled more than 16,000 miles by
foot and horse along winding rivers and game trails through
trackless country, much of it never previously penetrated by any
white man.)

"It is hardly too much to say that a mountain man's life was
skill," Bernard DeVoto asserted in *Across the Wide Missouri*. "He
not only worked in the wilderness, but also lived there and he did
so from sun to sun by the exercise of total skill. It was probably
as intricate a skill as any ever developed by any way of working
or living anywhere. Certainly it was the most complex of the
wilderness crafts practiced on this continent. The mountains, the
aridity, the distances, and the climates imposed severities far
greater than those laid on forest-runners, rivermen, or any of our
other symbolic pioneers."

No skill was more critical to a mountain man's safety and
longevity than an accurate reading of the "signs." In *Life in the
Far West* Ruxton gave an account of how the proper reading of a
sign as insignificant as a wood duck and her ducklings swimming
downstream could mean the difference between life and a terrible
death. Luke and Gonneville are experienced mountain men, while
La Bonté is the greenhorn still new to the ways of the West.

> Gonneville turned his head, and extending his arm twice
> with a forward motion up the creek, whispered, "*Les
> sauvages.*"
> "Injuns, sure, and Sioux at that," answered Luke.

Still La Bonté looked, but nothing new met his view but the duck with her brood, now rapidly approaching; and as he gazed, the bird suddenly took wing, and, flapping on the water, flew a short distance down the stream and once more settled on it.

"Injuns?" he asked. "Where are they?"

"Whar?" repeated old Luke, striking the flint of his rifle and opening the pan to examine the priming. "What brings a duck a-streakin' it down stream, if humans aint behint her? And who's thar in these diggings but Injuns, and the worst kind; and we'd better push to camp, I'm thinking, if we mean to save our hair."

In only one area did the Indian have a distinct advantage to the mountain man. His preferred weapon was the Hawken rifle which was accurate well beyond 100 yards. In the event of an Indian attack an experienced fighter could maintain a firepower of perhaps one shot every 30 seconds. Yet in that same time an Indian marksman could easily get off ten to 12 well-placed arrows. The Indian bow, accurate at 80 yards and deadly over a much greater distance, was more than a match for the Hawken rifle. It was not until the Colt revolver went into general production in 1846 that the West had a weapon with a firepower equal to the Indian's bow.

In *Adventures in Mexico and the Rocky Mountains* Ruxton painted a vivid word picture of the appearance of a typical mountain man: "The costume of the trapper is a hunting shirt of dressed buckskin, ornamented with long fringes; pantaloons of the same material, and decorated with porcupine quills and long fringes down the outside of the leg. A flexible felt hat and moccasins clothe his extremities. Over his left shoulder and under his right arm hangs his powder horn and bullet pouch. . . . Round the waist is a belt, in which is stuck a large butcher knife in a sheath of buffalo hide. . . . A tomahawk is often added; and, of course, a long heavy rifle is part and parcel of his equipment." (The characteris-

tic buckskin fringes along his sleeves and leggings were not merely for decoration; they also served as material to mend moccasins,
pack-saddles, or almost anything.)

Unlike other pioneers, the mountain man survived and prospered partly because of his ability to slough off his previous
cultural identity and adopt the customs, dress, and language of the
Indians. He was always much less civilized than earlier frontiersmen such as Daniel Boone, who liked to read *Gulliver's Travels*
around his campfire. The mountain man's costume, speech, outlook on life, and often enough his Indian squaw gave him a
decidedly savage aspect. Lewis Garrard, a Cincinnati youth who,
like Ruxton, traveled through the Far West in 1846 and lived with
the mountain men, described them at length in his book *Wah-to-
yah and the Taos Trail*:

> My companions were rough men—used to the hardships
> of a mountaineer's life—whose manners are blunt, and whose
> speech is rude—men driven to the western wilds with embit-
> tered feelings—with better natures shattered—with hopes
> blasted—to seek, in the dangers of the warpath, fierce excite-
> ment and banishment of care. . . . Yet these aliens from
> society . . . , who will tear off a bloody scalp with grim smiles
> of satisfaction, are fine fellows, full of fun, and often kind and
> obliging.

The Garrard passage hints at another important aspect of the
mountain man. By immersing himself in the destructive element,
he achieved perhaps the fullest measure of freedom any individual
has ever found in our country's history. There was no one to say
what he should do; no conventional rules of society restrained his
actions. He lived in his own Neolithic world, remote from the
early Industrial Age, which had bred him and unfettered by the
fixed taboos and rigid life patterns of his neighbors, the Indians.
The mountain man even escaped the strict puritanism of his age,
rejecting the sexual prudery of white women for the uninhibited

and spontaneous affections of the young squaws for whom prostitution was an integral part of the Indian economy. ("The girls of the Plains tribes were more fastidious in personal cleanliness than most American women of the period, especially the women of the frontier, and they were cannier with such feminine accessories as perfumes and adornments," insists historian DeVoto in *Across the Wide Missouri.*)

In 1846, when Ruxton journeyed through the Rocky Mountains, the era of the mountain men was in its twilight. Their period of flourishing had been remarkably short, about 20 years. Historian Dale Van Every estimates that their numbers never exceeded 500 at any one time. The total was perhaps 2,000. (The records suggest that one in four died at the hands of Indians.) Their way of life had been born out of a fashion, a seemingly insatiable demand in America and Europe for beaver-skin hats. The mountain men set their traps in virtually every stream in the western United States. During their heyday they sent 100,000 beaver skins a year back East. But in the 1830s the fickle winds of fashion changed. Beaver hats went out of style. Silk top hats became all the rage. The price of a beaver pelt plunged from $1 to $8. The beaver was saved from extinction, while the mountain man quickly faded into the pages of history and legend.

5

At Valverde Ruxton paid off his little Irishman and set out with a party of U.S. Army soldiers toward Santa Fe. In the far distance he saw the snowcapped peaks of the Rocky Mountains' Sangre de Cristo range, which overlook Santa Fe. He found Santa Fe to be "a wretched collection of mud houses," whose streets were full of drunken American soldiers. Soon afterward the Englishman rode into Taos and accepted an invitation to stay at the home of Stephen Lee, the town's sheriff. Among the first of the wild West towns, Taos was the favorite wintering hole of scores of mountain men, including such celebrities as Kit Carson (who retired there), Old Bill Williams, Jedediah Smith, and Jim Beckwourth. Ruxton mixed with the trappers and sampled the famous frontier beverage known as Taos Lightning. One evening he and three mountain men were watching a Mexican fandango when racial tensions got out of hand. Armed with bowie knives, the four of them quickly cleared the room of 20 Mexicans. When the Englishman made clear to his host his intention of crossing the Sangre de Cristos to winter on the northern side, Lee advised him that such a trip would be suicidal and pleaded with him to remain in Taos.

On January 1, 1847, against the advice of virtually everyone he consulted, Ruxton departed Taos in the company of a Pueblo Indian guide. He had shed his London clothes for the buckskin fashions of the mountain man. It was with genuine relief and great anticipation that he headed north. "I had now turned my back on the last settlement and felt a thrill of pleasure as I looked at the wild expanse of snow which lay before me, and the towering mountains which frowned on all sides," he wrote later, "and knew that now I had seen the last . . . of civilized man under the garb of a Mexican *serape*."

(Shortly after Ruxton's departure, as he struggled through snow, ice, and bitter cold, a large group of Pueblo Indians and local Mexicans attacked the American population of Taos. Charles Bent, whom General Stephen Kearny had appointed as New Mexico's first governor, was shot in his home. His district attorney was scalped alive and dragged through the streets before finally being dispatched. And Stephen Lee, Ruxton's host, retreated to his roof where he was shot and scalped. Only one American escaped the general massacre.)

Ruxton and his guide slowly made their way higher into the mountains along an old Ute trail. Emerging onto a high plateau they encountered large herds of antelope, some numbering in the thousands, which had been hunted so little they were almost tame. The graceful animals "trotted up to us, and with pointed ears and their beautiful eyes staring with eager curiosity, accompanied us for miles," Ruxton noted.

And everywhere were the wolves, so common that Ruxton rarely wasted a bullet on them. Whenever he butchered an antelope or deer he had shot, they sat patiently nearby, licking their chops in hungry anticipation. He stood in awe of their rapacious appetites. Once he killed a deer and then stood to one side to watch a pack of six wolves in action. Within five minutes there was nothing left but a well-picked skeleton. At night their eyes glowed like little coals in the darkness beyond the light of his campfire. One wolf stayed with Ruxton the entire way, trotting nearby, keeping the Englishman company. Ruxton became quite attached to the animal and put out meat for him each morning. "I had him twenty times a day within reach of my rifle, but he had become such an old friend that I never dreamed of molesting him," Ruxton wrote later.

The cold was so intense that Ruxton had to protect his pack animals with thick blankets each night. One night a wet sleet fell, and in the morning he discovered his animals hidden beneath mounds of ice. "We ourselves suffered extremely, turning constantly, and rolling almost into the embers of the scanty fire, and towards daybreak I really thought I should have frozen bodily," he recalled later. They frequently encountered snowdrifts 15 feet deep that forced them to dismount and beat a path through for the horses and mules using their own bodies. Game was scarce. And the few animals Ruxton shot were so gaunt they barely provided enough meat for one meal. But he pushed ahead and never once considered returning to Taos.

(While Ruxton labored through the frozen hell of the southern Rocky Mountains, a thousand miles to the west the Donner Party sat trapped in the snow-choked passes of the Sierra Nevada Mountains near Lake Tahoe. "Snowed all night & snows yet rapidly," Patrick Breen wrote in his diary. "Great difficulty in getting wood. John & Edwd. has got to get it. I am not able. Offered our prayers to God. . . . The prospect is appalling but hope in God.

Amen." Two days after Christmas some of the starving survivors in desperation dragged in the body of Patrick Dolan, cut strips from its legs and arms, and roasted them over a small fire. The ordeal of the Donner party had moved into its final and most terrible phase.)

In Ruxton's account of his own brutal journey across the Sangre de Cristos during one of the worst winters in memory we catch glimpses of the man's inner compulsions. Clearly, for him danger was a kind of drug that made him unfit for a more normal existence. On his travels he was keenly aware of the imminent and daily possibility of violent death. Such an awareness never overwhelmed him, as it might have a lesser man, but rather invigorated his senses and made him seem more alive. "That which does not kill us makes us stronger," Friedrich Nietzsche once said, and Ruxton would have agreed. What drew him to the mountain-man life was clearly much more than simple curiosity. He entered their world in the pursuit of absolute freedom and a hope of achieving a personal fulfillment to which the ordinary men of his time remained lifelong strangers. Few Englishmen had ever before been afforded comparable scope to indulge their deepest, most instinctive, and most commonly frustrated yearnings. Born of a need to pursue the freedom offered by the wilderness introduced to him by the James Fenimore Cooper's novels, Ruxton's nomadic impulses drew him north into the dangerous regions of the Rocky Mountains. There he would finally achieve his own manifest destiny.

After a hazardous and bitter struggle Ruxton reached the Huerfano (Orphan) River, then crossed the prairie to the St. Charles River, and finally arrived at the trading fort of Pueblo on the Arkansas River. There he spent the rest of the winter in the lodge of John Hawken, trapper, mountaineer, and nephew to the famous gunsmith in St. Louis. Pueblo was a winter home to a dozen or more mountain men, all unemployed since the price of beaver skins had plunged in the world market. The fort itself was a small, square, adobe structure with circular ramparts at the corners and a half-dozen little rooms in which the men lived. Their diet consisted entirely of game. Whenever their supply was exhausted, a hunting party left the safety of the fort with several pack animals and returned in two or three days loaded with buffalo or venison.

With his worn buckskin clothes, long hair, and wilderness skills, Ruxton was received by the mountain men as one of their own. Only his crisp British accent, clean-shaven face, and carefully cultivated mustache set him apart. In the fort's warmth and security he luxuriated in the companionship of men who had lived their adult lives in the most remote parts of the American West. He listened as they remembered a time when the beaver existed in such numbers as to be plucked from the streams like apples from the trees in Eden. They spoke in high-pitched voices, emphasizing each word as did the Indians whose dialects they heard more frequently than their own native tongue. As they cut slices of smoking buffalo meat off the big chunks roasting over the fire and wiped their greasy hands on their buckskins, they talked at length of the exploits of the most celebrated mountain men and recounted their own adventures. Later Ruxton faithfully recorded many of their stories, such as:

"Just by Little Arkansas we saw the first Injun. Me and young Somes was ahead for meat, and I had hobbled the old mule and was 'approaching' some goats [antelopes], when I see the critturs turn back their heads and jump right away for me. 'Hurraw, Dick!' I shouts, 'hyars brown-skin acomin,' and off I makes for the mule. The young greenhorn sees the goats runnin' up to him, and not being up to Injun ways, blazes at the first and knocks him over. Jest then seven darned red heads top the bluff, and seven Pawnees come a-screechin' upon us. I cuts the hobbles and jumps on the mule, and, when I looks back, there was Dick Somes ramming a ball down his gun like mad, and the Injuns flinging their arrows at him pretty smart, I tell you. 'Hurraw, Dick, mind your hair,' and I ups old Greaser and let one Injun 'have it,' as he was going plum into the boy with his lance. He turned on his back handsome, and Dick gets the ball down at last, blazes away, and drops another. Then we charged on 'em, and they clears off like runnin' cows; and I takes the hair off the heads of the two we made meat of; and I do b'lieve thar's some of them scalps on my old leggings yet."

Ruxton heard the sagas of the great Hugh Glass, whom historian Dale Van Every calls "the mountain man's mountain man, the single figure who most completely represented his kind." Glass's most celebrated exploit began in September 1823 when he suffered the disaster most dreaded by all mountain men: he was mauled by a wounded grizzly bear. He and several companions (including the 19-year-old Jim Bridger) were checking their traps for beaver when they spotted a large grizzly rooting in the dirt for nuts. Glass and another trapper stalked the bear and shot it at close range but failed to afflict a mortal wound. Enraged and in pain, the bear charged the two men. "Harraw, Bill," Glass shouted as he bolted, "we'll be made meat of as sure as shootin'!" Suddenly he tripped over a stone. The bear closed upon him. Glass fired his pistol into the bear's chest and then attacked it with his knife as the animal embraced him and started gnawing. When Glass's companions returned, they found the bear dead from knife wounds and Glass horribly mangled. He had suffered severe lacerations over most of his body and head. Bloody rib bones protruded through what was left of his buckskin jacket. His scalp hung across his face. When the injured man showed no signs of recovery, his companions took his rifle, knife, and other personal effects and abandoned him. Glass, however, was not dead. Somehow he summoned the strength to crawl to a stream and eat some wild cherries. He also ate the rotting bear meat. Driven by the passion to confront his faithless companions, Glass slowly made his way toward Fort Kiowa 100 miles away. He arrived six weeks later, looking, in the words of one contemporary observer, like "a lank cadaverous form with a face so scarred and disfigured that scarcely a feature was discernible." At the fort he found the trapper who had gone with him to shoot the bear. "Harraw, Bill, my boy," Glass demanded of the startled man, "you thought I was gone under that time, did you? But hand me over my horse and gun, my lad; I ain't dead yet by a damn sight!"

Throughout the winter Ruxton savored the free life of the mountain man. From his companions he learned how to "read signs" to know what lay ahead: "A turned leaf, a blade of grass pressed down, the uneasiness of the wild animals, the flight of birds, are all paragraphs . . . written in nature's legible hand and plainest language." His mentors taught him the proper way to take a scalp—"pass the point edge of a keen butcher-knife round the parting, turning it at the same time under the skin to separate the scalp from the skull." And they instructed him in the ways of Indians—how to tell an Indian's tribe by the style of his moccasins or his hair; and the difference between a white man's campfire and an Indian's (the former lays the logs over the flames whereas the Indian thrusts them in butt first). He listened to their stories of the Indian's love of gambling: in the frenzy brought on by high stakes braves sometimes wagered everything, including the scalps from their own heads.

Christianity was largely unknown among the mountain men. "There is no Sabbath west of the Mississippi," insisted the popular frontier wisdom. If a trapper wanted religion, he usually borrowed the philosophy of life and death from his neighbors, the Indians. The celebrated mountain man Old Bill Williams went west as a missionary, traded his Bibles for beaver traps, and took a squaw as his wife, yet he remained deeply spiritual. In the end he had convinced himself that after death he would return to earth as an elk and live in his favorite sheltered valley.

Such men clearly stood little chance of returning to civilization except for the briefest of visits. "It's hard to fetch breath amongst them big bands of corncrackers of Missoura," one trapper told

Ruxton. "Besides, it goes against nature to leave buffler meat and feed on hog; and them white gals are too much like picturs. . . . [Damn] the settlements, I say."

Ruxton clearly understood the role of the mountain man in the dynamics of American society during the second quarter of the nineteenth century. "These were the men whose hardy enterprise opened to commerce and the plow the vast and fertile regions of the West," he wrote in *Life in the Far West*. "Rough and savage though they were, they alone were the pioneers of that extraordinary tide of civilisation which has poured its resistless current through tracts large enough for kings to govern. . . . To these men alone is due the empire of the West— destined in a few short years to become the most important of those confederate states which compose the mighty union of North America."

Ruxton was also fascinated by the dark side of human nature he saw manifested among the mountain men. To his credit, he never romanticized them. He understood all too clearly that total freedom can corrupt as well as liberate the human spirit. If not an animal, the mountain man was at least a distant primitive, positioned well down on the scale of civilized development. In perhaps the most profound passage by any nineteenth-century observer on the mountain men and the broader moral implications of their way of life, Ruxton wrote in *Adventures in Mexico and the Rocky Mountains*:

> Constantly exposed to perils of all kinds, they become callous to any feeling of danger, and destroy human as well as animal life with as little scruple and as freely as they expose their own. Of laws, human or divine, they neither know nor care to know. Their wish is their law, and to attain it they do not scruple as to ways and means. Firm friends and bitter enemies, with them it is "a word and a blow," and the blow often first. They may have good qualities, but they are those of the

animal; and people fond of giving hard names call them
revengeful, bloodthirsty drunkards. . . . However, there are
exceptions, and I have met honest mountain men. Their animal qualities, however, are undeniable. Strong, active, hardy
as bears, daring, expert in the use of their weapons, they are
just what uncivilised white man might be supposed to be in a
brute state.

(At the same time Ruxton was making his epic journey across
North America, mountain man John Johnson was carving out
his own niche in Western folklore under the name of Liver-
Eating Johnson. Through the mists of time and legend we can
see that he was a man who would have fitted comfortably into
the world of both a Greek tragedy and a Stephen King novel. An
enormous man of 240 pounds with a great red beard, he once
killed five Sioux warriors in a camp brawl using only his fists. In
the spring of 1847 he returned from a trapping expedition to
find that Crow Indians had killed and scalped his pregnant wife,
a Flathead girl. Johnson vowed revenge upon the Crows. Soon
the news filtered through the West that Crow warriors were
turning up dead, scalped, their stomachs cut open and their liv-
ers gone. The legend of Liver-Eating Johnson spread. By the time
his blood lust had finally run its course, he was reputed to have
killed more than 300 Crows, scalped them, and eaten their liv-
ers raw. Johnson's actions would have repulsed but not surprised
Ruxton.)

On March 17 the ice on the Arkansas River "moved" for the
first time. The next day it was entirely broken up, a sure sign,
Ruxton was advised, that spring weather was on its way. By
March 24 the days had warmed sufficiently so that the river was
entirely clear of ice. Geese now made their appearance and provided the mountain men at Pueblo with a welcome diversion from
their winter diet of venison and buffalo meat. "The bluebird followed the goose," Ruxton noted, "and when the first robin was

seen, the hunters pronounced the winter at an end."

As the weather improved, Ruxton undertook solitary expeditions into the nearby mountains, leaving the Pueblo fort for days at a time. He camped deep in the Bayou Salado and found it a hunter's paradise. There he saw vast herds of buffalo ("the life and ornament of the boundless prairies") still existing after they had, even in 1847, been hunted to extinction on the midwestern prairie. "No animal requires so much killing as a buffalo," Ruxton insisted from extensive experience. "Unless shot through the lungs or spine, they invariably escape. . . . A bull, shot through the heart or lungs, with blood streaming from his mouth, and protruding tongue, his eyes rolling, bloodshot, and glazed with death, braces himself on his legs, swaying from side to side, stamps impatiently at his growing weakness, or lifts his rugged and marred head and helplessly bellows out his conscious impotence."

Ruxton pronounced buffalo meat the finest of all game flesh, an opinion shared by most hunters of the age. The Indians preferred their meat "ripe," letting it sit until it started to rot. On the other hand, mountain men frequently ate it raw. Ruxton once watched two trappers eating at opposite ends of a bloody buffalo intestine. "As yard after yard glided glibly down their throats. . . it became a great point with each of the feasters to hurry his operation, so as to gain a match on his neighbor," he reported. "Each, at the same time, exhorted the other . . . to feed fair. . . . The greasy [intestine] required no mastication and was bolted whole." Buffalo meat provided a complete diet. Both mountain men and Indians sometimes lived and thrived on nothing but the meat from fat buffalo cows for weeks on end. Trappers consumed prodigious quantities of the meat, often up to eight pounds at a sitting. "We live upon it solely," one wrote later, "without bread or vegetables of any kind, and what seems most singular, we never tire of or disrelish it."

(Buffalo meat was the mountain man's food of preference. But his survival, especially in a winter blizzard, often depended upon his ingenuity at discovering alternate food sources. Ruxton undoubtedly heard the stories about men who were alive only because they drank the blood of their horses, ate their moccasins, or resorted to cannibalism. "I have held my hands in an ant-hill until they were covered with ants, then greedily licked them off," one old trapper admitted. "I have taken the soles of my moccasins, crisped them in the fire, and eaten them. In our extremity the large black crickets which are found in the country were considered game. We used to take a kettle of hot water, catch the crickets and throw them in, and when they stopped kicking, eat them.")

One day Ruxton followed a small herd of deer over broken ground and suddenly came upon an Indian camp, the fire still smoking and the dried meat hanging from nearby tree branches. "Robinson Crusoe could not have been more thoroughly disgusted at his sight of the 'footprint in the sand,' than was I at this inopportune discovery," he wrote later. "I had anticipated a month or two's undisturbed hunting in this remote spot." A few minutes later he saw two Arapaho Indians emerge from the woods carrying a deer. He retired to his own camp several miles away and hoped he would remain undiscovered. However, the next day he awoke abruptly from a late-afternoon nap to discover to his horror that the mountain was on fire. A dense cloud of black smoke hung over all. He watched a mass of flame explode into the sky and roll fiercely up the stream toward his camp. He understood immediately what had happened. The Arapahos had picked up his "signs" and set the fire in an attempt to smoke him out. Ruxton quickly broke his camp and started toward safety on his horse with his mules behind. As he galloped out of the woods, the long dry prairie grass ahead exploded into flames. The Englishman raced directly into the wall of fire. Safely through on the other side, he turned back to survey the scene. The fire spread at least three miles on each side of the river where he had camped. The mountain above was one sheet of flame. (The fire traveled across 40 miles of prairie and burned for 14 days before it was finally extinguished.)

In the high-mountain wilderness Ruxton found himself in a natural setting so immense that it dwarfed man and his actions into utter insignificance.

> The perfect solitude of this vast wildness was almost appalling. From my position on the summit of the dividing ridge I had a bird's eye view, as it were, over the rugged and chaotic masses of the stupendous chain of the Rocky Mountains, and the vast deserts which stretched from their eastern bases; while, on all sides of me, broken ridges, and chasms and ravines, with masses of piled-up rocks and uprooted trees, with clouds of drifting snow flying through the air, and the [storm's] roar battling through the forest at my feet, added to the wildness of the scene, which was unrelieved by the slightest vestige of animal or human life.

The Rocky Mountains were nothing like the man-centered natural world Ruxton had experienced earlier in England and eastern Canada. He had traveled light years away from the wildness celebrated by the English Romantic poets. The American West subverted their comfortable assumptions about man and his place in the world. The Rocky Mountains offered no easy affirmation of a God-directed universe. The mountains, like the white trappers inhabiting them, were a profound experience for Ruxton, who found himself in a world that denied for man the assumptions about his importance and his nobility that gave meaning and significance to his efforts. In characteristic fashion, the Englishman accepted this natural world with all its moral and philosophical implications and drew both strength and inspiration from it. He wrote:

> Apart from the feeling of loneliness which any one in my situation must naturally have experienced, surrounded by stupendous works of nature, which in all their solitary

grandeur frowned upon me, and sinking into utter insignificance the miserable mortal who crept beneath their shadow;
still there was something inexpressibly exhilarating in the sensation of positive freedom from all worldly care, and a
consequent expansion of the sinews, as it were, of mind and
body, which made me feel elastic as a ball of Indian rubber,
and in a state of . . . perfect insouciance.

In early April Ruxton finally abandoned his solitary mountain
existence and with great regret headed back to Pueblo. There he
joined two trappers bound for Fort Leavenworth on the Missouri
River. The weather turned bad and rained for 30 days straight. On
May 3 the three arrived at Bent's Fort on the Arkansas River, the
Southwest's largest and most important fur-trading post. (Charles
Bent, the founder of the fort and first governor of New Mexico,
had been murdered in the massacre at Taos a few months earlier.)
From there Ruxton's small party rode with a military train of 20
wagons heading east. Also along was Lewis Garrard, an adven-
turesome young man from Cincinnati, who had gone West the
previous year looking for excitement. In his book *Wah-to-yah and
the Taos Trail* he remembered the Englishman: "George F.
Ruxton, the English traveler, with two men, here joined our party.
Mr. R. was a quiet, good-looking man, with a handsome mustache. He conversed well, but sparingly, speaking little of
himself."

On May 7, as Ruxton rode several miles ahead of the column,
he suddenly spotted by a river a cluster of white teepees, a
Cheyenne village in the distance. He visited there and learned that
all the young men were away on a buffalo hunt. "The lodges,
about fifty in number, were all regularly planted in rows of ten,"
Ruxton noted. "The chief's lodge was in the centre, and the skins
of it were dyed a conspicuous red. Before the lodges of each of the
principal chiefs and warriors was a stack of spears, from which
hung his shield and arms; whilst the skins of the lodge itself were
covered with devices and hieroglyphics, describing his warlike

achievements. Before one was a painted pole supporting several smoke-dried scalps, which dangled in the wind, rattling against the pole like bags of peas."

At noon on May 15 the military column arrived at Mann's Fort, which consisted simply of four log houses connected by angles of timber framework with loopholes for the cannons and rifles. The Pawnees had the fort under siege, killing any man who ventured more than several hundred yards away. A few days before, the Indians had speared one soldier within sight of 40 armed men; then, waving the bloody scalp aloft with yells of triumph, they retreated unharmed.

On leaving Mann's Fort, the wagon train struck out to the northeast over a tract of rolling prairie cut by many ravines. "We were now, day after day, passing through countless herds of buffalo," Ruxton recalled later. "I could scarcely form an estimate of the numbers within the range of sight at the same instant, but some idea may be formed of them by mentioning that one day, passing along a ridge of upland prairie at least thirty miles in length and from which a view extended about eight miles on each side of a slightly rolling plain, not a patch of grass ten yards square could be seen, so dense was the living mass that covered the country in every direction."

Here Ruxton also saw his first wagon trains heading West toward the new American territory of Oregon, bringing the settlers who followed on the heels of the mountain men. "Upwards of forty huge wagons of the Conestoga and Pittsburgh build and covered with snow-white tilts, were ranged in a semicircle, or rather a horse-shoe form, on the flat open prairie, their long 'tongues' (poles) pointing outwards; with the necessary harness for four pairs of mules, or eight yoke of oxen, lying on the ground before them, spread in a ready order for 'hitching up,'" he recalled later. "Round the wagons groups of teamsters, tall stalwart young Missourians, were engaged in busy preparation for the start, greasing the wheels, fitting or repairing harness, smoothing ox-bows . . . They were all dressed in the same fashion: a pair of 'homespun' pantaloons, tucked into thick boots reaching nearly to the knee and confined round the waist by a broad leather belt, which supported a strong butcher knife in a sheath. A coarse checked shirt was their only other covering, with a fur cap on the head."

Ruxton's Western adventure ended in Fort Leavenworth (near present-day Kansas City), then the most western of all U.S. Army garrisons. Established atop a high bank overlooking the Missouri River, it was hardly a fort as such, being four large wooden blockhouses placed at the corner of a square of frame buildings. Even so, Fort Leavenworth was an oasis of refined Eastern civilization in the middle of the Indian Territory. Most of the married officers had brought their wives with them. "I remember to have been not a little struck at the first sight of many very pretty, well-dressed ladies, who, after my long sojourn amongst the dusky squaws, appeared to me like the hour is of paradise," Ruxton admitted later. The white women, however, continually mistook the Englishman for an Indian chief.

In late June Ruxton booked passage on a steamboat to St. Louis. There he checked into the Planter's House, one of the city's finest hotels. The sudden return to civilization jarred his senses. He rediscovered the great joy of freshly baked bread. But his back, long accustomed to hard ground, rebelled at the unaccustomed softness of his first bed in ten months. He found chairs "a positive nuisance" and squatted cross-legged on the floor in his room. Forks were the "most useless superfluities," and he had always to fight a temptation to grab a leg of mutton mountain-man style and "butcher off a hunter's mouthful." His greatest ordeal was fitting once again into civilized fashions. "What words can describe the agony of squeezing my feet into boots, after nearly a year of moccasins, or discarding my turban for a great boardy hat, which seemed to crush my temples?" Ruxton lamented. "The miseries of getting into a horrible coat—of braces, waistcoats, gloves, and all such implements of torture—were too acute to be described."

Eight days after leaving St. Louis Ruxton was in New York City, boarding the ship *New World*. Thirty days later he was home in England, his long journey finally at an end.

6

In August 1847, as Ruxton's ship approached the English shore, General Winfield Scott's army, 12,000 strong, marched toward Mexico City along the road that Hernando Cortes had followed three centuries earlier. At the fortified pass of Cerro Gordo Captain Robert E. Lee outflanked a large group of Mexican troops, a brilliant operation in which Lieutenant Ulysses S. Grant and Captain George B. McClellan assisted. On August 20 the Americans fought a fierce battle at Churubusco and suffered 177 dead and 870 wounded. On September 13 the American army stormed their final obstacle, the fortified hill of Chapultepec, heroically defended by the young cadets of the Mexican military academy. On September 17 General Santa Anna surrendered. The "halls of Montezuma" had finally fallen to the forces of Manifest Destiny.

The Mexican War and the Oregon settlement together almost doubled the area of the nation, adding 1,200,000 square miles. These included a magnificent outlet to the rich Pacific trade; hundreds of millions of dollars in California gold (news of the first gold strike was just beginning to spread across the country as the treaty was signed); vast riches of silver in the territories of Colorado and Nevada; fertile farmlands that spread across a hundred horizons; great reserves, yet undiscovered, of oil; and the West itself, which was already establishing itself in the popular imagination as a state of mind as much as a geographical fact. This was truly a Golden Land, an American Eden.

The United States had won its war with Mexico at a monetary cost of $97,705,860 and a human cost of some 13,000 dead. (Only 1,721 died in battle; the others succumbed to injuries and disease.) There were other costs, less obvious at the time. "The war had opened a Pandora's box of evils for the United States," wrote historian Glyndon G. Van Deusen. "Out of it rose the specter of slavery extension, and out of this came bitter sectional strife, the disruption of [political] parties, the beginning of a series of strains and crises that were to culminate in the Civil War."

Ralph Waldo Emerson understood the broader implications of the conflict. "The United States will conquer Mexico," he had warned, "but it will be as the man who swallows the arsenic which brings him down in turn."

Thirteen years later the Southern guns that thundered at Fort Sumter in Charleston's harbor echoed Emerson's prophecy.

7

By mid-August George Ruxton was back in England. This time he fought off his chronic restlessness by working diligently to complete a book on his recent experiences. Sadly, all the journals, manuscripts, and notes relating to his trip had been lost while crossing the swollen Pawnee Fork of the Arkansas River on his way to Fort Leavenworth. He worked from memory and rough notes, which meant that he had to substitute his own impressions for the wealth of "scientific information" he had originally intended to include. The result was a much stronger narrative; *Adventures in Mexico and the Rocky Mountains* is one of the great travel books. "It is not often that one meets a hand equally practiced with the long rifle, bowie knife, and Colt's revolver and at the same time so apt with the pen," a critic for the *Westminster and Foreign Quarterly* enthused. Ruxton's achievement is all the more impressive when we remember that his formal education ended at the age of 16.

Ruxton's long stay with the mountain men had yielded such a wealth of material that he could use only a small fraction of it in his travel memoirs, so he began a novel. It provided him with the opportunity to enlarge upon the aspects of western American life that had appealed so strongly to his imagination. *Life in the Far West* appeared serially in *Blackwood's Edinburgh Magazine* in the summer of 1848. In his novel Ruxton presented the saga of the mountain men who first explored the West, assembling many of the stories he had heard in the evening sessions at Pueblo. He possessed an ear keenly sensitive to the subtle nuances of speech and the artistic skill to reproduce the unique dialect of the mountain men. His central character is an Easterner who goes West as a greenhorn but returns an experienced mountain man. The other characters are largely historical, based upon the mountain men he had met in his travels. (Bernard DeVoto called *Life in the Far West* "nine-tenths history.")

Ruxton was the first Englishman to write authoritatively and skillfully about this mysterious, faraway country. Both of his books were well received and enjoyed brisk sales. The American West fascinated the British public, who saw it as an exotic country full of strange animals and even stranger people. Nearly 2,000 years had elapsed since Europe and the British Isles had been so wild and new. Indians, in particular, enthralled them; the vision of natural man captured their imagination.

In the spring of 1848 Ruxton once again grew restless and yearned for new adventures in foreign lands. He petitioned the British government to commission him to search for the lost party of Sir John Franklin, which had disappeared on a search for the Northwest Passage. But in his heart he knew that his destiny lay in the American West. His thoughts returned with increasing frequency to his memories of "the welcome blaze of the campfire on a cold winter's night" and the rough conversation of his companions, the mountain men. He slowly grew to understand that his months in the Rocky Mountains had profoundly changed him. He had dressed in the buckskins of the Western frontier. And back in England he learned that he had absorbed many of the West's values as well. The composition of his two books no doubt helped him clarify his feelings. In *Adventures in Mexico and the Rocky Mountains* he wrote:

> Such is the fascination of the life of the mountain hunter that I believe not one instance could be adduced of even the most polished and civilised of men, who had once tasted the sweets of its attendant liberty and freedom from every worldly care, not regretting the moment when he exchanged it for the monotonous life of the settlements, nor sighing, and sighing again, once more to partake of its pleasures and allurements.

Ruxton was now a stranger in a strange land, more Indianized than even he had suspected. He had little in common any longer with the highly ordered and formal English society. He confessed to his editor at *Blackwood's* that he was "half froze for buffler meat and mountain doin's."

"Eastward I go only by force, but westward I go free," Thoreau had written. Across 5,000 miles of land and ocean, the lodestone of the West tugged powerfully at Ruxton's heart and soul. The open country, the freedom, the unknown beckoned him, and the pull of the American Eden finally proved irresistible.

Ruxton sold the book rights to *Life in the Far West* to raise travel money. He mapped out his itinerary: through New York to St. Louis and then on to Fort Leavenworth; down the Santa Fe Trail to the Arkansas River; then straight west to Bayou Salado in the Rocky Mountains for the winter; and in the spring across to the Great Salt Lake. Beyond lay California and Oregon, a whole new world to explore—"always supposing my hair is not lifted by Comanche or Pawnee on the scalping route of the Coon Creeks and Pawnee Fork," he excitedly advised his editor.

In August 1848 when Ruxton was in Buffalo, New York, on his way to St. Louis, a young man approached him, saying, "How do you do, Mr. Ruxton?" It was Lewis Garrard, who had been his companion on the ride from Bent's Fort on the Arkansas River to Mann's Fort. (The American knew Ruxton by his mustache.) "He did not recognize me," Garrard noted later. "My greasy buckskins, old wool hat, hickory shirt, and moccasins had been exchanged for more civilized habiliments. To aid his memory, I said—'Don't you recollect the wolf chase near Tharpe's bottom; the little sorrel mule, Bonita, and its owner stopping at Mann's Fort?' He then immediately called me by name. Retiring to one side, we had a talk of old scenes, his book, and other matters. . . . He was then on his way to the mountains—that afternoon he left."

On August 15 Ruxton arrived at the Planter's House hotel in St. Louis, but the city was in the grip of an epidemic of dysentery. Within a few days he had fallen ill. He seemed to recover, then suffered a relapse. He grew weaker, and died on August 29. Because of his books and the fact that he had made many friends in his two short visits to the city, the funeral was well attended. A hearse drawn by four horses led a procession of four mourning coaches, 16 private coaches, and a large crowd on foot. His body was buried beneath an acacia tree in the Episcopal Cemetery.

The Sioux Indians believed that a people without history were like a wind blowing on the buffalo grass. They pitied the early trappers because they brought with them few stories of their past and no historians to record their exploits for future generations. The Sioux need not have worried. Before the mountain men faded into history, they had found their Homer in the unlikely person of an Englishman who, as a boy, had skipped his studies to read the novels of James Fenimore Cooper.

National Portrait Gallery of London

Chapter

❦ 5 ❦

Richard Burton:
By Stagecoach Through the Far West

Early in the morning of August 7, 1860, the celebrated
English adventurer and explorer Richard Burton prepared
to embark on a lengthy stagecoach ride across the West
from St. Joseph, Missouri, to San Francisco, California. At that
time the United States was still a frontier nation. Settled America
continued to look westward toward dimly known mountain
ranges, vast forests, and immense prairies.

Burton's major goal was to add Salt Lake City to the other holy
cities he had visited—Mecca, Medina, Harar, Jerusalem, Rome,
and Benares. Probably the world's foremost authority on compar-
ative sexual customs, he wanted to investigate the Mormon
practice of polygamy and compare it to that of the Arabs and
Africans. With a Colt revolver strapped to his hip and an enormous bowie knife stuck in his belt, he also looked forward, as he
said, to "a little skirmishing with the savages."

Burton traveled without the prejudices or intentions of Frances
Trollope and Charles Dickens. He had little interest in American
manners, institutions, or politics. He concentrated instead upon
the exotic aspects of the Far Western experience—the Indians, the
outlaws, and the polygamous Mormons. Like most of the English
visitors before him, Burton later wrote a book about his experiences. The Mormon historian Fawn Brodie called his *City of
Saints and Across the Rocky Mountains to California* "the best
book on the Mormons published during the nineteenth century."
No other traveler chronicled his journey across America with such
erudition. Always the fastidious scholar, Burton missed nothing—

the languages and customs of the Indian tribes; the geography, geology, and botany of the land; the linguistic peculiarities of the Western settlers; the strengths and weaknesses of the frontier army. His keen eye caught it all.

All his life Burton exhibited an insatiable appetite for exploration. He had recently been the first white man to penetrate the vast wilderness of East Africa to search for the fabled headwaters of the Nile River, an expedition that had nearly cost him his life. Something in his nature drove him constantly to seek his destiny in the remote, dangerous, and unexplored regions of the world. (He once candidly confessed: "Men who go looking for the source of a river are merely looking for the source of something missing in themselves—and never finding it.") He regarded his impending journey through the Far West as a "vacation" after his African adventure.

Burton's real passion lay less in geographical exploration than in an examination of what Joseph Conrad later called the "heart of darkness." That which his contemporaries shrank from as bestial and perverse he investigated with enthusiasm and clinical detachment. In India he researched the ways to flay a man alive. In the Middle East he examined execution by impaling. In East Africa he diligently measured the length of penises among the various tribes. In West Africa he investigated human sacrifice. "His intellectual curiosity was astonishingly broad and deep rather than high," Burton's close friend Frank Harris recalled later in *Contemporary Portraits*. "He would tell stories of Indian philosophy or perverse Negro habits of lust and cannibalism, or would listen to descriptions of Chinese cruelty and Russian self-mutilation till the stars paled out. Catholic in his admiration and liking for all greatness, it was the abnormalities and not the divinities of men that fascinated him."

With his dark hair, enormous black mustache, and large, black, flashing eyes, Burton struck many people as satanic. (In fact, he once researched but never wrote a biography of Satan.) The poet Arthur Symons thought he possessed "a tremendous animalism, an air of repressed ferocity, a devilish fascination." The Arabist Wilfred

Blunt remembered his expression as "the most sinister I have ever seen, dark, cruel, treacherous with eyes like a wild beast's." He reminded Blunt of "a black leopard, caged but unforgiving." Burton had an extraordinary capacity for exerting his will over another person. He hypnotized his wife frequently to learn her innermost thoughts. "He used laughingly to tell everybody, it's the only way to get a woman to tell you the truth," she recalled after his death.

Explorer, soldier, diplomat, anthropologist, poet, author, archaeologist, scholar—Burton was a multifaceted genius. One of the greatest European linguists of his century, he was fluent in 29 languages and more than 40 dialects. An expert swordsman and marksman, he wrote the 15,000-word manual *A Complete System of Bayonet Exercise,* which the British Army adopted for general use. But he could cut a man down as swiftly with wit as steel. "This book has been carefully purged of everything useful," he once observed caustically in a review.

Perhaps no other British traveler of his century went to such extraordinary lengths to insure effective communication with the natives in the lands he visited. He began by eliminating the language barrier. During his early years in India, for example, in rapid succession he learned Sanskrit, Gujarati, Persian, Sindi, Punjabi, Telugu, Pashto, Multani, Armenian, and Turkish. ("Burton took to languages in India as other men to liquor, intoxicated by the sense of mastery and the exhilaration of unlocking mysteries," his late biographer Fawn Brodie observed.) Then, to achieve complete penetration of a foreign culture he often adopted a disguise. In 1853, when he decided to become the first Englishman to gain entrance to Mecca and Medina, the forbidden holy cities of Islam, he undertook elaborate preparations. He had himself circumcised, grew a beard, dyed his skin with henna stain, and studied Arab customs. He learned how to sit, eat, drink, walk, gesture, and pray as an Arab did. Then Richard Burton "disappeared" to be replaced by Mirza Abdullah, an Afghan doctor.

(It is a pity that George Ruxton never lived long enough to meet Burton, for the two were kindred souls. Both men thrived on danger.

They seized upon travel into remote wilderness areas as opportunities for self-denial and shaped their journeys into trials of manliness to heighten their enjoyment of life. And like Burton among the Arabs on his way to Mecca, Ruxton assumed the buckskins, dialect, and manners of the mountain men and became, in effect, one of them. Other travelers such as Mrs. Trollope and Dickens lacked this chameleon-like ability to shed their cultural coloration and pass undetected into an alien society.)

In 1856 Burton turned his attention to sleuthing what had become known in the nineteenth century as "the greatest geographical secret after the discovery of America"—the search for the legendary headwaters of the Nile River. "No unexplored region in our times, neither the heights of the Himalayas, the Antarctic wastes, nor even the hidden side of the moon, has excited quite the same fascination as the mystery of the sources of the Nile," historian Alan Moorehead observed in *The White Nile*. "For two thousand years at least the problem was debated and remained unsolved; every expedition that was sent up the river from Egypt returned defeated."

The Royal Geographical Society granted Burton funds for an expedition into east Africa to search for the sources of the Nile. As his companion, he selected John Hanning Speke, who had been with him on his ventures into Somaliland and Ethiopia. At 30 Speke was six years younger than Burton. He had spent ten years in the Indian Army, the last five on leave exploring remote parts of the Himalayas, even crossing the mountains into Tibet. On the eve of their departure Burton wrote in his journal:

> Of the gladdest moments in human life, methinks, is the departure upon a distant journey into unknown lands. Shaking off with one mighty effort the fetters of Habit, the leaden weight of Routine, the cloak of many Cares, and the slavery of Home, man feels once more happy. The blood flows with the fast circulation of childhood. Excitement lends unwonted vigour to the muscle, and the sudden sense of free-

dom adds a cubic to the mental stature. Afresh dawns the
morn of life. Again the bright world is beautiful to the eye,
and the glorious face of nature gladdens the soul. A journey,
in fact, appeals to Imagination, to Memory, to Hope—the sister graces of our mortal being.

On June 17, 1857, Burton and Speke landed on the coast of
present-day Tanzania, opposite the island of Zanzibar. In a coastal
village decorated with the bleached skulls of enemies atop high
poles they assembled their baggage train of 68 bearers and mule
drivers. Their supplies included great quantities of porcelain
beads, bolts of cloth, and coils of brass wire that functioned as
currency in the African interior. They marched along a trail well
worn by Arab slave-traders toward the Serengeti Plains through a
lonely countryside of low limestone ridges, thornbushes, and
baobab trees with fat tubs for trunks and antlers for branches.
Each village chief charged them an extravagant fee for passage
through his domain. After the Middle East with its history-saturated landscape, the barren African countryside disappointed
Burton. "Eastern and central inter-tropical Africa . . . lacks antiquarian interest," he wrote later. "It has few traditions, no annals,
and no ruins, the hoary remains of past splendour so dear to the
traveller and the reader of travels. It contains not a single useful
or ornamental work of art."

For seven months Burton's caravan marched across the empty
sprawl of eastern Africa and the Great Rift Valley. On a good day
they made six miles. The journey quickly degenerated into a desperate ordeal. Burton and Speke were both constantly ill from fevers
or inflammations of the eyes that left them nearly blind. The intense
humidity rotted their books, rusted their guns, and mildewed their
clothes. Swarms of vicious insects attacked them. Foul weather,
desertions, and a shortage of food added to their misery. Then, in
early February, they climbed a hill and looked upon a great lake.
Burton had discovered Lake Tanganyika, the longest—and after
Russia's Lake Baikal, the deepest—freshwater lake in the world.

The discovery electrified him. If a river flowed northward from this great lake, might it not be the source for the Nile River? They spent several weeks exploring portions of the lake. Local natives assured them that a large river to the north flowed into the lake, not out of it. "I felt sick at heart," Burton confessed.

Disappointed, the pair returned to the village of Ujiji (where some years later Henry Stanley would finally find Dr. David Livingstone). A discouraged Burton remained in camp while Speke led a small party northward to investigate stories of a second and larger lake. Burton's decision not to go cost him his place as one of his century's greatest explorers. After a surprisingly easy march of 225 miles Speke found himself standing on the edge of the second-largest freshwater body in the world. He named it Lake Victoria. He knew, instinctively but with absolute certainty, that he had made the greatest geographical discovery of his time. "I no longer felt any doubt that the lake at my feet gave birth to that interesting river, the source of which has been the subject of so much speculation and the object of so many explorers," Speke recalled.

Burton later haughtily dismissed his claims as mere guesswork unbacked by proper scientific investigation. Sick, exhausted, and hardly speaking to each other, the two men slowly retraced their route to the coast. On April 16 the pair arrived in Aden on the Arabian Peninsula. Burton tarried there a few extra days. Speke hurried back to London where he created a sensation with his unsupported claim that he had discovered the headwaters of the Nile River and insisted untruthfully that he, not Burton, had been the actual leader of the expedition. The Royal Geographical Society immediately voted funds for Speke to return to Lake Victoria to make further explorations. The damage was done. When Burton arrived soon afterward, he found Speke the hero of the day and himself a forgotten man. His bitterness over the betrayal burdened him for the rest of his life.

The African ordeal had taken a terrible toll on Burton's health. "I shall never forget him as he was then," Isabelle, his future wife, wrote later. "He had had twenty-one attacks of fever, had been partially paralysed and partially blind. He was a mere skeleton with brown yellow skin hanging in bags, his eyes protruding and his lips drawn away from his teeth."

A depressed Burton set about writing an account of his African expedition. His *Lake Regions of Central Africa* appeared the following year. The London papers were full of Speke's impending expedition to East Africa, and his quarrel with his former companion was now public knowledge. David Livingstone had also mounted a second expedition into the area. To Burton London became intolerable, and in late April 1860 he abruptly departed England for America. The original motivation for the trip is obscure. He appears to have gone there on the invitation of a close friend from his days in Aden, Lieutenant John Steinhauser, who suggested they "drink" their way through America. "I'll drink mint-juleps, brandy-smashes, whisky-skies, gin-sling, cocktail sherry, cobblers, rum-salads, streaks of lightning, morning-glory," Burton wrote in his journal. "It'll be a most interesting experiment. I want to see whether after a life of 3 or 4 months, I can drink and eat myself to the level of the aborigines." Almost no details of his early months in America survive. Apparently the pair traveled extensively throughout the States east of the Mississippi River. We do know that Burton called upon the Secretary of War John B. Floyd in Washington and obtained letters of introduction to the commanding officers at the major Army posts in the West.

In early August Burton appeared at the St. Joseph office of the Overland Stage Company and paid $175 for a ticket to Salt Lake City. His depression had lifted, largely at the thought of once again entering dangerous territory. The Far West in the late summer of 1860 looked increasingly grim. An Indian war had raged for several months throughout the Nebraska Territory. The Comanches, Kiowas, and Cheyennes were on the warpath. The Sioux were fighting their old foes, the Pawnee. "Horrible accounts of murdered postboys and cannibal emigrants, greatly exaggerated as usual for private and public purposes, filled the papers," he noted. The U.S. Army was busy on several fronts. It all looked like a glorious fray, and Burton longed to be in the midst of it.

2

"Where today is the Pequot? Where are the Narrangansetts, the Mohawks, the Pokanoket? They have vanished . . . as snow before a summer sun," the Shawnee chief Tecumseh declared, lamenting the catastrophic annihilation the whites had inflicted upon the Indian tribes of eastern America.

When George Ruxton traveled through the Far West in 1847, the fierce and proud Plains Indians appeared invulnerable. Wild, free nomads, they had developed into fierce and proud warriors. Incessant tribal conflict had honed the mounted brave into a formidable fighting man with skills of horsemanship far superior to those of the white cavalry who came later. Great herds of buffaloes provided the western Indians with abundant food and shelter. Their horses gave them the mobility to cover vast distances.

In 1847 the white settlement largely stopped at the Mississippi River. The several thousand whites who rolled westward in their covered wagons toward California and Oregon that year often saw their first Indians camped sociably around one of the frontier forts. The vastness of the distances and the sparseness of the Indian populations usually precluded frequent sightings along the trail. In many instances the Indians proved friendly to the whites, providing critical aid and assistance, which enabled them to complete their passage to the West Coast. Attacks on wagon trains were rare. (Historian John D. Unruh in *The Plains Across,* a study of the overland migration before the Civil War, computed the total number of emigrant deaths from Indian attack at just 362 between 1845 and 1860. This amounts to a mere 4% of the estimated 10,000 trail deaths.)

The next dozen years, however, brought dramatic changes. The numbers alone tell the story. The news of the gold strikes in

California provoked a flood of emigrants across the plains. On one day in 1850, August 14, the soldiers at Fort Laramie counted 39,506 overlanders in 9,927 wagons surging westward. By 1859 the number had dropped to 20,000 and then to 10,000 in 1860. The advancing white frontier, together with the vast increase in overland traffic, inevitably made the Indians uneasy. The influx of whites sharply reduced the numbers of buffalo, which was the economic basis of life for the Plains Indians; overgrazed the prairies; exhausted the small supply of available timber; and depleted water resources. The western Indians, who had already been compressed to make room for eastern tribes, now saw white farmers pouring into the country west of the Missouri River. Treaties were violated almost as soon as they were signed. Indians quickly learned that the federal government's primary responsibility was protection of the whites, not the rights and hopes of Indians. Armed conflicts between the two races increased dramatically throughout the 1850s. The myth of the Indian as "the noble red man" that had prevailed before 1850 soon gave way in the press to another stereotype, that of the bloodthirsty savage who must be exterminated at any cost.

By 1860 the West possessed a formidable array of villages, army forts, civilian trading posts, stagecoach stops, Pony Express stations, mining camps, ranches, and farms. In *The City of Saints* Burton summarized the precarious situation of the western Indians at the time: "The Indian race is becoming desperate, wild-beast like, hemmed in by its enemies that have flanked it on the east and the west and are gradually closing in upon it. The tribes can no longer shift ground without inroads into territories already occupied by neighbours, who are, of course, hostile. They are, therefore, being brought to final bay." When Burton's stagecoach rolled out of St. Joseph that August morning, the conflict between whites and Indians was still at the stage of skirmishing. The great Indian wars that ravaged the West for a quarter-century did not begin until a few years later. Nonetheless, the greatest hazard facing travelers on the frontier in 1860 came from Indians. Burned stage stations and scalped bodies were a common sight along the Overland Stage Company route. Passengers of both sexes traveled heavily armed.

One traveler to Colorado reported what happened when a force of 150 Indians besieged his stage. At first the passengers kept them at bay with heavy rifle and revolver fire. But the Indians brought forward a captured herder and staked him out on the ground in plain view of the whites. They slowly mutilated and then built a fire over the screaming victim. That night the stage passengers managed their escape and hurried to nearby Downer Station, only to discover, to their horror, that it was nothing but charred ruins. Scalped bodies, some with the arrows still sticking out, lay about. "The air of the plains is glorious, pure, and dry," the traveler noted matter-of-factly. "There is no odor to a dead body here, as it does not decay but simply dries up."

3

In 1860 St. Joseph boasted a population of 8,932 and successfully competed with Independence as a principal departure point for trips into the Far West. As a staging area, it served both greenhorns and seasoned travelers. Overlanders, confidence men, soldiers, and farmers jostled one another in the crowded streets. For those preparing to make the long trek west, St. Joseph represented a last opportunity to savor the benefits of "civilization." Ahead loomed hardship, deprivation, and danger.

In St. Joseph, Burton purchased a few necessities he hoped would make the long stagecoach ride endurable. (Passengers were allowed 25 pounds of luggage; excess baggage was charged at the rate of $1 a pound.) He bought a cache of tea, sugar, and cognac, having been advised such items were virtually nonexistent in the Far West. He packed a large supply of cigars ("the driver either receives or takes the lion's share") and quantities of matches for trade with the Indians. Other items included two thick pocket notebooks, a small sextant, compass, pocket thermometer, an umbrella, and a copy of Captain Randolph Marcy's *The Prairie Traveler: A Handbook for Overland Expeditions*. For protection he relied upon two Colt revolvers. "From the moment of leaving St. Joseph to the time of reaching . . . Sacramento the pistol should never be absent from a man's right side," he advised his readers. "Contingencies with Indians and others may happen when the difference of a second saves a life. The revolver should therefore be carried with its butt to the fore."

Burton's home for the next three weeks was a Concord stagecoach, manufactured by Abbot, Downing and Company of Concord, New Hampshire. Nine passengers rode inside, while a driver, guard, and two additional passengers sat on top. "A finished Concord coach was a thing of beauty," historian Oscar Winther observes in *The Transportation Frontier*. "In the case of . . . [the] Overland Stage Company the body of the coach was English vermilion; running gear, straw; leather upholstery and curtains, russet or black. . . . Scenic pictures decorated the door panels, and frequently the likeness of some contemporary actress was painted on either side of the footboard or driver's seat. On all mail-carrying coaches appeared in gold letters: 'U.S. Mail.' For ornamentation as well as use there were oil lamps on the upper sides. As a final step in manufacture the entire painted surface of the coach was given two coats of varnish. Concord coaches of the type used in the West weighed about twenty-five hundred pounds and cost about twelve to fifteen hundred dollars upon delivery."

In the spring of 1859 the Overland Stage Company inaugurated service between St. Joseph and San Francisco, traveling along the old Oregon Trail to Fort Laramie, then across the Rocky Mountains at South Pass to Salt Lake City and points west. Known as the Central Overland Trail, it was the most important route crossing the great expanse of western prairies and plains, and was the primary road for military and emigrant travel. The trip took an average of three weeks to Salt Lake City. Teams of mules were preferred over horses for their superior toughness, sureness of foot, and powers of endurance. Like most Western stagecoach lines, the Overland Stage Company was heavily subsidized by the federal government to carry mail. (The stagecoach was more glamorous than effective as a bond between the East and West, and within a decade the transcontinental railroad took its place.)

Burton's companions in the stagecoach included Lieutenant James J. Dana of the Fourth U.S. Artillery, who was traveling to Camp Floyd in the Utah Territory with his wife, Thesta, and two-year-old daughter, May. Early in the trip Burton won the affections of the parents when he presented little May with a carved ivory image, a souvenir from his recent African adventure. The other passengers included a federal judge, a marshal, and a U.S. Attorney. Burton was prepared to enjoy himself enormously, being attracted to those qualities of American life which had repelled Mrs. Trollope and Charles Dickens. He particularly liked the egalitarianism of the frontier society, praising "the unique sensation that all men are equal, that you are no man's superior, and that no man is yours."

Burton appeared for the departure wearing an old English tweed shooting jacket "with enormous pockets like a poacher's," a brown felt hat, and wool pants with their bottoms tucked into the tops of his boots. At 9:30 A.M. the driver snapped his reins and headed for Salt Lake City. The coach passed along the dusty roads of St. Joseph to the Missouri River, where a steam ferry conveyed them across to the opposite bank. Soon the driver shouted out "Emigration Road," and they were on their way West. Burton noted with approval that it was "a great thoroughfare, broad and well worn as a European turnpike or a Roman military route, and undoubtedly the best and longest natural highway in the world." For the next several miles they traveled through a tangled thicket of oak and elm trees. Suddenly they broke free, climbed a short hill, and looked across a vast expanse of grassland. Beyond lay the great American prairie.

Burton had earlier read Captain Randolph Marcy's warning in his copy of *The Prairie Traveler*: "On such a journey as this there is much to interest and amuse one who is fond of picturesque scenery and of wild life in its most primitive aspect. Yet no one should attempt it without anticipating many rough knocks and much hard labor."

For days the coach rolled through a thick tapestry of grass, already turning to ruddy yellow with the approach of autumn, and across graceful undulations of low-lying hills, which followed one after another to the horizon and then beyond. Burton soon developed a curious sensation that he was misplaced in the midst of "an ocean in which one loses the sight of land." He looked eagerly for the vast numbers of buffaloes he had read so much about but saw not a single one. The countryside was barren of wildlife, the result of thousands of busy hunters from hundreds of wagon trains. "These prairies are preparing to become the great grazing grounds which shall supply the unpopulated East with herds of civilized kine," he noted prophetically in his daily journal.

The tall grass of the prairie eventually gave way to the short grass of the Great Plains, and then to sagebrush and greasewood. The rivers grew fewer and farther apart. Vegetation seemed to confine itself to their unpredictable meanderings as they cut their way downward into the subsoil. The August heat was oppressive.

The big Concord stagecoach averaged 100 miles during each 24-hour period. The coach rocked wildly on its thoroughbraces, throwing Burton roughly up against the other passengers as the iron-tired wheels clattered noisily over the ruts in a perpetual cloud of choking dust. The trip soon settled into a numbing blur of endless stage stations, rapid changes of teams and drivers, and bone-jarring stretches of road that quickly produced an exhausted numbness. Sleep was impossible except for brief moments when he successfully blocked out the dust, motion, shouts of the driver, and constant rumble of the road. The heat of the day gave way to the chill of the night and clouds of mosquitoes. Thunderstorms added to the travelers' misery. "Gusts of raw, cold, and violent wind from the west whizzed overhead, thunder crashed and rattled closer and closer, and vivid lightning, flashing out of the murky depths around, made earth and air one blaze of living fire," Burton recalled later.

The drivers were hard-smoking, hard-drinking men. "I scarcely ever saw a sober driver," Burton insisted. "As for profanity—the Western equivalent for hard swearing—they . . . are not to be deterred from evil talking even by the dread presence of a 'lady.'" On occasion a driver invited Burton to ride up top in the box, a privilege granted only to the most distinguished passengers. Burton had a high regard for most of the drivers and found them intelligent, responsible, courageous, and good-humored.

Stage stations dotted the road every 15 miles or so. Most were simple frame, sod, log, adobe, or stone structures, offering few, if any, amenities. The Overland Stage Company maintained 153 stations along its central route, usually consisting of a stable for a dozen or so mules and horses and a crude hut where passengers dined and rested. Floors were hard-packed dirt, the windows simply holes in the walls without glass or curtains. Amenities such as shelves, cupboards, closets, and beds were rare. The dining table was often just a greasy board on uneven legs. A battered tin platter, a knife and fork, and a tin cup marked each place. Meals cost 50 cents and consisted inevitably of wretched coffee, greasy eggs, coarse bread, and fried bacon. Almost all the stations were filthy. In areas where Indian attacks were frequent they served double duty as forts. Protective walls surrounded the buildings, and narrow gun ports allowed effective fields of fire in all directions.

The Cold Springs station, the first beyond St. Joseph, served as Burton's introduction to all the others:

> The widow body to whom the shanty belonged lay sick with fever. . . . The ill-conditioned sons dawdled about, listless as Indians in skin tunics and pantaloons fringed with lengthy tags such as the redoubtable "Billy Bow-legs" wears on tobacco labels. And the daughters, tall, young women, whose sole attire was apparently a calico morning-wrapper, colour invisible, waited upon us in a protesting way. Squalor

and misery were imprinted upon the wretched log hut, which ignored the duster and the broom. Myriads of flies disputed with us a dinner consisting of doughnuts, green and poisonous with saleratus, suspicious eggs in a massive greasy fritter, and rusty bacon, intolerably fat.

Burton's detailed descriptions of the stagecoach stations convey vividly their drab monotony. Sleeping conditions were just as primitive. "Upon the bedded floor of the foul 'doggery' lay, in a seeming promiscuous heap, men, women, children, lambs, and puppies, all fast in the arms of Morpheus," he noted after one night spent in vain trying to get a decent sleep. Of another station he said: "I wish my enemy no more terrible fate than to drink excessively with M. Bissonette of M.B.'s liquor." Bathing facilities were nonexistent at the stations. Occasionally the driver would halt alongside a river or mountain stream and let his passengers rinse themselves quickly.

Burton traveled through a West that had changed profoundly in the 13 years since Ruxton's visit. Along with the tens of thousands of overlanders had come the outlaws, prostitutes, and general riffraff, who were already giving the West a reputation for "wildness." Many of the stations were located in country without law and without even the pretense of it. They proved perfect refuges for men wanted for murder and robbery. Lieutenant Dana recalled in later years that he and Burton had chatted with a young gunslinger named Wild Bill Hickok at the Platte River Station. Hickok worked for several years as a stage driver and station manager.

The most notorious of the station managers was Joseph (Jack) Slade, whose reputation for "deadly strife" had spread the length of the Central Overland Trail. For days the stage drivers had entertained Burton and the other passengers with tales of the infamous gunslinger. A strikingly handsome man, he was in later years reputed to have killed 26 men. Mark Twain left behind a full account of Slade's life and exploits in his early book, *Roughing It*. (In 1861 Twain traveled by Overland stage from St. Joseph to Virginia City, in the Nevada Territory.) Slade was born in Illinois, killed his first man while in his mid-twenties, and fled to St. Joseph. He soon gained a job with a wagon train bound for California. "One day on the plains he had an angry dispute with one of his wagon drivers, and both drew their revolvers," Twain recorded. "But the driver was the quicker artist and had his weapon cocked first. So Slade said it was a pity to waste life on so small a matter and proposed that the pistols be thrown on the ground and the quarrel settled by a fist-fight. The unsuspecting driver agreed and threw down his pistol—whereupon Slade laughed at his simplicity and shot him dead!"

Later Slade secured work as a division agent for the Overland Stage Company. In 1860 he worked west of Fort Laramie out of the Horseshoe Station where, Burton thought, "an ominous silence" prevailed. The homicidal Slade with his low cheekbones and thin lips fascinated the Englishman. Slade joined the passengers at the dinner table, a revolver on his hip and a bowie knife in his belt. "He had lately indeed had a strong hint not to forget his weapon," Burton noted. "One M. Jules, a French trader, after a quarrel . . . walked up to him and fired a pistol, wounding him in the breast. As he rose to run away, Jules discharged a second which took effect in his back." (The Frenchman fled to the Rocky Mountains. Later Slade tracked him down, bound him to a post at the Rocky Ridge station, and used his arms and legs for target practice before finally shooting him through the head. Then he did something which ensured him a permanent place in Western legend: He cut off Jules's ear and used it as a watch fob.)

Burton met Slade's wife and found her "like the other women in this wild part of the world generally—cold and disagreeable in manner, full of 'proper pride,' with a touch-me-not air." She permitted the women passengers to sleep in the house but told the men they must find places as they could outside. They slept in a barn "hardly fit for a decently brought-up pig." Several drunken fellows sprawled over the only available bunks. The floor was damp. No door blocked the cold night wind. "Into this disreputable hole we were all thrust for the night," Burton complained. "Amongst us, it must be remembered, was a federal judge, who had officiated for years as a minister at a European court. His position, poor man, procured him nothing but a broken-down pallet."

(As a footnote to the above, Slade's violent drunkenness finally brought him afoul of some local vigilantes. On March 10, 1864, they put an end to his career as a gunfighter when they hanged him. His distraught wife berated his executioners for not having the courage to shoot him dead rather than hang him like common thief.)

As crude as they were, the stage stations were social oases among the vast empty spaces. Rarely did Burton see other human beings as the coach rolled from station to station. For days they passed through a countryside "inhabited only by wolves and antelopes, hares and squirrels, grasshoppers, and occasionally an Indian family." There were two brief encounters with Pony Express riders who galloped past the lumbering Concord coach with scarcely time to shout greetings. "The riders are mostly youths, mounted upon active and lithe Indian nags," Burton reported. "They ride 100 miles at a time—about eight per hour—with four changes of horses and return to their stations the next day." The Pony Express had started service only five months before. Each letter they carried cost its sender $5 a sheet.

Occasionally Burton saw wagon trains, "those ships of the great American Sahara. . . . They are not unpicturesque from afar, these long winding trains, in early morning like lines of white cranes trooping slowly over the prairie." On August 16, at the Platte River, Burton's coach passed a column of 24 rattling, weather-beaten, canvas-topped covered wagons full of Mormon emigrants from England, "wending their ways toward the Promised Land." The trail captain turned out to be a nephew of the prophet Brigham Young, a blond-haired young man with a heavy beard, suitably armed with the universal revolver and bowie knife. The good spirits and excellent health of the group impressed Burton.

However, mismanagement, incompetence, and inexperience were often more typical of the overland experience and proved the ruin of many a wagon train. Burton described one such group they briefly encountered. On August 22 he noted in his pocket journal: "We passed several families and parties of women and children trudging wearily along. Most of the children were in rags or half nude. All showed gratitude when we threw them provisions. The greater part of the men were armed, but their weapons were far more dangerous to themselves and their fellows than to the enemy." At one station an overlander begged some cloth to make a burial shroud for his child, who had been accidentally shot that afternoon. The station crew contemptuously turned him down, insisting to Burton that such accidents were a common event, two or three happening every month. "We were now in a region of graves," Burton noted, "and their presence in this wild was not a little suggestive."

Burton, however, was much more interested in the American Indians and saw in them a kindred people to the desert Bedouins he admired so highly. "Both have the same wild chivalry, the same fiery sense of honour, and the same boundless hospitality," he noted with approval. "Elopements from tribe to tribe, the blood feud, and the vendetta are common to the two. Both are grave and cautious in demeanour and formal in manner—princes in rags or paint. The Arabs plunder pilgrims; the Indians, bands of trappers. And both rob according to certain rules."

When Burton left St. Joseph, he was resolved to break his trip to Salt Lake City at any time that a good opportunity for Indian fighting presented itself. Eager to see action, he showed his letters of introduction from the Secretary of War to the commanding officers of all the forts along the Central Overland Trail. One day the driver pointed out the place where Indians had massacred a troop of 30 soldiers in 1854. At Fort Kearny Burton learned a major action had just been fought against a large body of Comanches, Kiowas, and Cheyennes. After he heard the details of the fighting and the casualties suffered by the Indians, he concluded there was little chance of additional fighting in the near future in that region and reboarded the stage in the hopes of seeing "independent service" on the road.

Burton the Indian fighter was disappointed. The future held

Indian scares but no Indian fights. But Burton the anthropologist found plenty to interest him. The coach sometimes passed pretty Indian encampments in the distance, their idyllic tranquillity seemingly undisturbed by the clashes elsewhere between soldiers and braves. "These Indian villages are very picturesque from afar when dimly seen dotting the verdure of the valleys and when their tall white cones, half hidden by willow clumps, lie against a blue background," Burton noted. "The river side is the savages' favourite site; next to it the hill foot where little clumps of three or four tents are often seen from the road, clustering mysteriously near a spring. Almost every prairie-band has its own way of constructing lodges, encamping and building fires, and the experienced mountaineer easily distinguishes them."

One day Burton watched with keen interest the migration of an entire Dakota Indian village across the prairie. The warriors on horseback headed up the column, each brave armed with a small tomahawk that he carried with a powder horn in his belt, while a long tobacco pouch made from antelope skin hung from his other side. Across their shoulders they carried their bows, arrows, and shields made from buffalo hide. A few had guns. Behind came the women, children, and ponies dragging travois holding the tribe's heavier items. Burton studied the women closely. "The grandmothers were fearful to look upon, horrid excrescences of nature," he concluded. "The middle-aged matrons were homely bodies, broad and squat like the African dame after she has become *mère de famille*. Their hands and feet were notably larger than those of the men, and the burdens upon their backs caused them to stoop painfully." The young Indian girls, however, completely captured Burton's fancy. He observed with obvious relish their "large and languishing eyes," flawless teeth, shiny black hair, and trim figures. Most wore bracelets of brass wire, bead sashes around their waists, scarlet leggings, and costly moccasins.

That same evening the coach stopped for several hours at the Diamond Springs Station. Burton found a group of soldiers sitting around, drinking a homemade brew they called "lightning-bug," and telling Indian stories. The station keeper told them about an old mountain man whom the Indians had killed a few days before. Married to two squaws, he had sat in his tent drinking with several Cheyennes, "a tribe famous for its ferocity and hostility to whites," when the Indians asked him if he feared death. The mountain man shrugged his shoulders and replied philosophically, "You may kill me if you like." His drunken guests immediately leaped up and hacked him to death. Burton studied the reaction of the men at the station to the tale and drew his own conclusion: "In these regions the opposite races regard each other as wild beasts; the white man will shoot an Indian as he would a coyote. He expects to go under whenever the 'all-fired, red-bellied varmits' . . . get the upper hand."

Throughout his stagecoach journey Burton's inquisitive mind sought information on all aspects of Indian culture. He asked hundreds of questions. Nothing escaped his attention. And his constant comparisons with the ethnology of other native peoples give Burton's discussion of American Indian life a richness lacking in other overland accounts.

On the importance of the buffalo to Indian society: "The horns and hoofs make glue for various purposes, especially for feathering arrows; the brains and part of the bowels are used for curing skins; the hide clothes the tribes from head to foot; the calf-skins form their saddle blankets; the sinews make their bowstrings, thread, and finer cord."

On the position of women among Indians: "They place their women in the most degraded position. The squaw is a mere slave, living a life of utter drudgery."

On marriage among Indians: "Marriage is a simple affair with them. In some tribes the bride . . . is carried off by force. In others the man who wants a wife courts her with a little present and pickets near the father's lodge the number of horses which he supposes to be her equivalent. As amongst all the savage tribes the daughter is a chattel, an item of her father's goods, and he will not part with her except for a consideration."

On Indian dining customs: "They have no regular hours for meals or sleep. . . . The women rarely sit at meals with the men. In savage and semi-barbarous societies the separation of the sexes is the general rule, because, as they have no ideas in common, each prefers the society of its own."

The Indian custom of scalping particularly fascinated Burton. His discussion of that "solemn rite" covers three pages in *The City of Saints*. As an introduction, he catalogued the various early European people who practiced scalping and offered up numerous anthropological conjectures as to the source of the custom in primitive societies. He then gave readers a detailed description of the proper way to take a scalp. (After making the initial cuts, the Indian "sits on the ground, places his feet against the subject's shoulders by way of leverage, and holding the scalp-lock with both hands he applies a strain which soon brings off the spoils with a sound which, I am told, is not unlike 'flop.'")

Scalplocks were popular souvenirs with foreign visitors, who frequently paid $50 and more for a fancy one. Burton advised his readers how to distinguish a true scalp from a fake one intended for the tourist trade: "It must be remembered by 'curio' hunters that only one scalp can come off one head: namely, the centre lock or long tuft growing upon the coronal apex with about three inches in diameter of skin. This knowledge is the more needful as the western men are in the habit of manufacturing half a dozen cut from different parts of the same head."

Burton the linguist was keenly interested in the Indian system of sign language, which allowed members of one tribe to communicate readily with those of another. He diligently studied the various gestures, learned the tribal variations, and in less than a month had made himself fluent in Indian sign language.

A military man, Burton used his stops at the various forts to appraise the condition of the American frontier army. In 1860 the federal government maintained 7,090 enlisted men and officers in the West, largely to control the Indians and provide protection for the emigrant caravans. Occasionally Burton's stagecoach passed Army columns patrolling the Central Overland Trail in defensive formations—small groups of troopers, rifles at the ready, riding the flanks of the main body, while individual soldiers rode ahead as lookouts. Often the men did not look like soldiers at all. A regulation uniform was hardly to be seen. The men wore slouch hats, buckskin or woolen trousers and shirts, and sometimes moccasins rather than boots. Most sported beards to protect their faces against sunburn and windburn.

On August 23 Burton's Overland stage pulled into Fort Bridger in the Wyoming Territory for a 45-minute stop. He passed the time chatting with the officers and drinking toddies. "The officers complained very naturally of their isolation and unpleasant duty, which principally consists in keeping the roads open for, and the Indians from cutting off, parties of unmanageable emigrants who look upon the Federal army as their humblest servants," he noted.

Burton never ceased to be amazed at the magnificence of the Western scenery. A highlight was the passage across South Pass over the Continental Divide. The driver briefly stopped the coach to let his passengers enjoy the view. "That evening the Wind River Mountains appeared in marvelous majesty," he wrote later. "The huge purple hangings of rain-cloud in the northern sky set off their huge proportions. . . . The mellow radiance of the setting sun diffused a charming softness over their more rugged features, defining the folds and ravines with a distinctness which deceived every idea of distance. And as the light sank behind the far western horizon, it travelled slowly up the mountain side, till, reaching the summit, it mingled its splendours with the snow—flashing and flickering for a few brief moments."

On August 25, after 19 days in his stagecoach, Burton caught his first glimpse of Salt Lake City lying in the distance like an Eden newly made—"a lovely panorama of green, azure, and gold land as fresh as if it had come from the hands of God." He was overwhelmed with emotion. He had come once again to a holy city at the end of a long and dangerous journey.

4

"Going amongst the Mormons!" an American acquaintance had protested to Burton in New Orleans. "They are shooting and cutting one another in all directions. How can *you* expect to escape?"

In 1860 fear and hatred of the "White Indians," as Mormons were sometimes called, ran high. Three years before, a group of Mormon fanatics had murdered 120 men and women from a wagon train in the infamous Mountain Meadows Massacre. President James Buchanan hurried four regiments to Utah. "This is the first rebellion which has existed in our territory," he declared, "and humanity itself requires that we should put it down in such a manner that it shall be the last." Brigham Young, the living prophet of Mormonism, managed to negotiate an uneasy peace. But the soldiers remained, garrisoned at Camp Floyd to the west of Salt Lake City, until they were recalled at the outbreak of the Civil War.

No other American religious minority suffered such persecution in the nineteenth century as did the members of the Church of Jesus Christ of Latter-Day Saints, in large part because of their practice of polygamy. Persecution drove them westward from central New York to rural Illinois, and finally on to the arid wastes of the Great Salt Lake Basin. The Mexican War had opened vast new territories for eventual settlement. The first overlanders were Mormons under the leadership of Brigham Young, who sought a land so inhospitable and isolated that no one else would want it. (George Ruxton had encountered their first migration in the early spring of 1847 when they wintered over on the banks of the Arkansas River.) In the barren land of the Ute Indians the Mormons hoped to make a refuge from their enemies and worship

without fear of persecution. A virgin land promised new begin-
nings and a place where they could control their own destiny.
Beyond beckoned California, but Brigham Young refused to be
tempted. "Like the Adam of Mormon theology, Young chose a
world of struggle and growth over an easy but static Eden," historian Leonard Arrington observes in *The Mormon Experience*.

The isolation was, of course, short-lived. In January 1848 John
Sutter discovered gold in his millrace, unleashing one of the greatest migrations in history. The Mormon pioneers suddenly found
themselves athwart the national highway to California. Salt Lake
City became a halfway house, the most important stop between St.
Joseph and the West Coast. Thousands of overlanders paused there
to rest, recuperate, reprovision, and reoutfit. The Mormons, in
turn, prospered as they catered to the needs of the gentile throngs.

In England the Mormons were considered a great curiosity. A
writer for *The Times* of London thought them "the most singular
phenomenon of modern times." Mormon missionaries actively
recruited throughout England, sending 16,356 new converts to
Utah between 1850 and 1860. "Mormonism is emphatically the
faith of the poor," Burton observed. And it was among the
wretched poor in the English slums that the Mormon missionaries
preached their message of spiritual rebirth in America with the
greatest success. In 1863 Charles Dickens visited some 800
Mormon emigrants aboard the ship *Amazon* docked in London.
He noted their "great steadiness of purpose and much undemon-
strative self-respect" and expressed astonishment at the "universal
cheerfulness." Like Dickens, Burton was keenly interested in
learning more about Mormonism. "Having read and heard so
much about Utah as it is said to be, I was anxious to see Utah as
it is," he told Brigham Young during their first meeting.

Salt Lake City was home to some 9,000 people when Burton
arrived. There he enjoyed his first comfortable lodgings and decent
food since leaving St. Joseph. Gracious hostesses in clean dining
rooms served him ample portions of fresh vegetables, new pota-
toes, buttered bread, and freshly baked pastries. He learned that

much of the fine furniture in his hotel and the private residences he visited had been scavenged from along the Central Overland Trail after the pieces had been abandoned by weary California-bound emigrants. And he quickly discovered that in the isolation-induced inflation of the city no coins under a quarter circulated.

During his three-week stay in Utah Burton immersed himself in Mormon culture. He met all important church officials and interviewed everyone from Brigham Young to a field hand, attended church services and dances, visited a penitentiary, browsed the shops, accompanied the governor of the Utah Territory and his wife on a bathing expedition to the Great Salt Lake, studied the Ute language, and read prodigious amounts of Mormon and anti-Mormon literature.

Burton's meeting with Young took place in the study of his Beehive House in the company of various church elders. He noticed that Young kept a revolver and rifle within easy reach of his desk. Burton came away impressed. "The Prophet is no common man," he concluded. "He has none of the weakness and vanity which characterise the uncommon man. . . . There is a total absence of pretension in his manner, and he has been so long used to power that he cares nothing for its display. The arts by which he rules the heterogeneous mass of conflicting elements are indomitable will, profound secrecy, and uncommon astuteness." Young also liked Burton and later took him on a tour of the city. When the Englishman asked if he could be admitted to the church, the prophet replied with a chuckle: "I think you've done that sort of thing once before, Captain."

For all its gracious refinement, Salt Lake City still showed the effects of its frontier environment. Burton was taken to the spot where shortly before his arrival two men with reputations for horse stealing had been mysteriously gunned down. The bodies were later put on public display as a warning. He detected a broad tolerance in the community for vigilante actions to keep the peace. Six weeks earlier another horse thief was summarily shot to death when he was discovered rustling some stock. "In a place where, amongst much that is honest and respectable, there are notable exceptions, this wild, unflinching, and unerring justice, secret and sudden, is the rod of iron which protects the good," Burton noted approvingly. "During my residence in the Mormon City not a single murder was . . . committed. The three days I spent in Carson City witnessed three."

Nonetheless Burton quickly came to feel cramped in the puritanical confines of a Mormon culture that prohibited liquor, gambling, and sensuality in all its aspects. "I reached this place about a week ago and am living in the ordour of sanctity," he complained in a letter to a friend. And in *The City of Saints* he admitted: "A Moslem gloom, the result of austere morals and manners and of the semi-seclusion of the [opposite] sex, . . . hangs over society."

A major reason for Burton's visit to Salt Lake City was his fascination with polygamy. Unlike Mark Twain, Horace Greeley, Ralph Waldo Emerson, and other visitors who preceded or followed him, he brought to bear on the practice a vast background of personal experiences and study among the polygamous peoples of Africa and the Middle East. In eastern Africa he had visited a tribe where the chief kept many wives but gouged out the eyes of his subjects who failed to adhere to a strict puritanical code. And during Burton's trip to Mecca he had used his disguise of an Afghan doctor to penetrate the harem on numerous occasions.

Mormon polygamy (or "pluralism," as the church called it) both fascinated and repulsed the American people. In fact, perhaps no more than 20% of the church's population ever lived in polygamous families. And even there the reality was one of strict sobriety, not the boisterous sensuality of the popular imagination. The Mormon family was every bit as Victorian as its more orthodox counterpart in New England. The Mormons were quick to answer their critics by pointing out that polygamy was an established institution with ancient roots, popular in Old Testament days, and insisting that it was a practical and honorable way to provide marriage and motherhood to thousands of deserving women who would otherwise be condemned to long years of "painful" spinsterhood. Such justifications, however, fell on deaf ears.

"This was fairy-land to us, to all intents and purposes—a land of enchantment, and goblins, and awful mystery," Twain wrote in *Roughing It* of his 1861 visit to Salt Lake City, poking considerable fun at Mormon polygamy. "We felt a curiosity to ask every child how many mothers it had, and if it could tell them apart. . . . With the gushing self-sufficiency of youth I was feverish to plunge in headlong and achieve a great reform here—until I saw the Mormon women. . . . The man that marries one of them has done an act of Christian charity which entitles him to the kindly applause of mankind, not their harsh censure—and the man that marries sixty of them has done a deed of open-handed generosity so sublime that the nations should stand uncovered in his presence and worship in silence."

Burton approached Mormon polygamy with far more tolerance than did most of his contemporaries. "Man is by nature polygamic, whereas woman, as a rule, is monogamic and polyandrous only when tired of her lover," he often insisted. "The man loves the woman, but the love of the woman is for the love of the man." In *The City of Saints* he reviewed the common Mormon justifications of polygamy and then suggested several of his own. "To the unprejudiced traveller it appears that polygamy is the rule where population is required," he wrote. "The other motive for polygamy in Utah is economy. Servants are rare and costly; it is cheaper and more comfortable to marry them." Burton was quick to see that Mormon polygamy offered few sensual excitements. "A *ménage à trois*, in the Mormon sense of the phrase, is fatal to the development of that tender tie which must be confined to two," he insisted. "In its stead there is household comfort, affection, circumspect friendship, and domestic discipline."

As Burton's departure drew closer, he became increasingly concerned about reports of hostile Indian actions in the deserts west of Salt Lake City. Three stage drivers had been murdered in separate attacks. Federal soldiers had reportedly slain 17 Indians in several bloody encounters. Burton prepared for the final portion of his trip by "shingling off" his hair to make his head unappealing to any would-be scalp hunters. He laid in a small supply of biscuits, butter, tinned food, whiskey, tea, and sugar against the inevitable hardships of the Overland Stage stations' dining fare.

Burton left Salt Lake City on the morning of September 20. Instead of traveling by stagecoach he had decided to try his hand at trail riding. He paid $150 to accompany a man named Kennedy, an Irish speculator driving 33 horses and mules to California. On a recent trip Ute Indians had attacked Kennedy's outfit and driven off two of his horses. They shot one horse out from under him and put a bullet through his right arm. In the company of several heavily armed cowboys, Burton departed the Mormon capital on the back of mule ("here worth $240 and 'bound' to fetch in California $400"). They quickly covered the 30 miles to Camp Floyd, where he met with Porter Rockwell, the former bodyguard to the Mormon leader Joseph Smith and a man famed throughout the Utah Territory for innumerable killings. He and Burton drank whiskey together and exchanged stories. Rockwell advised the Englishman about Indian tactics and cautioned him about the dangers ahead. "Finally he comforted me with an assurance that either the Indians would not attempt to attack us and our stock—ever a sore temptation with them—or that they would assault us in force and 'wipe us out,'" Burton noted.

From Camp Floyd the small group, with their herd of stock and several wagons, made their way across the forbidding desert of western Utah. Evenings were spent at Overland Stage Company stations. By day they traveled through a landscape as bleak as the far side of the moon. "All was desert," he wrote later. "The hair of this unlovely skin was sage and greasewood. It was warted with sand-heaps; in places mottled with bald and horrid patches of salt soil, whilst in others minute crystals of salt, glistening like diamond dust in the sunlight, covered tracts of moist and oozy mud." In late afternoon they arrived at the station, which proved to be a hole four feet deep and roofed over with split cedar trunks, manned by two men and their bulldog. Here, as at the other stations, there was considerable talk of Indian attacks and casualties. Much of the violence had been provoked by the whites who often shot braves on sight and raped Indian women for sport. Only the Mormons escaped the Indian wrath. "The Mormons treat their step-brethren with far more humanity than other western men," Burton noted. "They feed, clothe, and lodge them, and attach them by good works to their interest."

The dawn of October 5 brought a driving wind, snow, and hail. The group took breakfast at a log cabin, which, like most stations in the region, showed signs of a recent Indian attack. Later that morning they rode nervously through a rugged canyon. ("An uglier place for sharpshooting can hardly be imagined.") Burton caught sight of two fires high up a nearby hillside, which were suddenly extinguished. "Indians," he shouted to his companions. They whipped their animals to a frenzy to escape an ambush. When they arrived at the next stage station, they were horrified to find that the Indians had been there only a few days before. All that remained was a chimney, charred posts, and several mutilated bodies. "One fellow's arm projected from the snow," Burton observed grimly.

Burton's group passed into the Nevada Territory, a surrealistic landscape of life-threatening desert littered with hundreds of abandoned wagons. It was like traveling through an enormous graveyard. Every few yards they passed the skeleton of some animal, its dust-coated skin stretched tightly over empty ribs. (One emigrant counted 4,960 dead horses, 3,750 dead oxen, and 1,061 dead mules on a 40-mile stretch of the Carson Desert. When Twain traveled the same route the following year, he noted: "It would hardly be an exaggeration to say that we could have walked the forty miles and set our feet on a bone at every step!")

On October 19 Burton and his companions rode into Carson City, the capital of the Nevada Territory and a wide-open silver-mining town. He had heard stories along the trail of the wild times in that lawless city with its reputation for being a place "where revolvers are fired even into houses known to contain 'ladies.'" When Burton visited there, Carson City was a town of some 2,000 people with a main street of white frame stores and board sidewalks that creaked when he walked along them. Violence was a daily fact of life. Three men died in gunfights during Burton's three-day sojourn. However, he doubted whether anyone would be charged for the murders and cited the following story to suggest why: "A man was [acquitted] of killing his adversary after saying to bystanders, 'Stoop down while I shoot the son of a [bitch].' Counsel for the people showed *malice prepense*; counsel for defense pleaded that his counsel was *rectus in curia* and manifestly couldn't mean a man but a dog. The judge ratified the verdict of acquittal." But the first signs of increased respectability were already appearing—brick buildings and tidy picket fences around some of the houses.

Carson City and its satellite Virginia City sat in the midst of the richest ore-bearing region of the United States—Nevada's Comstock Lode. The first ore sample shipped west to an assayist in Grass Valley, near Sacramento, California, showed $3,876 in silver and gold per ton. A newspaper report of the discovery appeared on July 1, 1859, and sparked a hysterical rush from the nearby California gold fields, a mere 100 miles away. George Hearst, the father of newspaper tycoon William Randolph Hearst, was one of the first to arrive and bought the silver mine that formed the basis for that family's fortunes.

The discovery of the Comstock Lode marked a turning point in the development of the American mining industry. "No California mining venture of the 1850s had demanded such a huge investment, none had been conducted on such a flamboyantly large scale, none had required such a rapid advance in engineering and technology," insists historian Rodman W. Paul in *Mining Frontiers of the Far West*. "The foothills of the Sierra Nevada were in fact a basic school in which the Far West studied the fundamentals of a new profession. Having mastered there the initial exercises, Californians were ready to graduate to the Comstock Lode, which became for them an advanced school in which they discovered how to mine in depth and on a large scale, how to use powerful and intricate machinery and large numbers of employees, and how to cope with metals more complex than free gold." By the end of the nineteenth century Americans were the world leaders in the extraction of precious metals.

Burton declined to linger in Carson City. Instead he boarded a stage for California and then caught a train into San Francisco "where a tolerable opera, a superior supper, and the society of friends made [my] arrival exceptionally comfortable." San Francisco in 1860 was a bustling metropolis of 56,800, one that had been transformed from a rowdy gold rush town into a city whose sophistication rivaled that of cities back East. He spent ten days there. "Temptingly near" were the giant sequoias, Yosemite Valley, Los Angeles, and Vancouver Island. But Burton was too wearied to do any more traveling. "For eight months I had lived on board steamers and railroad cars, coaches, and mules," he confessed. "My eyes were full of sight-seeing, my pockets empty, and my brain stuffed with all manner of useful knowledge. It was far more grateful to *flaner* about the stirring streets, to admire the charming faces, to enjoy the delicious climate, and to pay quiet visits like a 'ladies' man' than to front wind and rain, muddy roads . . . rough teamsters . . . and the solitude of out-stations."

Before Burton departed San Francisco on November 15 on the clipper ship *Golden Age*, he observed the critical American presidential election. Abraham Lincoln had won the Republican Party's nomination on the third ballot. With his humble birth, homely wit, and skill in debate he appealed to the same sort of Northerner who had once voted for Andrew Jackson. Out of 4½ million votes cast, Lincoln received 1,866,452. In a field of four candidates, this was sufficient to make him President. His election precipitated a civil war that was perhaps inevitable.

Part

3

The Civil War

A house divided against itself cannot stand," Abraham Lincoln proclaimed in 1858 during one of his campaign debates against Stephen A. Douglas, as both men ran for the U.S. Senate seat from Illinois. (Lincoln lost that election.) "I believe this government cannot endure half slave and half free." A moderate on the issue of slavery, Lincoln accepted the institution of slavery where it existed in the Southern states but opposed the admission of additional slave states into the Union.

Abolitionist extremist John Brown had little patience for such moderation. He sounded the alarm to his followers: "These men are all talk. What is needed is action. Action!" On October 16, 1859, he and 18 well-armed supporters captured the Federal arsenal at Harpers Ferry, Virginia, hoping to spark a slave revolt. Robert E. Lee, a colonel in the U.S. Army, led the detachment of Marines sent to recapture the building. Brown failed, was hanged in early December, and in short order became a martyr for the abolitionists and a murderous villain for the Southern true believers.

The creep toward civil war became a rush in the 1850s. In 1852 Harriet Beecher Stow published *Uncle Tom's Cabin,* a melodramatic novel in which she depicted slavery as a passion play with a cast of saintly blacks and sadistic whites. The book raised emotions to new heights on both sides of the Mason-Dixon Line, selling more than 300,000 copies in the first year of publication.

The drums of war sounded ever louder as the decade wore on. The acquisition of new Federal territories, especially as an aftermath of the war with Mexico, made slavery a national problem, subject to increasing debate in the halls of Congress. The nation expanded state by state across the continent, with each addition carefully contrived to preserve the unstable balance between free soil and slave. But the reality was that the climate and geography of much of the western territories excluded slavery. Nonetheless, the westward extension of slavery led ultimately to the Civil War. That was fought, Lincoln would later insist, so that Americans could decide, once and for all, whether a nation "conceived in liberty and dedicated to the proposition that all men are created equal . . . can long endure."

The Western world in mid-century was experiencing profound changes as many nations became progressively industrialized. America was just beginning to exploit its own immense agricultural potential and was simultaneously expanding its factory system. New railroad trunk lines, constantly being pushed westward, were tying the Upper Mississippi Valley securely to the North. In 1850, for the first time, the value of manufactured goods exceeded the output of agriculture. A new industrial state was rapidly being created, one in which slavery had no place because it was uneconomical and morally unacceptable. In 1860 the North boasted more than eight out of the country's ten factories, more than 70 percent of railroad mileage, all of the country's fighting ships, and most of the money supply.

In 1860 the South remained determinedly agrarian, producing vast quantities of cotton for the world's textile industry beyond its borders, chiefly in the Northern states, England, and France. Against the industrial might of the Northern states, the South could offer only its sectional faith and a vigorous will to fight regardless of the odds.

The result was what historian Bruce Catton in his *Centennial History of the Civil War* called "a state of highly unstable equilibrium." And then he elaborated:

Everything seemed to be turning into something different. A simple pastoral society was developing great cities, a network of mines and factories, powerful combinations of production and trade and finance. Smallness was giving way to bigness, loosely held political controls were growing stronger and more centralized, revolutionary readjustments in almost every aspect of national life were beginning to take place. The Industrial Revolution was under way, and it could not be stopped.

Into this mix poured tens of thousands of new German, Irish, and Italian immigrants, in such great numbers that many Americans felt overwhelmed and threatened. One result was the formation of the Know-Nothing Party, whose platform exhibited a strong Southern bias and called for the exclusion of Catholics and other "foreigners" from public office. In the elections of 1852 their candidates captured numerous local and state elections across the country from New Hampshire to Texas. Yet all this was to no avail. The census of 1860 showed that of 31 million people in this country, 4,136,000 were foreign-born, and the overwhelming majority of these lived in the Northeastern and Mid-Western states. Very few had settled in the South.

"The story of 1860 is the story of a great nation, marching to the wild music of bands, with flaring torches and with banners and with enthusiastic shouts, moving down a steep place into the sea," Bruce Catton wrote. There were 18 free and 15 slave states at the time. In the tumultuous election of that year most people voted their emotions, dividing their votes among four political parties. The Republicans had nominated Abraham Lincoln; the Constitutional Union Party, John Bell; the Northern wing of the Democratic Party, Senator Stephen A. Douglas; and its Southern wing, John C. Breckinridge, the current vice president.

Breckinridge carried every cotton state, along with Delaware and Maryland. Douglas ran second to Lincoln in the popular vote but carried only Missouri. Virginia, Kentucky, and Tennessee went for Bell. Lincoln carried every free state and rolled up a large majority in the electoral college.

On December 20, the state legislature in South Carolina, without a debate, voted 169 to zero to secede from the Union. When the news was announced in Charleston, bells were rung, cannons were fired, parades filled the streets, and people turned out to celebrate their state's new status as an independent nation. The state's political leaders insisted that the military forts near Charleston, which had been built and maintained by the federal government, now belonged to South Carolina. A delegation was quickly dispatched to Washington to arrange for their transfer.

On April 12, 1861, at 4:30 A.M., the first shot of the Civil War was fired against Charleston's Fort Sumter. The two sides exchanged fire throughout the day. The next day the fort's commandant, out of ammunition, surrendered his small detachment. When the news reached nearby Georgia, the Reverend Charles C. Jones exclaimed, "All honor to Carolina! I hope our state may emulate her bravery and patriotism and her self-sacrificing generosity. The conduct of the government of the old United States towards the Confederate States is an outrage upon Christianity and the civilization of the age."

The rebels had fired on the American flag. That was enough to arouse "a whirlwind of patriotism," as Emerson described it, in the Northern states. "Now we have a country again," he wrote. "Sometimes gunpowder smells good."

Both sides went eagerly to war, expecting the action to be over in a matter of months. When the war finally concluded in 1865 four years later, more than 600,000 American men lay dead and the Southern states had been ravaged. In that course of time we decided, as a nation, once and for all what kind of country we were going to be.

When news of what was going on in America after the election of 1860 reached London, the editors of the *Times* realized that there was a fine row brewing on the opposite side of the Atlantic, and they had better send a reporter who knew the military business. They chose William Howard Russell, their top war correspondent. He reached Washington in March, after

Lincoln's inauguration, arriving in that strange twilight when the new administration had been installed but Fort Sumter had not yet been fired upon, and nobody knew quite what was going to happen.

Russell set out on a six-week tour of the Southern states. Fort Sumter fell as he made his way to Charleston. He found himself the only non-Southern reporter filing stories from the Confederacy. He arrived back in Washington in time to catch the battle of Bull Run, the first major engagement of the war, and he described in vivid detail the chaos of that encounter. His collected dispatches to the *Times* are a picture book of what the war looked like in its earliest stage.

Chapter

§ 6 ¿

Bull Run Russell

The year begins with feelings of enmity & apprehension," a New York Episcopal minister wrote anxiously in his diary on the first of January in 1861.

South Carolina had recently seceded from the Union. The Federal government was opposing it, though few could agree on what form that opposition ought to take. Other Southern states appeared certain to follow South Carolina's lead. Most Americans hoped for a compromise, but Congress had thus far failed to reach one, and the president-elect opposed compromise. "Hold firm, as with a chain of steel," Lincoln wrote to a friend in the House.

The steady drift toward separation and war was subject to curious eddies and countercurrents, and the pattern refused to become clear. A political settlement began to look increasingly unlikely. Grown paranoid over its ever-dwindling minority status in population and representation in Congress, and further excited by the relatively small but extremely vocal abolition movement in the North, the Southern states and their leaders saw only two choices: either forfeit slavery and the shadow issue of state rights or else attempt to leave the Union. While a few talked of armed conflict and a military buildup in Charleston harbor had begun, war did not appear inevitable, necessary, or even probable to most observers. It seemed unlikely that one state, or even several states, could oppose the might of the Federal government for long.

On January 9 Mississippi became the second state to secede and was quickly followed by Florida, Alabama, Georgia, and Louisiana. The rush of events left many Americans feeling frus-

trated and confused. Questions proliferated. Were the states actually gone? If so, for how long? Could anything be done? Would the
border states follow? What about president-elect Lincoln—would
he take immediate action after assuming office or would he wait?

Colonel Robert E. Lee was stationed at a frontier post near San
Antonio in January 1861. In a letter to one of his sons he
expressed his fear that the country could experience no greater
calamity than a dissolution of the Union. "Secession is nothing but
revolution," he wrote. "The framers of our Constitution never
exhausted so much labour, wisdom, and forbearance in its formation, and surrounded it with so many guards and securities, if it
was intended to be broken by any member of the Confederacy at
will. . . . Still, a Union that can only be maintained by swords and
bayonets, and in which strife and civil war are to take the place of
brotherly love and kindness, has no charm for me. If the Union is
dissolved, the government disrupted, I shall return to my native
state and share the miseries of my people."

On February 4 the representatives of the seceded states assembled in Montgomery, Alabama. Four days later they adopted the
Constitution of the Confederate States of America, and on the next
day elected Jefferson Davis as their president. The ties that bound
the Union together were quickly being snapped, one by one.

William Tecumseh Sherman, a former army officer and now the
superintendent of the Louisiana State Military Academy, watched
with anguish as events unfolded. He listened to the reckless brava-
do of his colleagues who urged a course of war. "You people of
the South don't know what you are doing," he shouted at them
one night. "This country will be drenched in blood, and God only
knows how it will end. It is all folly, madness, a crime against civilization! You people speak so lightly of war; you don't know
what you're talking about. War is a terrible thing! You mistake,
too, the people of the North. They are a peaceable people but an
earnest people, and they will fight, too. They are not going to let
this country be destroyed without a mighty effort to save it."

Then Sherman made a prophecy. "You are bound to fail," he told his listeners. "Only in your spirit and determination are you pre-pared for war. In all else you are totally unprepared, with a bad cause to start with. At first you will make headway, but as your lim-ited resources begin to fail, shut out from the markets of Europe as you will be, your cause will begin to wane. If your people will but stop and think, they must see that in the end you will surely fail."

2

By 1860 travel books on America had become a staple of the British publishing industry. The British reading public showed an insatiable demand for books about the American people and their customs, democracy, inventions, slavery problem, and Indians, and about the West. When news of the political events following the presidential election of 1860 reached London, the editors of *The Times* of London decided that a fine war was in the making and they had better send a top reporter to the States to cover the outbreak of hostilities. They chose William Howard Russell (1820–1907), a man who had earned himself a place in the history books as the world's first war correspondent for his cov-erage of the Crimean War. He had already demonstrated an extraordinary ability to describe in vivid detail the confusion and turmoil of a military campaign and project its result with a high degree of probability.

"Mr. Russell of *The Times*" was the title Russell preferred. But he seemed to pick up a new nickname after each military cam-paign he covered. Crimea Russell. Balaclava Russell. Bull Run Russell. He answered to them all. In later years he was knighted and became Sir William. The marble legend at the base of the stat-ue marking his grave in London's St. Paul's Cathedral says simply: "The First and Greatest of War Correspondents."

"What distinguished Russell was that he remained an open-eyed and frank critic when those whom he criticised might have made it much more comfortable for him to shut his eyes or hold his tongue," the editor of the *Manchester Guardian* wrote of Russell shortly after his death. "He was an entirely honourable and patriotic journalist, and it probably never occurred to him to ask himself whether the conclusions he came to would accord with the popular passions of the moment."

Russell owed his success not to any advantages of birth but rather to certain qualities of his character—a capacity for concentrated hard work, dedication to the job at hand, respect for the truth, and high moral courage. Other war correspondents have been finer writers, but few have had the influence of Russell in shaping the political events of his country. His dispatches from Crimea ultimately toppled a government, while his reports from America helped keep Britain from intervening in the Civil War on the Southern side.

A stocky Irishman born outside Dublin, the young Russell was enamored of military life, often getting up at dawn to watch the soldiers drilling at nearby barracks. Later he toyed with the idea of becoming a doctor. But then a cousin, who worked as a reporter in London, hired him to cover the violence in the Irish elections of 1841. Russell quickly demonstrated initiative, reasoning that the one place where most participants in the election would eventually end up was the hospital. He stationed himself in the casualty ward, where he interviewed the candidates and their opponents as they were carried in. *The Times* prominently ran two of his articles. John Delane, the paper's editor, invited the young man to London for an interview and quickly concluded a freelance arrangement for his services. Within a few years Russell had forced his way onto the paper in a full-time position by a strategy of cunning, persistence, and solid reporting. *The Times* was Britain's most prestigious and influential paper, so powerful that its editor often knew of important news before the government did. Its circulation was four times greater than the combined total of its three chief competitors.

The outbreak of the Crimean War in 1853 marked the turning point in Russell's life. Ambitious to expand the Russian empire, the czar ordered his army against the crumbling Ottoman Empire, "the sick man of Europe," with the purpose of securing as much of the Balkans as possible. A chief goal of British foreign policy had been to determine how best to defend British economic and political interests in India from Russian expansionism. To this end England hoped to maintain Turkey as a buffer zone. In early 1854 both England and France entered the war on the side of Turkey. The public enthusiasm for the war surprised everyone. "The war is popular beyond belief," Queen Victoria wrote.

The mounting war fever generated an unprecedented demand for news from the front. "The excitement, the painful excitement for information, beggars all description," observed one minister of government. In past wars British editors had either relied upon official military dispatches or employed junior officers to send letters from the battlefronts. The editors at *The Times* decided that these traditional solutions were wholly inadequate and opted instead to send Russell to Crimea to be the British public's eyes and ears. This was, after all, still an age when armies were small, professional bodies, entire battles could be viewed from a nearby hilltop; and a competent correspondent might know as much about what was going on as a general. Russell thus became the first correspondent in history to accompany an army into battle.

On April 5 Russell arrived at Gallipoli, where he stayed for some time amid all the noise and excitement of preparations for war. Unlike other journalists, who would have felt they must write about the war or nothing, he perceived correctly that everything was interesting and relevant. He set out to write an account of day-to-day events as he saw them, describing the scenes and circumstances, the forces, strategies, and personalities involved. He also reported the incompetence and mismanagement that threatened to bring chaos to the war effort and undermine the army's morale. No provisions had been made for the arrival of an army in Turkey. Food supplies were practically nonexistent. The little meat available to the soldiers had the texture of "coarse mahogany." Soldiers had been issued only a single regulation blanket to protect them against the freezing nighttime cold. On April 30 he wrote to *The Times*: "There are no fuses for such shells as we have, and we have plenty of fuses for shells which we have not. There are lots of 13-inch shells and no fuses for them, and there are lots of 10-inch fuses and no shells for them. . . . Who sent them out, or who kept them back? Who are the traitors, or the knaves, or the fools?"

Russell saw his first battle on September 20 when Cossacks charged the British position at Alma. Shells burst around him, while bullets ricocheted about his feet. Astride his broken-down horse, scribbling as fast as he could, his only concern was finding the best spot from which to view the fighting. Sometimes the difficulties appeared insurmountable. Later he recalled the terrible actions of that day:

"How was I to describe what I had not seen? Where learn the facts for which they were waiting at home? My eyes swam as I tried to make notes of what I heard. I was worn out with excitement, fatigue, and want of food. I had been more than ten hours in the saddle; my wretched horse, bleeding badly from a cut in the leg, was unable to carry me. My head throbbed, my heart beat as though it would burst. I supposed I was unnerved by want of food and rest, but I was so much overcome by what I saw that I could not remain where the fight had been closest and deadliest. I longed to get away from it—from the exultation of others in which thought for the dead was forgotten or unexpressed. It was now that the weight of the task I had accepted fell on my soul like lead."

Russell was too exhausted to write his account that night. He slept fitfully and feverishly, lying on the ground under a commissary tent. When he awoke the next morning, in the early light he saw soldiers carrying off wounded Russians, digging graves, picking up the dead, and collecting arms. Later that day he wrote his dispatch on pages torn from an old notebook, using for a desk a plank laid across two casks.

A month later Russell was present at the disastrous charge of the Light Brigade, the war's most infamous incident. He described the entire debacle in the vivid details readers of *The Times* had come to expect from his dispatches. "At ten minutes past eleven our Light Cavalry Brigade advanced," he wrote. "They swept proudly past, glittering in the morning sun in all the pride and splendour of war. . . . At the distance of 1,200 yards the whole line of the enemy belched forth, from thirty iron mouths, a flood of smoke and flame. The flight was marked by instant gaps in our ranks, by dead men and horses, by steeds flying wounded or riderless across the plain. In diminished ranks, with a halo of steel above their heads, and with a cheer which was many a noble fellow's death cry, they flew into the smoke of the batteries; but ere they were lost from view the plain was strewn with their bodies. Through the clouds of smoke we could see their sabers flashing as they rode between the guns, cutting down the gunners as they stood. We saw them riding through, returning, after breaking through a column of Russians and scattering them like chaff, when the flank fire on the hill swept down. Wounded men and dismounted troopers flying towards us told the sad tale. At thirty-five minutes past eleven not a British soldier, except the dead and the dying, was left in front of the Moscovite guns."

Two weeks later Russell's 6,000-word account of the daring but futile cavalry charge appeared in *The Times* and sent an entire nation into mourning. His dispatch is generally credited with inspiring Lord Alfred Tennyson's famous poem, "The Charge of the Light Brigade."

Russell settled down at Balaclava with the army. Day by day he chronicled the misery and horror that quickly overtook the British forces with the onslaught of a terrible winter. He felt duty-bound to report the facts rather than what the authorities wanted the British public to know. Disease and exposure devastated the army because of a totally archaic and outdated military system. By January 1855, 13,076 British soldiers lay sick. The deaths from battle casualties were less than one-eighth of the loss from the sufferings of winter. There was a general shortage of boots, greatcoats, medicines, and shelter. Officers clothed themselves in rabbit skins, and their men in bread bags and rags. In this state the army in the open trenches was constantly exposed to continuous artillery fire and freezing storms.

In his dispatches, Russell lashed out at the indifference of the British authorities to the army's medical needs. Wounded and ill soldiers could look forward to no hospitals, no medicines, and no doctors. They died with no effort being made to save their lives. "The sick appear to be tended by the sick," he wrote, "and the dying by the dying." He pleaded for doctors to aid the stricken troops but even more desperate, he insisted, was the need for nurses. "Are there no devoted women among us," he asked, "able and willing to go forth and minister to the sick and suffering soldiers?" Back in London, Florence Nightingale read his dispatches and promptly organized a corps of 38 nurses to tend the men in Crimea. Her efforts marked the beginning of nursing as a recognized profession.

Russell's frank reporting of the scandalous conditions in Crimea provoked a storm of protest in England and inflamed popular opinion against the government, which found it increasingly difficult to ignore the truth. *The Times* reporter, insisted one military authority, had awakened "the conscience of the British nation to the sufferings of its troops." Other British armies had suffered terribly at the hands of incompetent superiors. But for the first time the story was being told while it was happening and while there was still an opportunity to do something about it. In early 1855 the government resigned. When the new secretary for war, the Duke of Newcastle, visited Crimea, he told Russell, "It was you who turned out the Government."

Russell was not only the first correspondent to understand that inefficiency and suffering were as newsworthy as great victories, but also the first to realize that his profession wielded immense power. In his hands reports from the field became a force before which generals quailed.

In the fall of 1855 Russell returned to London and found himself hailed as a hero. Lord Palmerston, the new prime minister, invited him to breakfast. And Trinity College in Dublin awarded him an honorary doctor of laws degree. Now that he had demonstrated his brilliance as a war correspondent, the *Times* took advantage of every opportunity to use him. When the Indian

Mutiny broke out in 1857, he went there to cover the action for his paper. This he did with a sense of moderation and humanity, which seemed—in the inflamed India of 1858—to be close to treason. The influence of his dispatches was immense, and he is generally given credit for the policies of clemency and justice which ended the mutiny.

Russell's dispatches from two major conflicts had made clear to the military establishment in Britain that they had committed a dangerous mistake in tolerating him and his colleagues. But by then it was too late. The war correspondent had become a fact of modern warfare. In 1861 when the American Civil War erupted, 500 of them turned out to report the conflict on the Northern side alone.

3

The Civil War was the most dramatic and significant event in the history of the United States as an independent nation. It was the climax of a half-century of social, political, and economic rivalries growing out of an economy half slave and half free. In the scope of its operations and in the magnitude of its cost in human life and financial resources, the war exceeded all previous such conflicts.

The Civil War was both the first conflict to receive the onslaught of the press in vast numbers and the first to be covered extensively by war photographers. The *New York Herald* alone fielded 63 men and spent a million dollars covering the war. Most European papers sent correspondents, and many devoted as much space to the war as did the American press. Some 50,000 miles of telegraph wires meant that editors received their correspondents' dispatches from the front within hours instead of days. As a result, the reporting of the Civil War became both more extensive and more immediate than ever before.

Within short order these changes redefined journalism. "It was during the Civil War," *The New York Times* noted in 1901, "that the New York newspapers gained their first realizing sense of two fundamental principles that made them what they are today— first, the surpassing value of individual, competitive, triumphant enterprise in getting early and exclusive news, and second, the possibility of building up large circulations by striving increasingly to meet a popular demand for prompt and adequate reports of the day-to-day doings of mankind the world over."

Among this army of correspondents, William Howard Russell was a giant towering over pygmies. The vast majority of them were uninformed, dishonest, unethical, and partisan. None had any previous experience at war reporting. Almost all were appallingly ignorant of military strategy and history. Few had any skills as writers. Many were quick to invent incidents. Most saw their responsibility largely in terms of maintaining the morale of both the soldiers and the civilians back home. "It is not within the province of your correspondent to criticize what has been done by the army or navy," wrote one. "Nor will he state occurrences which it may be unpleasant to read."

As war approached, a groundswell of support for the South flowed through Britain. On many occasions the United States had offended British sensibilities by seeming to threaten Canada. Many Englishmen welcomed the impending civil war as a means of removing a potential threat to British North America. In 1861 some 20% of the British population was directly or indirectly dependent on the prosperity of the cotton manufacturers, who were in turn dependent upon the American South for 80% of their supplies. This clear commercial relationship provoked considerable Southern sympathy on the part of wide segments of the British population.

The Times determined to send Russell to America to cover the outbreak of hostilities. A pro-Southern sentiment was strongly entrenched among the newspaper's editors. "Why should we be so very anxious to see the Union preserved?" one of them insisted. "What has it done to command our sympathy?" And another admitted, "The Northern government and its policy are an abomination to me, and I greatly enjoy to hear them abused."

Russell, on the other hand, professed complete impartiality. "No man ever set foot on the soil of the United States with a stronger and sincerer desire to ascertain and to tell the truth, as it appeared to him," he wrote later. "I had no theories to uphold, no prejudices to subserve, no interests to advance, no instructions to fulfill. I was a free agent, bound to communicate to the powerful organ of public opinion I represented, my own daily impressions of the men, scene, and actions around me, without fear, favour, or affection of or for anything but that which seemed to me to be the truth."

Russell sailed for America on March 3, 1861. On March 16 he reached New York, where he was welcomed as "the most famous newspaper correspondent the world has ever seen." One of the New York reporters gave his readers this word picture of the celebrated guest: "He has short iron locks parted down the middle, a grayish mustache, and a strong tendency to double chin, a very broad and very full but not lofty forehead: eyes of a clear, keen blue, sharply observant in their expression. . . . You must imagine this portly and pleasant-looking gentleman dressed in the extreme elaboration of Piccadilly full evening dress, his massive throat encased in the neatest and most dazzling of snowy ties; his broad chest making an immense display of fine linen; his waistcoat a miracle of embroidered silk, dark in color save where illuminated by flowers or traversed by his heavy watch-chain."

Russell was amazed to learn of the contempt in which most New Yorkers held Lincoln. Virtually everyone he met tried to convince him that "the respectable people were disgusted at the election of such a fellow as Lincoln as their President." They spoke of the new cabinet officers as undistinguished and obscure men and the president as a mere "rail-splitter."

Russell arranged a visit with Horace Greeley. The famous newspaper publisher and abolitionist approved Russell's plans to head South as quickly as possible. "Be sure you examine the slave pens," he urged the Irishman. "They will be afraid to refuse *you*, and you can tell the truth."

On March 25 Russell boarded the train for Washington and

found his sleeping car full of "rowdies, whiskey, and fighting." Several of these were office-seekers, hoping to get appointments from the new administration. One of them, a big man with a broken nose and numerous rings, jewels, chains, and pins, took Russell aside and informed him, "I'm going to Washington to get a foreign mission from Bill Seward [the new Secretary of State]. I won't take Paris, as I don't care much about French or Frenchmen. But I'd just like to show John Bull how to do or maybe take Japan if they are very pressing."

All official Washington made itself available for Russell. He, after all, represented *The Times,* then indisputably the most famous and powerful newspaper in the entire world. "I think I never felt so much as in this matter the enormous power *The Times* has," an English historian observed in 1863. "Not from the quality of its writing . . . but from its exclusive command of publicity and its exclusive access to a vast number of minds." Both Northern and Southern leaders clearly understood that England's role in the coming conflict could prove decisive. If she decided to intervene with her navy, then she could guarantee a Southern victory. If she stayed neutral, then Lincoln and his advisers were confident of victory. Both sides carefully courted Russell throughout his stay in America. But he was determined to see and judge everything for himself.

On his first evening in Washington Russell was introduced to the powerful Secretary of State, William Henry Seward: "A well-formed and large head is placed on a long, slender neck and projects over the chest in an argumentative kind of way, as if the keen eyes were seeking for an adversary." Seward appeared unperturbed by the secession of the Southern states. "Why, I myself, my brothers, and sisters have all been Secessionists—we seceded from home when we were young, but we all went back to it sooner or later," he reassured his guest. "These States will all come back in the same way."

The next day Seward took him to the White House and introduced him to Lincoln. "Soon afterward there entered with a shambling, almost unsteady gait a tall, lank, lean man, considerably over six feet in height with stooping shoulders, long pendulous arms, terminating in hands of extraordinary dimensions, which, however, were far exceeded in proportion by his feet," Russell wrote later in his dispatch back to London. "He was dressed in an ill-fitting, wrinkled suit of black which put one in mind of an undertaker's uniform at a funeral. . . . The impression produced by the size of his extremities and by his flapping and wide projecting ears may be removed by the appearance of kindliness, sagacity, and the awkward bonhomie of his face."

Seward introduced them.

"Mr. President, allow me to present to you Mr. Russell of the London *Times*."

"Mr. Russell, I am glad to make your acquaintance and to see you in this country," Lincoln replied in a friendly manner. "The London *Times* is one of the greatest powers in the world—in fact, I don't know of anything which has more power, except perhaps the Mississippi. I am glad to know you as its minister."

Official Washington assiduously courted the correspondent. The next evening he returned to the White House to attend Lincoln's first official dinner party, the only man there who was not a member of the cabinet. He met Mrs. Lincoln for the first time, and observed, "She is profuse in the introduction of the word 'sir' in every sentence, which is now almost an Americanism confined to certain classes." He noted with keen interest the President's skill in using anecdotes to make his point.

The most immediate problem confronting the new president was what to do regarding Fort Sumter, in Charleston harbor, one of four Federal forts still flying the Union flag in Confederate territory. The garrison there had originally occupied the more vulnerable Fort Moultrie. Then on December 26, six days after South Carolina had seceded, U.S. Army Major Robert Anderson evacuated his eighty-two men to the stronger fortress three miles out in the harbor. President James Buchanan had tried to reinforce the Federal troops but Charleston gunners fired on the supply ship and forced it back. Though Confederate guns ringed Fort Sumter, they had not yet fired on the soldiers there. However, Confederate authorities refuse to allow the garrison to buy food in the local markets. On the day after his inauguration Lincoln received a dispatch from Major Anderson informing him that he had provisions for six weeks at best. That meant the new president had just over a month to decide whether to send supplies (an act which almost certainly would provoke an armed response) or let the fort surrender.

In his first letter back to the *Times* Russell described at length the curious phenomenon of Washington at the beginning of a new administration when the city was under siege from thousands of office-seekers. "All the hotels are full of keen gray-eyed men, who fondly believe their destiny is to fill for four years some pet appointment under Government," he wrote. "At the very moment when the President and his Cabinet should be left undisturbed to deal with the tremendous questions which have arisen from their action, the roar of office-seekers dims every sense and almost annihilates them."

He visited the Capitol building, its cupola still under construction, and observed meetings of both the House and Senate. The obscene yellow tobacco stains on the white marble staircases and the noisy informality of the chambers displeased him. He thought the senators looked more like "a gathering of bakers or millers."

Next came several days of interviews with important civilian and military officials in the new government. He found no unity among the Northerners, no fixed purpose, and little understanding of the crisis. The military preparations he observed were amateurish at best. Naval and army officers were resigning *en masse* to accept service in the rebel army.

The mood of the Southerners was markedly different, as he learned when he spent an evening with a delegation from Jefferson Davis to Washington to negotiate the terms of secession. He found them united and determined, optimistic about their chances in an armed conflict, and contemptuous of Northerners, whom they believed to be morally degraded by trade and industry. They regarded Lincoln as a fool and thought Seward the ablest as well as the least honorable of their enemies. They were also unwavering in their support of slavery.

The encounter convinced Russell that war was inevitable. "I fear, my friend, you are going to immortal smash," he wrote pessimistically to an American friend the next day. "That little lump of revolutionary leaven has at last set to work in good earnest and the whole mass of social and political life is fermenting unhealthily. . . . The world will only see in it all the failure of republican institutions in time of pressure as demonstrated by all history— that history which America vainly thought she was going to set right and re-establish on new grounds and principles."

On the morning of April 12 war between the States suddenly erupted as Southern gunners began a bombardment of Fort Sumter after learning of Lincoln's decision to reinforce the garrison. The siege lasted 34 hours. The next day Major Anderson surrendered to the vastly superior Confederate forces. Some 4,000 artillery shells had been fired, but not a single soldier killed. On April 14 Major Anderson formally surrendered the fort when the Confederates permitted him to fire a final 50-gun salute to the Union flag, an ember fell into some powder. One soldier was killed in the explosion, and five were injured. Private Daniel Hough thus became the first fatality of the Civil War.

Everywhere throughout the South news of the fall of Fort Sumter provoked cheering crowds, clanging church bells, and thunderous salutes. The same news electrified and united the North. Lincoln's call for 75,000 volunteers on April 15 met with immediate success. "The indifference, the Southern preference, the indecision which prevailed when you were here are vanished," a friend in New York City wrote to Russell. "The attack on Sumter and the call of the President swept them away in a single night, and now no man dare avow himself a traitor." On April 19 Lincoln ordered a naval blockade of the Southern states.

Russell departed Washington on April 13 determined to use his own eyes and ears to test the feeling of the South. From Norfolk he traveled by train through dismal swamps, like Martin Chuzzlewit's Eden, with log cabins flying the new Confederate flags, to Goldsborough, where for the first time he saw the war fever sweeping the South. A mob surged through the streets. The shouts for Jeff Davis and the Southern Confederacy overpowered the discordant bands playing "Dixie."

"Here was the true revolutionary furor in full sway," Russell wrote home to his editor. "The men hectored, swore, cheered, and slapped each other on the backs; the women in their best, waved handkerchiefs and flung down garlands from the windows. All was noise, dust, and patriotism."

On April 16 Russell arrived in Charleston where he met the hero of the hour, Confederate General Pierre Beauregard, who had commanded at the siege of Fort Sumter. "You shall go everywhere and see everything," the general reassured his visitor. "We rely on your discretion and knowledge of what is fair in dealing with what you see."

Charleston was still celebrating the fall of Sumter. The streets were crowded with lanky soldiers wearing clanking spurs and sabers, awkward squads marching to and fro, drummers beating calls and ruffles, and groups of slaves delighted with the glare and glitter. Every house seemed to fly a Confederate flag. A new doggerel rhyme was popular. Everywhere Russell heard people singing the refrain:

"With cannon and musket, with shell and petard,

We salute the North with our Beau-regard."

Everyone was of the opinion that the war would be over in a few months. Most were optimistic that England would maintain a policy of neutrality at first but would quickly come into the conflict on the side of the Confederacy. "When John Bull begins to want cotton he'll come off his perch," Russell was told. He was to hear this opinion throughout his travels in the South—cotton was king, and in the end England would bow before his throne.

"The utter contempt and loathing for the venerated Stars and Stripes, the abhorrence of the very words United States, the intense hatred of the Yankees on the part of these people, cannot be conceived by anyone who has not seen them," Russell wrote home in a dispatch. "I am more satisfied than ever that the Union can never be restored as it was."

Russell visited Fort Sumter, which now flew the Confederate

flag, its walls largely undamaged by the bombardment. He was more interested in accessing the readiness of Southern forces in the area. The general lack of discipline among the troops was quickly apparent. He saw a number of rough, long-haired fellows in coarse gray tunics lying across hay bales smoking cigars on the deck of a ship carrying gunpowder. A major approached them.

"Gentlemen," he asked them courteously, "you'll oblige me by not smoking over the hay. There's powder below."

"I don't believe we're going to burn the hay this time, kernel," one soldier replied. "And anyway we'll put it out afore it reaches the 'bustibles."

To Russell's disgust the major simply grumbled and walked away.

In South Carolina Russell found the most extreme and fanatical secessionists. In a dispatch back to London he noted: "Nothing I could say can be worth one fact which has forced itself upon my mind in reference to the sentiments which prevail among the gentlemen of this State. I have been among them for several days. I have visited their plantations. I have conversed with them freely and fully. And I have enjoyed that frank, courteous, and graceful intercourse which constitutes an irresistible charm of their society. From all quarters have come to my ears the echoes of the same voice. That voice says, 'If we could only get one of the Royal race of England to rule over us, we should be content.'"

Mary Boykin Chesnut, the wife of a Confederate colonel, observed Russell often during his visit to Charleston. Later she wrote in her diary: "Russell, the English reporter for *The Times*, was there. They took him everywhere. One man studied up his Thackeray to converse with him on equal terms. Poor Russell was awfully bored, they say. He only wanted to see the Forts and get news that was suitable to make an interesting article. Thackeray was stale news over the water."

Later, after Russell's account of his visit had appeared in *The Times*, she noted: "Charleston's people are thin-skinned. They shrink from Russell's touches. I find his criticism mild. I expected so much worse. Those Englishmen come, somebody says, with their three P's—Pen, Paper, and Prejudices. . . . He let us off easily."

Russell's travels took him through the Deep South to New Orleans and up the Mississippi River to Cairo and then back to Washington. Everywhere Southerners evinced a spirited optimism about the outcome of the war, joking about "old Abe Lincoln's paper blockade." The workmanlike enthusiasm of their preparations for the impending struggle impressed him. "There is no people in the world so crazy with military madness," he advised his readers. He was the only non-Southern journalist traveling through the South at this time, and his lengthy dispatches to the *Times* were as eagerly read in Washington as London.

At Montgomery Russell called on Jefferson Davis, the president of the Confederate States of America. Davis was born in a log cabin in Kentucky, less than 100 miles from Lincoln's birthplace. He had served seven years as a colonel in the army and seen action during the war against Mexico. He was wounded in the foot, returned home on crutches, and at victory banquets heard himself pronounced a military genius and the hero of the South.

"He did not impress me as favorably as I had expected, though he is certainly a very different looking man from Mr. Lincoln," Russell reported to his readers. "He is like a gentleman—has a slight, light figure, little exceeding middle height, and holds himself erect and straight. . . . Wonderful to relate, he does not chew and is neat and clean-looking, with hair trimmed and boots brushed. The expression of his face is anxious. He has a very haggard, care-worn, and pain-drawn look, though no trace of anything but the utmost confidence and greatest decision could be detected in his conversation."

Russell toured several large plantations and studied the slavery system. A Georgian planter advised him, "When people talk of my having so many slaves, I always tell them it is the slaves who own me. Morning, noon, and night I'm obliged to look after them, to doctor them, and attend to them in every way." At a plantation in Mississippi where Russell dined one evening, his host informed him proudly that the light-skinned slave serving them was a son of the former president Andrew Jackson. In Alabama he stayed with an Irish planter who had come to America a poor and friendless youth but now lorded over two large plantations totaling 22,000 acres and worth $500,000. "It is as easy to persuade the owner of such wealth that slavery is indefensible as to have convinced the Norman baron that the Saxon churl who tilled his lands ought to be his equal," Russell observed.

He was much affected by a slave auction in Montgomery. "The auctioneer was an ill-favoured, dissipated-looking rascal," he reported. "A stout young Negro, badly dressed and ill-shod, stood with all his goods fastened in a small bundle in his hand, looking out at the small and listless gathering of men. . . . 'A prime field hand!' the auctioneer called out. 'Just look at him—good-natured, well-tempered; no marks, nary signs of bad about him! Only nine-hun-ther-ed and fifty dol'rs for 'em!'" The man sold for $1,000. Russell overheard two men next to him talking. "That nigger went cheap," one said. "Yes, sir! Niggers is cheap now—that's a fact."

Russell listened to the many arguments the Southerners made for slavery. He believed that the system debased both slave and slave-owner alike. He understood that the real reason for the system was economic and railed against those who justified it on religious grounds. He made no attempt to hide his abolitionist views from his Southern hosts and often engaged them in spirited arguments over the wisdom of secession. "Russell is fighting secession sword in hand," observed a Northerner who watched him in action. "He attacks these gentlemen with great vigour—stigmatizes the whole movement as impolitic and suicidal and invariably has the best of the argument."

In the third week of May Russell arrived in New Orleans. He found the city streets full of Turcos (Turkish troops), Zouaves (French infantrymen), and Chasseurs (light cavalry). Building walls were covered with placards of volunteer companies. He went into a store to buy some shirts but discovered the seamstresses and tailors so busy sewing uniforms and Confederate flags they could not take his order. He read in the papers that persons expressing the opinion that the South would lose the war were receiving six-month jail sentences.

Russell made his way up the Mississippi River, interviewing both military and civilian leaders and visiting military fortifications. On a floating hospital near Memphis he found scenes reminiscent of Crimea. Scores of soldiers suffering from fever and dysentery lay on their stretchers without a soul to help them. Russell moved among them with his medicine chest, ministering to them as best he could. He bent over one man, whom dysentery had reduced to a mere skeleton. The soldier eagerly grabbed his arm. "Stranger," he pleaded, "remember, if I die, that I am Robert Tallon of Tishomingo County and that I died for States' Rights. See, now, they put that in the papers, won't you? Robert Tallon died for States' Rights." He quickly learned why the soldiers lacked medical attention. All the Southern doctors wanted to enlist in the army as colonels at the least and "wield the sword instead of the scalpel."

On June 19, to his considerable relief, Russell stepped off the steamboat at Cairo, Illinois, and was once again back in Northern territory. He returned to Washington on July 3. The city had undergone major changes since his last visit. Army camps with hundreds of tents set in neat lines ringed the country's capital. The fields around Washington resounded with shouts of command and the tramp of men. Hundreds of artillery pieces were jammed into parks near the camps, and long trains of canvas-covered army wagons filled the open spaces in the suburbs.

Within a few hours of his arrival Russell was meeting with Seward. "Well, Mr. Secretary," he advised him, "I am quite sure that if all the South are in the same mind as those I met in my travels, you will have many battles before they submit to the Federal Government." Seward was unswayed and continued to take the optimistic view that the Southern states would quickly return to the Union. He also advised his British visitor that if England provoked a war, the North would not shrink from it.

"I could not," Russell observed in his dispatch, "but admire the confidence—may I say coolness?—of the statesman who sat in his modest little room within sound of the enemy's guns, in a capital menaced by their forces, who spoke so fearlessly of a war with a

Power which could have blotted the paper blockade of the Southern forts and coast in a few hours, and, in conjunction with the Southern armies, have effected the occupation and destruction of the capital."

Russell next met General Irvin McDowell, the commander of the Army of the Potomac. McDowell was a 41-year-old Ohioan who, after graduating from West Point, had gone on to become an instructor in tactics at the Academy. He had served with distinction in the Mexican War. Blue-eyed, square-jawed, bearded, and heavy-set, he gave the appearance of self-confidence. In his personal habits he was strictly a puritan. He neither drank nor smoked, refusing even tea and coffee. The general greeted Russell warmly and talked freely with him about military matters. "I declare I am not quite easy at the idea of having your eye on me," he admitted, only half-joking, "for you have seen so much of European armies, you will, very naturally, think little of us, generals and all."

The assessment was correct. McDowell took him on a tour of the camps. "I was not favourably impressed with what I saw," Russell wrote in his dispatch to his paper, "for I had expected to find upwards of 100,000 men in the highest state of efficiency, whereas there were not more than a third of the number, and those in a very incomplete, ill-disciplined state." He noted that the Northern volunteers possessed none of the swashbuckling brava-do of their Southern counterparts. He saw many serious deficiencies, including an absence of cavalry, a hodgepodge of artillery pieces with few gunners who knew how to employ them effectively, no reserve ammunition, and inadequate transport.

During the tour Russell heard occasional shots in the camps. "What's that?" he asked an officer. "They are volunteers shooting themselves," the soldier replied. Later Russell reported that answer to Lincoln, who replied, "Well, that seems to be a waste of good mater-ial in every way." The accidents were caused by carelessness but they were numerous. "In every day's paper there is an account of deaths and wounds caused by the discharge of firearms," he observed.

General McDowell admitted to Russell that he did not possess a single reliable map of Virginia. Nor did he have the intelligence capability to develop such a map. He knew little or nothing of the country before him and had no solid information on the Southern deployment near Manassas, 30 miles away.

The politicians and Northern papers were strident in their calls for military action against the South. Lincoln yielded to the pressure and against the advice of his generals ordered McDowell to attack the Southern army near Manassas Junction, Virginia. Because the battle took place on a Sunday, a great many Washington residents packed picnic lunches and accompanied the Union army for the sport of watching the first major engagement of the Civil War. Numerous ladies were present, dressed in their colorful summer frocks. The two armies clashed on a plateau near a small stream called Bull Run. The troops of both armies were inexperienced, the officers so unused to handling large numbers of men, the opposing flags so similar, and the uniforms so varied that a scene of extraordinary confusion took place. The lack of preparation, discipline, and equipment that Russell had observed earlier had its impact on the Union soldiers. Southern reinforcements prevented an early Union victory. The Union lines buckled and then fell back into a retreat. The retreat quickly became a rout.

Russell missed the actual battle. In the early dawn of July 21 he left Washington in a horse-drawn gig and made his way along a road clogged with traffic for the battlefield some 30 miles away. By 9:00 A.M. he was close enough to hear the thudding sounds of canons in the distance, "like taps with a gentle hand upon a muffled drum." He soon encountered a body of armed soldiers, bayonets glittering in the sunlight through the clouds of dust, plodding along laughing. They were the 4th Pennsylvania Regiment, marching away from the front because their three-month enlistment time was up.

Russell hurried toward the sound of guns and was quickly within sight of the battle. The nearby woods echoed to the roar of cannons. Through his binoculars he watched the thin lines of blue smoke and heard the sound of rolling musketry that marked a skirmish. White puffs of smoke burst high above the treetops.

The nearby hillsides were covered with spectators from

Washington. One man approached Russell. "Are we really seeing a battle now?" he asked. "Are they supposed to be fighting where all that smoke is going on? This is rather interesting, you know."

A lady with opera glasses was quite beside herself whenever there was an unusually heavy discharge of artillery. "That is splendid!" she cried. "Oh my! Is that not first-rate? I guess we shall be in Richmond this time tomorrow."

An officer galloped up to the crowd. "We've whipped them on all points," he shouted. "We have taken all their batteries. They are retreating as fast as they can and we are after them."

Russell rode on another three miles toward the fighting. He reached a bridge and was surprised to see ahead several wagons rushing down the road away from the battlefield. Numerous soldiers ran alongside. "Turn back! Turn back! We are whipped!" the drivers shouted to the crowd. A few minutes later Russell hailed an officer riding swiftly toward the rear, an empty scabbard hanging at his side.

"What is the matter, sir?" Russell demanded. "What is this all about?"

"Why, it means we are pretty badly whipped," he gasped. "That's the truth."

The panic spread. The troops and wagons moving toward the battle turned back. Another officer confirmed that the Union army had been beaten on all fronts. Russell hurried to a nearby cornfield and watched in amazement as hundreds of Union soldiers ran toward him, flinging their coats, blankets, guns, caps, bayonets, and packs to the ground. They were convinced that Southern cavalry were hot on their heels.

Russell gave up as hopeless his effort to reach the front and found himself swept along in the flood of panic-stricken humanity. He was separated from his gig but managed to find a horse. "The runaways ran alongside the wagons, striving to force themselves in among the occupants, who resisted tooth and nail," he recalled later in his dispatch. "The drivers spurred and whipped and urged the horses to the utmost of their bent. I felt an inclination to laugh, which was overcome by disgust, and by that vague sense of something extraordinary taking place which is experienced when a man sees a number of people acting as if driven by some unknown terror. . . . It never occurred to me that this was a grand debacle. All along I believed the mass of the army was not broken, and that all I saw around was the result of confusion created in a crude organisation by a forced retreat."

Russell felt certain that McDowell would be able to regroup his forces and prevent the Confederates from advancing on Washington. But he saw no sign of any attempt to stop the rout. That, if anything, became worse. "I was trotting quietly down the hill road beyond Centreville when suddenly the guns on the other side, or from a battery very near, opened fire, and a fresh outburst of artillery sounded through the woods," he wrote later. "In an instant the mass of vehicles and retreating soldiers, teamsters, and civilians, as if agonised by an electric shock, quivered throughout the tortuous line. With dreadful shouts and cursings, the drivers lashed their maddened horses and, leaping from the carts, left them to their fate and ran away on foot. . . . The firing continued and seemed to approach the hill, and at every report the agitated body of horsemen and wagons was seized, as it were, with a fresh convulsion."

Such were the scenes that Russell saw that Sunday. After riding until midnight he finally reached Washington and the comfort of his rooms. He tried to write his report but fell asleep at the table. He awoke about 6:00 in the next morning. Rain was falling in torrents. He looked out his window and saw the street filled with muddied soldiers returning from Manassas. Looking closely at them, he noticed that they belonged to various regiments. Many were without knapsacks, belts, and muskets. Some had neither greatcoats or shoes. Others were covered with blankets.

Russell hurried outside and stopped an officer who had lost his sword. An empty sheath dangled from his side.

"Where are all these men coming from?" he asked.

"Well, sir," the officer replied slowly, "I guess we're all coming out of Virginny as fast as we can, and pretty well whipped, too."

"What! The whole Army, sir?"

"That's more than I know. They may stay that like. I know I'm going home."

No one in Washington had ever seen such a spectacle before. Thousands of demoralized soldiers, most of them dirty and hungry, many without arms or even uniforms, continued to stream for several days across the Potomac bridges into the capital. The casualties had been high. The Union forces suffered 2,700 men dead or wounded and the Confederates almost 2,000. McDowell lost the battle, not because of faulty tactics—Sherman later claimed that Bull Run was "one of the best-planned battles of the war"—but because of the failure of his green and untested troops and a lack of proper intelligence. Lincoln refused to blame McDowell. Instead, he blamed himself for yielding to the politicians and sending an unready army into battle. But in the shock and anger of defeat the country needed a scapegoat. McDowell had to go. Within four weeks his command was suspended, and he was later transferred to the Pacific coast.

Ten days after the defeat Russell sat with McDowell at a table under a tree in front of his tent. "Cast down from his high estate," he wrote, "placed as a subordinate to his junior, covered with obloquy and abuse, the American general displayed a calm self-possession and perfect amiability which could only proceed from a philosophic temperament and a consciousness that he would outlive the calumnies of his countrymen. He accused nobody; but it was not difficult to perceive he had been sacrificed to the vanity, self-seeking, and disobedience of some of his officers, and to radical vices in the composition of his Army."

A few days later Russell fell ill. He consulted a doctor, who prescribed powders in mint juleps. "Now mint juleps," he explained to his readers, "are made of whiskey, sugar, ice, very little water, and sprigs of fresh mint, to be sucked up after the manner of sherry cobblers with a straw. 'A powder every two hours, with a mint julep. Why, that's six a day, doctor! Won't that be—eh?—won't that be rather intoxicating?' 'Well, sir, that depends on the constitution. You'll find they will do you no harm, even if the worst takes place.'" Russell spent the next ten days in an alcohol-induced haze brought on by the mint juleps, and the doctor declared that he had thus saved the life of the celebrated correspondent.

When Russell returned to his journalistic duties, he found that life in Washington had returned to normal. Squads of soldiers patrolled the streets. Guards stood at every corner. And a rigid system of passes had been established.

Within a month of the Union defeat at Manassas copies of *The Times* with Russell's lengthy dispatch on the battle arrived in the States from England. Delane, his editor, had sent him congratulations on the dispatch, saying, "I can't describe to you the delight with which I, and I believe everybody else, read your vivid account of the repulse at Bull Run and the terrible debacle which ensued. My fear is only that the U.S. will not be able to bear the truth so plainly told."

The American public eagerly awaited the account. "We scarcely exaggerate the fact," insisted *The New York Times*, "when we say, the first and foremost thought on the minds of a large number of our people after the repulse of Bull Run was, What will Russell say?" Newspapers across the country reprinted the dispatch on their front pages, often accompanying it with violent denunciations and personal abuse. None of the papers seemed interested in the fact that numerous Union officers who had participated in the battle pronounced Russell's account both accurate and moderate. The *Chicago Tribune* claimed that Russell had not been there and fabricated the entire account. The *New York Herald* editorialized, "As for running away, Mr. Russell himself set an example, and riding on a foaming steed, was foremost in the line of retreat."

Nor was Russell's account any more popular in the Southern states. Mary Boykin Chestnut of Charleston, who had observed his visit with such interest earlier that year, read his account and then wrote in her diary: "Russell, I think in his capacity as an Englishman, despises both sides. He derides us equally, North and South. He prefers to attribute Bull Run to Yankee cowardice rather than to Southern courage. He gives no credit to either side. After all, we are mere Americans!"

The storm of passion raised by his article stunned Russell. "I knew that there would be a certain amount of risk," he advised his readers, "but I confess I was not by any means disposed to think that the leaders of the public opinion would seek the small gratification of revenge and the petty popularity of pandering to the passions of the mob by creating a popular cry against me."

In the months following the publication of his Bull Run article Russell suffered constant vilification both in the press and at the numerous social engagements he attended. Angry strangers accosted him on the streets and in bars. Once a soldier leveled his rifle at him while he was touring an Army camp. "The torrent is swollen today by anonymous letters threatening me with bowie-knife and revolver, or simply abusive, frantic with hate, and full of obscure warnings," he noted in his diary on August 23.

The experience taught the *Times* correspondent an important truth about America. "The Americans, with all their faults, are a prodigious fine people and I cannot help admiring many things about them," he wrote to his editor. "It is their cursed Press. I say not so because it has abused me, but because I really believe it is a curse conducted as it is, which renders the country so obnoxious."

Russell returned to England in the spring of 1862. After reporting the rout of the Federal troops at Bull Run, he found that the military authorities had turned against him. They denied him permission to accompany the Union troops in any further engagements. He had been sent to America to report the military operations. That clearly became impossible under the new restrictions. It is regrettable that the United States lost the services of its most worthy chronicler at this critical time in its history.

"Many think the contest is now over," he had observed prophetically in an earlier dispatch. "I, on the contrary, am persuaded this prick in the great Northern balloon will let out a quantity of poisonous gas and rouse the people to a sense of the nature of the conflict on which they have entered."

Out of Bull Run would come an effort so prodigious that simply to make it would change America forever. In the dust, smoke, and panic of defeat an era had come to an end.

Part

§ **4** ॐ

The Rise of Modern America

On July 4, 1876, the people of America celebrated the country's centennial anniversary with unbridled enthusiasm and optimism. In that 100 years the country had grown from a population of 4 million to one of 40 million, from 13 states to 38. The major focus of the festivities was the Centennial Exposition, which boasted 249 structures on 285 acres in Philadelphia's Fairmouth Park. President Ulysses S Grant officially opened the exhibition on May 10. Over the next six months some 10 million people paid the admission of 50 cents to stroll through the exhibits and gape in wonder at the hundreds of modern marvels on display, including Alexander Graham Bell's telephone and the Scholes-Glidden typewriter. In fact, the dawning Age of Technology was a major theme of the Centennial Exposition. The large Machinery Hall, for example, featured a mind-boggling collection of saws, lathes, presses, pumps, and mills, all powered by a 2,550-horsepower Corliss steam engine.

On June 25, 1876, in a distant part of America far from the bright lights and modern marvels of the Centennial Exposition, Lieutenant Colonel George Armstrong Custer and 250 of his men were killed at the Battle of the Little Big Horn, Montana Territory, when their planned ambush of a sleeping Indian encampment became a battle with overwheming numbers of Sioux and Northern Cheyenne (who were wide awake). The details of that infamous day, describing the battle as just the reverse of what it actually was, reached the East Coast during the week of July Fourth. The festive crowds in Philadelphia were stunned when they heard the news. The nation sank into mourning, and church bells ran out the *Te Deum* in cities, towns, and villages nationwide. (Custer's "last stand" is frozen in time as a defining moment in American history. In actual fact, it was not even a battle but rather a large skirmish, and one that settled nothing and changed nothing.)

Within a generation of Lee's surrender at the Appomattox Court House, the United States had become the world's foremost industrial power. The end of the Civil War marked much more than the military and political victory of the North. It also signified the triumph of a new business class, whose ethics would soon come to permeate all aspects of the American society and in the process transform the United States from an agrarian society to a maturing industrial nation. The portion of American society engaged in agriculture dropped from 61% in 1860 to 37% in 1900. American railroads, stretching a quarter of a million miles in 1900, had expanded eight-fold since the Civil War and connected giant, electrically lighted cities with downtown skylines increasingly dominated by towering skyscrapers made possible by Otis's invention of the hydraulic elevator. The influence of the old agrarian-minded statesmen of the prewar generations yielded to that of a new and expanding urban middle class, particularly those men whose wealth was rooted in wartime opportunities and continued to grow in the burgeoning economy of the postwar decades.

A new American age implied new or different Americans. Between 1866 and 1900 more than 13 million immigrants entered the United States and included for the first time large numbers of Italians, Slavs, and Jews. Their presence exploded the populations of American cities and enriched urban culture, while simultaneously sparking an ethnic backlash.

The decade of the 1870s was a time of easy money, a laissez-faire attitude of the government toward business, and a relaxation of morals in politics, business, and personal behavior. Those years became known as the "Gilded Age," thanks to Mark Twain and

Charles Dudley Warner in their novel *The Gilded Age,* published in 1873. Colonel Beriah Sellers, the novel's chief character, epitomized the perennial business optimism and fever for speculation during the era. Magnificent dreams, enormous private projects, and lush profits seemed very American in their boldness and scope.

"The social philosophy of the age was summed up in three words—preemption, exploitation, and progress," Arthur Ekirch, Jr., observed in his fine book, *The Decline of American Liberalism.* "Although America, as it moved forward to conquer the last frontiers to the west, still accounted itself individualistic and democratic, individualism was being simplified to 'the acquisitive instinct,' while progress was becoming synonymous with the pre-emption and exploitation of the public domain by large-scale business interests aided by government subsidies."

With the rich resources of the trans-Mississippi West now open to private exploitation, the businessman suddenly had singular opportunities to achieve a measure of personal wealth undreamed of just a few decades earlier. Hundreds of thousands of Americans surged across the Great Plains and Western states, homesteading farms, exterminating the millions of buffalo and replacing them with cattle, staking mining claims for gold and silver deposits, and binding the Mississippi Valley to the West Coast with iron rails.

Post–Civil War America alarmed the Indians of the trans-Mississippi West, many of whom still maintained their nomadic hunter lifestyle. The U.S. Census Bureau estimated in 1870 that of the 383,712 Indians, 234,740 still roamed freely across the western territories and states. What threatened their world was the rapid influx of pioneers with their eyes fixed on Indian lands. Settlers expected U.S. Army troops to support their countrymen by forcing the Indians off their traditional land. When Indian resistance grew in frequency and intensity, federal officials decided they had no choice but to subdue the Indians to make the West safe for the nation's expansion.

The western Indians had been relatively peaceful until 1860.

Then, in response to the advance of white settlers into the upper Mississippi and Missouri territories, the Sioux of the Dakotas went on the warpath, devastating the Minnesota frontier and killing and capturing almost 1,000 white people. And thus began the great Indian wars which lasted well into the 1870s. The federal government's insistence upon concentrating the Western Indians on small reservations kept the conflict alive. No less an authority than George Custer admitted in an article he wrote for an Eastern magazine, "If I were an Indian, I would certainly prefer to cast my lot . . . to the free open plains than submit to the confined limits of a reservation, there to be the recipient of the blessed benefits of civilization with its vices thrown in."

The U.S. Army, with its previous military experience limited to the campaigns of the Civil War, found itself poorly equipped psychologically to defeat the elusive, unorthodox Plains fighters who often had no permanent villages to attack or crops to destroy. But time was on the side of the Army. "You cannot stop the locomotive any more than you can stop the sun or moon, and you must submit and do the best you can," General William Tecumseh Sherman warned an assemblage of Indians at Medicine Lodge, Kansas, in 1869. "Our people in the East hardly think of what you call a war here. But if they make up their minds to fight you, they will come out as thick as a herd of buffalo, and if you continue fighting, you will be killed." By 1880, after almost 300 years of conflict, the Indian Wars finally were resolved, not by power-sharing but by subjugation of the Native Americans.

Between 1870 and 1900 the U.S. government issued more than 500,000 patents for new inventions. Advances in science and technology were an integral part of the American transformation into a modern industrial nation. Electrical appliances, the telephone and telegraph, the factory system, and mass transportation transformed the lives of millions of Americans.

Among the many inventions that took Americans giant strides forward into modern ways of living, few affected the West as much as did the refrigerated railroad cars. Transporting hundreds of thousands of pounds of freshly killed beef from Chicago to the Eastern cities, they accelerated the slaughter of more than 50 million buffaloes and their replacement throughout the Great Plains and Western states by cattle, and stimulated the great cattle drives of the 1870s. In 1871 alone, more than 600,000 head were driven north to the railheads and transported to slaughterhouses, and then their beef was shipped in refrigerated railcars to the Eastern markets.

As manufacturers brought forth a torrent of mass-produced consumer goods, new sales approaches were developed. Singer began offering installment buying for purchasers of their popular sewing machines. Mail-order buying swept the nation and proved a boon for people living in isolated farming communities. The ponderous Sears-Roebuck catalogs were as ubiquitous as Bibles in many households. Materialism also commercialized aesthetic values, spawning a culture of bad taste, which Oscar Wilde was quick to denounce during his 1882 lecture tour.

"The Gilded Age was transitional, but the velocity and variety of change set it apart from its predecessors," historian H. Wayne Morgan has observed. "In a broad sense, it was the first 'modern' American generation."

Irishman Frank Harris, our next traveler, participated in the greatest man-controlled migration of animals the world has ever known and left us perhaps the finest account of a post–Civil War cattle drive. Oscar Wilde's yearlong tour of America in 1882 covered some 15,000 miles and took him to 60 cities and towns in all regions of the country. He found a confident, prosperous America largely recovered from the ravages of the Civil War and moving swiftly into world prominence and a modern age.

Chapter

§ 7 §

Frank Harris:
Confessions of a Cowboy

E arly in 1872 eight American cowboys crossed the Rio Grande into Texas, driving ahead of them a herd of 1,500 longhorn cattle they had rustled several days before from a large hacienda in Mexico. A few hours later a group of 20 armed Mexicans overtook them and demanded the return of their cattle. The Americans refused, and the situation quickly became tense. Threats were exchanged. Suddenly, the cowboys drew their revolvers and fired on the Mexicans. Two Mexicans fell dead to the ground and another four were wounded. The others fled back toward the border.

"After the battle we all adjourned to Locker's [Saloon] and had a big drink," one cowboy wrote later. "Nobody took the fight seriously; whipping [Mexicans] was nothing to brag about. But Rossiter thought that a claim should be made against the Mexican Government for raiding United States territory; [he] said he was going to draw up the papers and send them to the state district attorney at Austin. The proposal was received with whoops and cheers. The idea of punishing the Mexicans for getting shot trying to recapture their own cattle appealed to us Americans as something intensely humorous. All the Texans gave their names solemnly as witnesses, and Rossiter swore he would draw up the document. Years afterwards [I learned] that Rossiter had got forty thousand dollars on that claim."

The observer of that scene of frontier violence was Frank Harris, an English youth who had run away from home at the age of 14 and traveled to America, where he had a series of extraordinary adventures. For a time in New York he had worked as a sandhog deep in the underwater muck of the East River, laying the foundations of the Brooklyn Bridge. Later, as a night clerk in a Chicago hotel, he met three cowboys who made a good living driving longhorn cattle out of Texas up the Chisholm Trail. Enthralled, he listened to their tales of buffalo hunts and Indian fights. He made up his mind to become a cowboy and thus spent two years on the Western frontier. He tamed wild horses, branded cattle, fought Indians, saw saloon fights, and took up the fine art of cattle rustling. Later he witnessed the great Chicago fire. His experiences were to affect him profoundly. He would return to England thoroughly Americanized.

Harris's life (1856–1931) holds a dreadful fascination. A short, dark man, pugnacious and unable to check his insults, he combined tactlessness with a commanding voice. Once in a London restaurant he was heard by all to say, "No, my dear Duke, I know nothing of the joys of homosexuality. You must speak to my friend Oscar about that." Then, in the silence that followed he added in a loud voice: "And yet, if Shakespeare had asked me I would have had to submit."

Harris counted among his acquaintances such luminaries as Thomas Carlyle, George Merdith, Robert Browning, Captain Sir Richard F. Burton, Algernon Swinburne, and Guy de Maupassant. "Frank Harris has been received in all the great houses in London—*once!*" Oscar Wilde remarked wittily. (Later he dedicated *An Ideal Husband* to his friend and future biographer Harris.)

"Frank was a man of splendid visions, unreasonable expectations, and fierce appetites," George Bernard Shaw, his friend for 40 years, observed. "He blazed through London like a comet, leaving a trail of deeply annoyed persons behind him."

"Frank Harris is the most dynamic writer alive," the English biographer Hesketh Pearson insisted in 1923, adding that his "appeal is to the men and women who have lived, not drifted through life."

One of the great editors of his age, Harris took over the *Evening News* at 27 and made its circulation soar by writing about sex and brawls. Later, when he edited the *Saturday Review,* he took the opposite tack. By hiring Shaw, Max Beerbohm, and H.G. Wells as writers, he made its coverage of the arts the best in any English-language publication. As a writer Harris was prolific, versatile, and full of personal involvement. He published some 25 volumes in all, including one novel, a collection of short stories, and two biographies. Generally, he was a man whose ambitions exceeded his talent and energy, doomed always to remain a minor writer.

Only in *My Life and Loves,* his five-volume autobiography, did Harris break new ground and rise to greatness, fulfilling Shaw's prophecy in 1915: "Your most interesting book will be your autobiography." In it Harris determined to set down freely and honestly the truth about himself without fear or compromise. He had no intention of writing a discreet memoir. Mixed in with the accounts of his meetings and friendships with Walt Whitman, Karl Marx, Henry James, Richard Wagner, John Ruskin, and others, he penned the most fully detailed and frankly worded account of his sex life that any literary figure has ever written. His sexual recollections began with his peering up girls' dresses in his first school and continued through his explorations in a lifeboat on his way to America to the various kinds of affairs one might expect. But his life, and therefore his autobiography, went further. He also described, for instance, the procurement of girls at an Italian village for the joint delight of his guests and himself, and a succession of 12-year-old prostitutes in Bombay. He narrated all his encounters graphically but offered no moral judgments about them. He wrote of sensual experience as part of the human experience. He lived, he worked, he ate, he slept, and he fornicated. For Harris sex was neither dirty or self-consciously beautiful. It simply *was.*

(Any biographer of Harris has to deal with the persistent charges that he sometimes falsified events in his life. "As I came to maturity I found that my memory . . . began to colour incidents dramatically," he freely admitted in *My Life and Loves.* Certainly, in recounting the events of his own life he revealed an excellent sense of narrative drama; the events and people come alive for the reader. As with all his nonfiction, we have to ask how much of it is true.

(Professor John F. Gallagher, who edited the scholarly edition of *My Life and Loves,* wrote in his introduction to that book: "There is the question of whether Harris invented sex episodes in the hopes of increasing sales or heightening effect, or whether his memory played him false in recalling details. It does not seem likely that a man who could accurately quote at length, say, from Swinburne's *Anactoria* and from Macaulay's essay on history fifty years after reading them would find it difficult to remember the faces and anatomies of women. And those persons still alive who knew him best deny there was any necessity for invention by him.")

Harris was born James Thomas Harris, probably in 1856, in Galway on Ireland's western coast. His mother died when he was five. His father held a minor commission in the Royal Navy and was often away from home, and father and son were together only on rare occasions. Harris attended a series of schools. In all it was a restless life, rootless, with no continuity and few friends. "I often used to think that no one cared for me really," he recalled later in *My Life and Loves,* "and I would weep over my unloved loneliness." His chief interests were sex, sports, and books of romantic adventure. Like George Ruxton before him, he found himself ensnared by James Fenimore Cooper's tales of frontier adventures and began to dream of faraway places.

Harris's unhappiness grew after his father enrolled him at Ruabon, on the border between England and Wales. Like many British schools of that era, Ruabon had organized traditional fagging into a rigid pyramid of chiefs, monitors, and sub-monitors, who were with the younger boys and who presumably guided their footsteps during most hours of the day and night. Harris had to endure a claustrophobic existence of rigid discipline and stupid punishments. He saw himself as a caged bird, he wrote later, and longed to be free. He became increasingly preoccupied with thoughts of America and its vast plains, herds of buffalo, wild Indians, and cowboys. In his American dreams he always saw himself as a combination of Horatio Alger and William Cody, making a great deal of money quickly and enjoying splendid Western adventures. The modest windfall of a second prize in a school composition contest suddenly gave him the means of escape. With £15 cash in his pocket he set out in 1870 for Liverpool to book passage for America. "I was trembling with excitement and delight," he recalled later. "I was going to enter the real world and live as I wished to live. I had no regrets, no sorrows. I was filled with lively hopes and happy presentiments."

Harris quickly checked the steamship offices and found a ship sailing to New York the next afternoon. He paid £4 for a steerage passage. A steward showed him a chalked circle on one deck, his place for duration of the transatlantic voyage. In his excitement Harris had neglected to bring the necessary mattress and two blankets. A few hours later the ship's doctor, a young man with a nonchalant manner and reddish hair, questioned him at length.

"Where's your father or mother?" he asked.

"Haven't got any," Harris replied.

"Do they let children like you go to America?" the doctor persisted. "What age are you?"

Harris, lying, gave his age at 16, and asked, "How does it matter to you? You are not responsible for me, thank God."

"I am though," the doctor said, "to a certain degree, at least. Are you really going to America on your own?"

"I am."

"What to do?" the doctor persisted.

"Anything I can get."

"Hm, I must see to this."

The doctor took the young Irish boy under his wing, and Harris spent the next two hours in the doctor's cabin reading Macaulay's essays on British history. When the doctor returned, Harris recited much of Macaulay's chapter on Warren Hastings by heart. The older man was impressed and quickly arranged for a demonstration of Harris's extraordinary memory in the lounge. The amused passengers passed a hat, took up a collection, and presented Harris with a first-class ticket. An older gentlemen from New York even offered to adopt him. But as Harris observed later, "I had not got rid of one father to take on another, so I kept as far away from him as I decently could."

During the voyage Harris experienced his first sexual conquest. Her name was Jessie Kerr, and she was the pretty daughter of the ship's chief engineer. Sixteen years old, she was free and easy in manner, and he lost no time in making her acquaintance. Soon the couple was meeting daily, whenever Jessie could escape from her father's watchful eye. Harris quickly set about trying to seduce her. His seduction of Jessie was little more than a commonplace exhibition of boyhood lust. Later in his life, Harris insisted that lust was as important a reality as love and we should accept it as such without trying to hide it under more poetic names.

"I had learned enough now to go slow and obey what seemed to be her moods," Harris recalled later in *My Life and Loves*. "Gently, gently, I caressed her sex with my finger till it opened and she leaned against me and kissed me of her own will, while her eyes turned up and her whole being was lost in thrills of ecstasy. When she asked me to stop and take my hand away, I did her bidding at once and was rewarded with being told that I was a 'dear boy' and 'a sweet,' and soon the embracing and caressing began again. She moved now in response to my lascivious touchings, and when the ecstasy came on her, she clasped me close and kissed me passionately with hot lips and afterwards in my arms wept a little, and then pouted that she was cross with me for being so naughty. But her eyes gave themselves to me even while she tried to scold."

Jessie thus became the first in Harris's long list of amours. In his lovemaking Harris was as direct and impatient as he was to be in his working life. For him there were no preliminaries, no wooing, no courtship. The simple act of desiring a woman aroused him to the act itself. The fact that most of his women proved easy conquests tells us volumes about his forceful personality.

Twelve days after departing Liverpool, Harris arrived in New York City. "What an entrance to a new world!" he recalled later. "A magnificent and safe ocean port which is also the meeting place of great water paths into the continent. No finer site could be imagined for a world capital. I was entranced with the spacious grandeur, the manifest destiny of this Queen City of Waters."

2

In 1870, when Harris arrived in New York City, modern America was in the process of being born. The Civil War was over. The North had won. Slavery had been abolished. General Ulysses S Grant was president, and the Industrial Revolution was reshaping the American landscape. In the East, the smoke from thousands of factories and mills blackened the skies. In the West, the Union Pacific and Central Pacific railroads had been joined at Ogden, Utah, the previous year. U.S. Army troops strove to keep order over vast territories. The Comanche and Sioux Indians waged a courageous but futile war against the encroaching civilization. Herds of cattle began filling the void left in the Great Plains by the slaughter of hundreds of thousands of bison.

Unbridled capitalism reined supreme throughout the land, while scandals rocked the Grant administration. In 1869 two New York stock gamblers, Jay Gould and Jim Fisk, had tried to corner the gold market and almost succeeded, nearly bringing the whole financial system to its knees. "Boss" Tweed's gang was busy stealing $100 million from New York City. Corruption and scandal seemed to be everywhere. Well did Mark Twain call this the Gilded Age, for when the gilt rubbed off one only found base brass. It was a time of materialism run amuck.

Of all this young Harris knew nothing. He only knew that he had arrived at last, a pilgrim in the promised land. Later he affirmed that the American sky, higher and wider than the sky of Europe, lifts the heart to idealism. He recalled his feelings that first day in *The Bomb,* his novel about a young immigrant who falls in with a group of Chicago anarchists: "The May morning had all the beauty and freshness of youth; the air was warm, and yet light and quick. I fell in love with the broad, sunny streets. The people, too, walked rapidly. The street cars spun past.

Everything was brisk and cheerful. I felt curiously exhilarated and lighthearted."

Harris set about immediately looking for a room. An Irish-born housewife befriended him and insisted he spend nights with her and her husband, also Irish, until he got on his feet. "Ye're a child an' don't know New York," Mary Mulligan told him in her thick Irish brogue. "It's a terrible place and you must wait till Mike comes home. . . . He will put ye on yer feet. Sure he knows New York like his pocket, an' yer as welcome as the flowers in May." He insisted upon paying her $3 a week for his room and board.

Early the next morning Harris set out to search for a job. Like the heroes in the Horatio Alger stories, he began proving himself in the humble role of a bootblack. He spotted a shoeshine stand with three customers and only one bootblack. He offered his services. The man quickly agreed to teach him the trade in exchange for half the money Harris made. In two hours he had collected $3, enough to cover his weekly room and board. America did indeed appear to be a land of plenty. "The last anxiety left me," he noted.

Later that same day Harris heard great news from Mike Mulligan. Men were wanted to work under the water in the iron caissons of Brooklyn Bridge, for wages of $5 a day. "Five dollars!" cried Mary. "It must be dangerous or unhealthy or somethin'— sure, you'd never put a child to work like that." But the idea of danger appealed to the young Irishman almost as much as the pay. That next day Harris presented himself at the construction site and was quickly employed as sandhog to work in the underwater muck of the East River where the foundations of the bridge were to rest.

Brooklyn then was still a city unto itself, the third largest in America. Some 400,000 people lived in 25 square miles. Manhattan was only two miles away, but accessible only by one of the 13 huge ferries that made almost 1,000 crossings every 24 hours. In January 1870 the first caisson had been sunk under the supervision of Washington Roebling, a Prussian-born engineer.

The completed bridge was opened in 1882. But in late 1870 construction was still in its earliest stages, with excavations being dug for the deep foundations.

The caissons that Roebling employed were like enormous diving bells made of wood and iron and shaped like gigantic boxes with heavy roofs, strong sides, and no bottoms. Filled with compressed air, they were sent to the bottom of the river by the weight of large stones on their roofs. The compressed air kept the river water out, helped support the boxes against the pressure of the water and mud, and made it possible for the workmen inside to dig out the riverbed. An air lock allowed workers to get in and out of the sealed chamber. When the caissons finally hit bedrock, excavation would stop, the interiors would be filled with concrete, and the entire structures would become the foundations for the bridge's pillars.

Work in the caissons was exhausting, often crippling, and sometimes fatal. The bends—that awful twisting of the flesh caused by the release of nitrogen bubbles in the blood after a return to normal air pressure—were a constant danger. Dizziness and deafness were cumulative, even if one escaped the bends. Two hours was the maximum of any one shift, and even so the men were troubled by headaches, buzzing ears, and a curious dragging of the limbs, as though they had lead weights strapped on them.

Harris worked two shifts for $5, driven by the thought that in a month he could make enough money to live on for a year. In his autobiography *My Life and Loves* and his novel *The Bomb* he left behind the fullest, most detailed accounts we have of this stage in the construction of the Brooklyn Bridge:

"When we got into the 'air-lock' and they turned on one air-cock after another of compressed air, the men put their hands to their ears and I soon imitated them, for the pain was very acute. Inside, the drums of the ears are often driven in and burst if the compressed air is brought in too quickly. I found that the best way of meeting the pressure was to keep swallowing air and forcing it up into the middle ear. . . . When the air was fully compressed, the door of the air-lock opened at a touch and all went down to work with pick and shovel and on the gravelly bottom. My headache soon became acute. The six of us worked naked to the waist in a small iron chamber; in five minutes the sweat was pouring from us, and all the while we were standing in icy water that was only kept from rising by the terrific air pressure. . . . After two hours' work down below we went up into the air-lock room to get gradually 'decompressed,' the pressure of air in our veins having to be brought down gradually to the usual air pressure. The men put on their clothes and passed round a bottle of schnapps; but though I was soon as cold as a wet rag and depressed and weak to boot, I would not touch the liquor. In the shed above I took a cupful of hot cocoa, which stopped the shivering, and I was soon able to face the afternoon's ordeal."

Harris resolved to prove himself and did the work of two men. "You're the best in the shift," his foreman told him, "the best I've ever seen, a great little pony."

After six days Harris had terrible shooting pains in his ears and was told he might go deaf. Mary Mulligan fixed up a remedy— "a roasted onion cut in two and clapped tight on each ear with a flannel bandage." It worked like magic and within minutes his pain subsided. A few days later an Italian worker in his shift came down with the bends. He writhed about on the floor while blood spurted from his nose and mouth. A shocked Harris noted that "his legs were twisted like plaited hair." Harris quit the job after he had finished his month. With $150 in his pockets, he felt like a rich man.

Harris set himself up as a bootblack and soon had a loyal clientele. His regular customers included a Chicago businessman named Kendrick. One day Harris absentmindedly quoted a Latin passage from Virgil. Struck by his words, Kendrick took a deeper interest in the thin, rather ragged young boy who shined his shoes with such intensity. "Bootblacking's not your game," Kendrick told him. "How would you like to come to Chicago and have a place as night clerk in my hotel?" Harris never hesitated. Three days later he and Kendrick boarded a train for Chicago.

"My first round, so to speak, with American life was over," he wrote later. "What I had learned in it remains with me still. No people is so kind to children and no life is easy for the hand-workers; the hewers of wood and drawers of water are better off in the United States than anywhere else on earth. To this one class, and it is by far the most numerous class, the American democracy more than fulfills its promises. It levels up the lowest in a most surprising way. I believed then with all my heart what so many believe today, that all deductions made, it was on the whole the best civilization yet known among men."

3

In the Chicago of 1870 the older life of the East and the raw life of the West met and mingled. Texas cowboys rubbed shoulders with New York bankers. The outlying streets were full of blowing dust or flowing mud, yet concrete sidewalks had recently appeared in some of the fashionable districts. Avenues such as Michigan and Wabash had been widened into drives. A network of horse-drawn streetcars extended over the city. Some 2,500 gaslights illuminated the streets with more brilliance than in most Eastern cities. Home to 300,000 people, Chicago was also the major meat-packing center in the country. Such men as Philip D. Armour and Gustavus F. Swift had based their fortunes on the lucrative contracts of the Civil War period. By the 1870s they were cooperating to dominate the market and fix prices.

Chicago was noted, too, for its spectacular fires. In 1868 a fire on Lake Street had caused more than $2 million in damages. By 1871 the city was paying more for fire insurance than it collected from state, county, and municipal taxes. Of the city's 60,000 buildings, 40,000 were constructed of wood. Most had roofs made of felt and tar or wooden shingles. Housed in one of the city's few fireproof buildings, the *Tribune* published an editorial calling the majority of Chicago's buildings a "cheat, a snare, and a lie."

Harris went to work as the night clerk at the Fremont House, a "good but second-rate hotel" located near the Michigan Street depot. He immediately set about learning the good and bad points of the hundred bedrooms. When guests arrived, he met them at the entrance and found out what they wanted. When they were on edge and short-tempered, he tried to soothe them. In this he succeeded. After the first week Kendrick told him that a dozen visitors had already praised him highly. "You have a dandy night clerk," they had told him. "Spares no pains . . . pleasant manners . . . knows everything . . . *some* clerk; yes, sir!" The hotel management increased his salary from $40 to $60 a month. Harris redoubled his efforts and soon was keeping the books as well. Kendrick raised him to $100 a month. "Pay, like water, tends to find its level!" he concluded.

In early June 1871 Harris's life suddenly took a dramatic change. Three strangers checked into the Fremont House, all cattlemen. They signed their names on the registry as Reece, Dell, and Ford. Reece and Dell were both British, who always dressed in brown riding boots, Bedford cord breeches, and dark tweed coats. Ford was American, six feet tall with a hatchet-thin, bronzed face. They were cattleman who made a lucrative business by buying cattle on the Rio Grande for a dollar a head, and driving them to market in Kansas City, and selling them for $15 or $20 a head. "Of course, we don't always get through unscathed," Reece told Harris. "The Plains Indians—Cherokees, Blackfeet, and Sioux—take care of that. One herd in two gets through and that pays big."

The three cattlemen took a liking to the young Irishman, who had grown six inches during his time in America and now looked older than his years. Harris, in turn, fell under their spell as he listened to their stories of cattle punching, Indian fights, and life on the range. He determined to go on the trail with them after they left Chicago, if they would have him. Reece taught him some basic riding skills, and Ford finally gave his consent. Harris had saved $1,800 and agreed to go into partnership with the men on buying cattle.

On June 10 the four men boarded a train in Chicago and the next day disembarked at Kansas City, then the gateway to the Western frontier. They picked up three more men belonging to their outfit: Bent, a Civil War veteran; Charlie, a handsome American youth, more than six feet tall, strong and light-hearted; and Bob, a short man, half Mexican and half Indian, who rarely spoke except to curse Americans in Spanish. Harris stopped at a store to purchase a Colt revolver, Winchester rifle, shotgun, and some appropriate clothes with Reece's expert advice.

At 4:00 the following morning Harris and the six cowboys rode out of Kansas City toward the southwest. By the fourth day they had left all roads and homesteads behind and were on the open prairie, riding through buffalo grass and sagebrush, averaging 30 miles a day. Ford appointed Harris the hunter after discovering he possessed a sixth sense for direction, which always brought him back to the group. Harris savored his new life.

"After breakfast about five o'clock in the morning, I would ride away from the wagon till it was out of sight and then abandon myself to the joy of solitude with no boundary between plain and sky," he recalled later in *My Life and Loves*. "The air was brisk and dry, as exhilarating as champagne, and even when the sun reached the zenith and became blazing hot, the air remained lightsome and invigorating. . . . Game was plentiful. Hardly an hour would elapse before I had got half a dozen ruffled grouse or a deer, and then I would walk my pony back to the midday camp, with perhaps a new wild flower in my hand whose name I wished to learn."

After a ten-day ride the group reached Reece's Texas ranch set in the midst of 5,000 acres of prairie, a large frame building that housed 20 men. Revolvers and rifles of a dozen different varieties, along with skins of mink and beaver, decorated the walls of the parlor. Buffalo and bear skin rugs covered the floor. Nearby was a great brick stable, constructed English style. A stream ran within 300 yards of the buildings.

Two days later the cowboys set out from the ranch for the Rio

Grande 1,200 miles away. Two wagons, each drawn by four mules, carried all their supplies and food. Their goal was to purchase 6,000 head of cattle at a dollar a head and drive them to Kansas City, the nearest railhead. With them was Harris, the bootblack-sandhog-desk-clerk-turned-cowboy. The summer sun had already begun to brown his face and hands. Leather chaps protected his legs. A six-shot Colt revolver rode his hip.

"That first ride into the Southwest was of the essence of romance," Harris recalled later. "It was a plunge a thousand miles into the unknown. It was like an old border foray, with enough strangeness to interest and enough danger to warm the blood."

4

The best-advertised feature of the life of the post–Civil War West was the cattle business. Authors as diverse as Theodore Roosevelt and Zane Grey, and painters such as Frederick Remington and Charles Russell, have given it a permanent place in American mythology. Later, Hollywood made the Western cowboy film a staple of American entertainment for five decades. All this—despite the fact that the cattle business in the distinctive form that included the long drive lasted less than two decades.

Except for the horse, no animal played such a critical role in the shaping of the mythology of the American West as the Texas longhorn, a breed of cattle so important to the early ranching industry that it influenced every phase of the development of the southwestern United States. Longhorns made up the great herds that cowboys drove from Texas to Kansas for shipment east by rail. It was chiefly longhorns that filled the void when the great herds of buffaloes were killed off and the Indians confined to reservations. Without the longhorn, it is doubtful that the cowboy would have become an American myth. "The Texas longhorn made more history than any other breed of cattle the civilized world has known," insisted the great Western historian J. Frank Dobie in his book *The Longhorns*.

What is a longhorn? The Texas Longhorn Breeders Association offers up the following description in its literature: "Texas longhorns are big, raw-boned, and rangy, with slabbed sides and a squarish look. They have long legs, with the huge forequarters making the front legs seem shorter. The head is large and long, giving the eyes a wide-spaced appearance. The neck is short and stocky. In color they do not rival a rainbow; they eclipse it, although the hues are more akin to muted earth tones. They range from black to white, solid and dotted, splashed and spotted, with all the colors in between—mulberry, speckled, and ring-streaked blue, slate or the highly prized mouse color, duns, and browns, yellows and creams, all the spectacular shades of red. No two are exactly alike in color."

Their great horns are their most striking characteristic, and these frequently reach six feet from tip to tip but can be longer. Two animals on exhibit in Chicago at the Columbian Exposition of 1893 boasted spreads in excess of nine feet.

The stock that produced these longhorns came to this country from Spain, one of several places in Europe and Asia where the wild auroch—ancestor of all today's domestic cattle—is believed to have been first tamed. Christopher Columbus brought the first longhorns to Santo Domingo on his second voyage to the New World. When Cortez moved into Mexico, he took with him calves from these animals. When Coronado set out in 1540 in search of the Seven Cities of Cibola, he had 500 head of longhorns with him. More came with the Spanish priests who followed. Many of these animals escaped into the wild, where they survived and multiplied. In 1767 a Frenchman who crossed Texas noticed, west of the Brazos River, "horned cattle, originally tame, that long since have become wild and now roam in large herds all over the plains."

Their value in the pre–Civil War years lay almost entirely in their hides and tallow. And sport. Game hunters found the wild longhorn cattle more challenging than many other commonly hunted species in the West. "I should be doing an injustice to a cousin-germane of the buffalo did I fail to mention as game the wild cattle of Texas, animals miscalled tame but fifty times more dangerous to footmen than the fiercest buffalo," enthused hunter-author Colonel R.I. Dodge in 1876.

Hardy, aggressive, and adaptable, the longhorns were well suited to the rigors of life on the ranges of the southwestern United States. "Under primitive conditions only the fittest survived; predatory animals and the adversities of climate promoted selective breeding," Dobie writes. "Left to make their own way, the cattle developed hardihood, fleetness, and independence. They grew horns to fight off wolves, to hook down succulent mistletoe out of trees, and to sweep out of the way thorned branches protecting sparse tufts of grass on the parched ground."

When the Civil War ended in 1865, Texas soldiers returned to find their ranches in ruin, their livestock scattered, and the state bankrupt. But all across the open bush country roamed millions of wild longhorns. And back East people clamored for beef. The longhorn quickly became the basis for a Texas cattle industry that soon led the war-ravaged state out of its depression.

The post–Civil War cattle drives, celebrated in such classic films as Howard Hawks's *Red River,* began in the spring of 1866, when the first large herds of longhorns were driven along the legendary Chisholm Trail toward the railhead in Abilene, Kansas. This was the beginning of the greatest controlled movement of cattle in history. Within the next 20 years cowboys drove more than 10 million longhorns north out of Texas to fatten on lush Midwestern grasses or be shipped directly by rail to the beef-hungry East. Others were driven to the northern Plains states to stock range left empty by the slaughter of the buffaloes. In 1884 alone more than 4 million longhorns arrived in Kansas from Texas. Cattle moving shoulder-to-shoulder backed up 40 miles on some of the trails.

And yet by 1920 the breed stood on the edge of extinction, reduced to a few hundred head scattered across the remote bush country of Texas. The longhorn did not go, like the passenger pigeon and the buffalo, in a senseless, wasteful slaughter. Rather it fell victim to changing fashions within the cattle industry. "The longhorn came to be outlawed not only by economy but by a rage for standardized, uniform stock," observes Dobie. "Durhams, followed by Polled Anguses and Devons, were at first the principal importations. Then the Hereford was settled upon as the breed best adapted to the range. The time came when, to bring a price justified to the raiser, a crop of calves had to look as nearly alike as possible, be as uniform in age, color, and conformity as a flock of lambs." After longhorns lost their commercial value, ranchers ceased to waste rangeland or effort on those "worthless animals."

By 1925 the situation had deteriorated to the point where several concerned Texas congressmen managed to move a bill through Congress authorizing the establishment of a herd of longhorns at the Wichita Mountains National Wildlife Refuge near Cache, Oklahoma, to preserve the species from extinction. In 1927 U.S. Forest Service employees Will Barnes and John Hatton, armed with a description of the longhorn "type," set forth on a 5,000-mile search for purebred longhorns. It was not an easy task. After inspecting more than 30,000 head of Texas cattle, Barnes and Hatton located only 20 cows, three bulls, three steers, and four calves—this in an area where longhorns once existed by the millions.

The first herd assembled at the Witchita refuge was scrubby, mean, irritable, and ready to fight at the slightest provocation. All the animals were wild. Many had never likely seen a human being before. From this first government herd came the foundation stock for one other refuge herd and for small private herds.

And so the longhorn was saved. In the 1930s and 1940s various ranchers started breeding programs of their own, drawn to the longhorn for reasons of sentiment and nostalgia. The longhorn, after all, was as much a part of Texas history as the Alamo. When a group of breeders formed the Texas Longhorn Breeders Association in 1964, there were fewer than 1,500 genuine Texas longhorns in existence. That has changed rapidly in the past

decade. Today there are over 70,000 purebred longhorns registered with the association and more than 2,500 breeders. The
longhorn has returned with a vengeance.

5

Harris quickly discovered an essential feature of trail riding:
boredom. The ordinary life of the cowboy was reasonably
dull. After sunset the group of ten sat around the campfire chatting
reflectively. They had three subjects of primary interest: women
and what to do with them, religion, and the relationship between
management and labor. When the arguments finally petered out,
Bent brought out his worn deck of cards and the men gambled
until late in the evening.

A break in the routine came one morning while Harris was collecting dried buffalo chips for the cook's fire. As he stooped to
pick up one large chip, a little prairie rattlesnake struck him suddenly on his thumb. He quickly crushed its head with his boot
heel, bit out the flesh around the two tiny puncture holes, and
then stuck the open wound in the red embers to cauterize it. The
others did not take the injury as casually as Harris did. They knew
how dangerous any rattlesnake was—particularly a young one
that hadn't yet learned to control the flow of its venom. Ford filled
him with whiskey and walked him back and forth in the camp. A
great urge to sleep came over him. He felt himself going numb and
deaf. Ford and Reece kept him walking for two hours until the
effects of the poison finally wore off.

In time Reece's party reached Texas and encountered their first
towns. Each man demanded to be paid his wages, slicked himself
up as much as possible, and headed for the first saloon. Within an
hour they were crazy drunk and looking for Mexican prostitutes
with whom to spend an hour or a night. Harris refused to accompany them to the saloon and begged the young Charlie not to play
the fool. "That's what I live for," he shouted and rode off. They

soon paid for their indiscretions. Charlie was the first to come down with a severe case of gonorrhea, which laid him up for a month. One by one the other cowboys fell ill with the same disease.

Reece and Ford spent their days buying cattle and within a month had assembled a herd of 6,000 animals. Harris bought 500 head with his own money. By late July they started up the trail, driving the huge herd ahead of them. Cautiously they skirted Indian Territory. "The God damned Americanos lose them all now," gloated Bob, the Mexican. "One single Indian can stampede the whole herd, pouf! Then what you got?"

A week later Harris noticed the cattle were uneasy. He mentioned the fact to Bob. "Indians," the Mexican told him. That night Harris was off duty, but he circled the uneasy herd as usual. Suddenly about midnight an Indian leaped up, shouted an ungodly yell, and waved a sheet. Harris fired his rifle wildly, and the Indian ran away. The cowboys soon quieted the cattle.

With no further close calls, Reece's men brought the herd safely to Kansas City and sold one-fourth of the cattle at $15 a head. They reached Chicago in early October and put the rest of their herd in the yards near the Michigan Street depot. Once again Harris found himself back at the Fremont House. The next day they sold another half of the herd. Harris sold 300 of his animals for $4,500, and now counted himself a wealthy man.

Throughout the summer of 1871 Chicago had experienced the driest weather in the city's history. From the fourth of July to the first of October less than an inch and half of rain had fallen, when normally eight to nine inches could be expected. The city's factories, frame houses, wooden pavement, and plank sidewalks were dangerously dry.

On the night of Saturday, October 8, the sound of fire alarms abruptly awakened Harris out of a deep sleep. His youthful curiosity aroused, he hurriedly dressed and rode out to watch a fire raging out of control on the West Side. Harris counted more than 50 fire trucks and crews fighting the flames. The fire consumed four blocks of buildings before it was finally brought under control. The next morning Harris excitedly gave a full account of the night's events to Reece and Ford. "To my astonishment, no one seemed to pay any attention," he recalled later. "A fire was so common a thing in the wooden shanties on the outskirts of American towns that nobody cared to listen to my epic."

That night Harris once again heard the alarm bills ringing about 11:00 P.M. He quickly dressed, strapped on his revolver, and rode to the fire. While still far away, he understood that this fire was much more serious than that of the previous night. A gale-force wind blew across the city and whipped up the flames. Despite the firemen's best efforts the flames spread quickly, leaping from building to building, swallowing one block after another. The heat became so intense that the fire trucks could not get within 200 yards of the blaze. A great roar began to build in intensity.

"[One] thing I noticed almost immediately," Harris wrote later, "the heat was so terrific that the water decomposed into its elements and the oxygen gas in the water burned vehemently on its own account. The water, in fact, added fuel to the flames. As soon as I made sure of this, I saw that the town was doomed and walked my pony back a block or two to avoid flying sparks."

Harris could not know that the fire had started in the barn of Mrs. Patrick O'Leary. One of her five cows had kicked over a lamp when she returned to her house to get some salt for an ailing animal. The firemen who responded to the alarm were still exhausted from fighting the previous night's. Two other barns, a paint shop, and a shed quickly caught fire and burned fiercely. Suddenly, a mass of burning material from one of the burning barns whirled four blocks through the air and landed on the steeple of St. Paul's Catholic Church. The flames quickly spread to a nearby lumber mill and ignited a thousand cords of kindling intended for Chicago stoves, 500,000 feet of furniture lumber, and 750,000 wooden shingles. By then the great Chicago fire was unstoppable.

For most of the night Harris watched the inferno rage out of control, destroying a swath of buildings over a mile wide. Once he came upon a dozen men holding a looter. While he watched, appalled, the angry crowd lynched the thief from a nearby lamppost. "It filled me with rage," he wrote later. "It seemed a dreadful thing to have done. The cruelty of the executioners, the hard purpose of them, shut me away from my kin."

Harris made his way cautiously across town to the lakeshore, arriving there shortly after sunrise. He estimated the crowd of men, women, and children there at more than 100,000. For the first time, he was able to get a visual perspective on the immensity of the conflagration. "Behind us roared the fire," he recalled in *My Life and Loves*. "It spread like a red sheet right up to the zenith above our heads, and from there was borne over the sky in front of us by long streamers of fire like rockets. Vessels four hundred yards out in the bay were burning fiercely, and we were, so to speak, roofed and walled by flame. The danger and uproar were indeed terrifying and the heat, even in this October night, almost unbearable."

Harris wandered through the crowd on the beach. He noted how the people came together to help one another in the emergency. Many men were busy erecting temporary shelters for their wives and children. One man had brought four barrels of water to the beach and posted a sign that read: WHAT DO YOU THINK OF OUR HELL? NO DRINKS LESS THAN A DOLLAR.

Harris remembered the cattle and hurriedly rode back to the Michigan Street stockyards. The longhorns were milling about wildly in their pens. Harris quickly let down several bars. Soon the panic-stricken cattle burst through the fences and stampeded through the streets. Harris, on his horse, managed to drive 672 head out of the city into the country. He arranged with a farmer to keep his cattle there for a week at $1 a head. Later that day he met up with Reece and Ford and told them what he had done. They were delighted. "One thing is certain," Ford said, "six hundred head of cattle are worth as much today in Chicago as fifteen hundred head were worth before the fire, so we hain't lost much."

The next day Harris led Reece and the others back to the farm, where they ran into trouble almost immediately. The farmer claimed they had struck a bargain for $2 a head. His son and an Irish helper backed him up. Then, Reece and Ford checked the cattle and counted only 600 head. More than 50 had disappeared. The farmer insisted Harris had counted wrong. Ford checked a nearby stable and found another 30 longhorns, and the cowboys began to drive the herd off the farm. The farmer tried to block their way. Ford looked at him for a while and then told him very quietly, "You have stolen enough cattle to pay you. If you bother us, I will make meat of you—see!—cold meat." The farmer stepped aside and said nothing more. The next day Ford sold the herd to two hotel proprietors for a huge markup. He paid Harris another $1,500 as his share.

When the fire finally burned itself out, it had destroyed 2,124 acres within the city, made 90,000 people homeless, and destroyed property worth $200 million, one-third of the wealth of Chicago. The experience had changed Harris in important ways. He had gone into it an Irish boy and come out of it a proud American. "The courage shown by the common people in the fire, the wild humor coupled with the consideration for the women, had won my heart," he wrote later. "This is the greatest people in the world, I said to myself, and was proud to feel at one with them."

6

Anticipating a long Kansas winter, in Chicago Harris bought a few books, including Thomas Carlyle's *Heroes and Hero Worship* and John Stuart Mill's *Political Economy*. Back on the ranch, he spent six weeks learning how to break horses under Reece's wise supervision. As the harsh winter weather closed in on the ranch, outdoor work practically ceased. Harris passed his time reading his books. Of more immediate interest were three recently published medical books devoted largely to sexual matters. Harris memorized them and then quoted long passages to the other cowboys at every opportunity, quickly gaining a reputation for astounding wisdom. On the whole, however, it was a dull and unprofitable winter. He had long ago exhausted the rather superficial information of his associates.

As soon as winter broke, Reece ordered the group back to San Antonio, Texas, to purchase additional cattle. However, he soon found that the price had doubled and he had enough money to buy only 3,000 head. Harris offered up $3,000 of his own money and joined Reece as an equal partner.

Harris also learned another important truth about life on the Western frontier. The line between the law-abiding citizen and the criminal was, at best, fuzzy. Many a cowboy lapsed now and then into cattle rustling. Reece ordered his cowboys across the Rio Grande and deep into Mexico, where they raided a large ranch and made off with 1,500 head of cattle. Whatever moral objections Harris might have had were quickly overcome by the prospect of easy money and the thrill of driving by night a herd of stolen cattle. Everything went according to plan until the second night. Suddenly a shot in front stampeded the cattle. Harris quickly rode out to one flank of the herd while Charlie took another, using their long whips to control the animals. The murmur of hooves became a thunder, and then they were all racing hard across the empty bush country. Harris heard another gunshot and looked behind him in time to see a man riding hard down him. He drew his revolver and got off a quick shot. The man and his horse went down. He never knew whether he had wounded or killed him. Harris hurried after the herd. The excitement, tension, and struggling mass of dark animals needed all his attention. Eventually, they made it back safely to Texas, where Harris received a lesson in the fine art of changing brands.

In late July they began once again the long, hard, dangerous drive to the north. Harris promised his cowboys a one-third share in the profits to make them even more diligent in the care of his cattle. The organization of a trail herd was quite predictable. Two cowboys, known as "pointers," rode in the lead, or "point," of the herd. These posts of honor were always occupied by experienced riders whose duty it was to direct the herd, to prevent mix-ups with other herds on the trail, and to head off threatened stampedes. At an appropriate distance behind the pointers came the "swing riders," followed in turn by the "drag riders," whose business it was to look out for the calves and the spent, injured, and lazy cattle. The hands with the least experienced usually worked the drag. The trail boss usually rode ahead of the herd unless he decided to ride back to talk to his men. The cowboys kept the herd in formation along the trail by riding along the sides, pressing inward. They averaged 12 to 15 miles a day.

The days fell quickly into a familiar routine. Shortly after daybreak the cowboys started the herd moving along the trail. Periods of controlled grazing alternated with several hours of trailing. In the meantime the cook drove his chuck wagon ahead to make camp at a suitable site, preferably one with plenty of water. In the evening the cowboys circled the herd, forcing them into a compact mass for the night. Four night watches were set, the first till 10:00 P.M., the second till midnight, the third till 2:00 A.M., and the last until dawn. After breakfast the routine began all over again.

"Other old-timers have told all about the stampedes and swimming rivers and what a terrible time we had," cowboy E.C. Abbot recalled in *We Pointed Them North*, "but they never put in any of the fun, and fun was at least half of it."

On this trail ride, unlike that of the previous summer, Indians proved a constant threat. One night a group of Indians, their faces and hands smeared with phosphorous, suddenly appeared weaving white sheets and successfully made off with 1,000 head of cattle and 100 horses. Groups of Indians continued to follow the herd staying just beyond the range of the cowboys' Winchesters. Several mornings when Harris rode out to hunt game, Indians ambushed him and chased him back to the herd. The Indians grew more numerous and became bolder with each passing day.

One afternoon Reece counted more than 100 Indians and understood they were getting ready for a major attack. Bob remembered a scrub-oak forest five miles away that would provide good cover. Brent and Charlie, the best shots in the group, stayed behind to give the others cover. Within a couple of hours they had the cattle safe in the woods. The cowboys took up their positions near a shallow creek as the Indians came into view. All the cowboys admitted their situation looked desperate. The Indians refused to make a frontal assault. Instead they lay siege to the camp, attacking at night, cutting out small groups of cattle, and giving the cowboys no chance to sleep. The battle went on for days. Finally, Reece knew they would never make it north without help. Someone had to ride to Fort Dodge, more than 200 miles away and bring back soldiers. The choice fell upon Harris, the worst shot among them but also the man with the keenest sense of direction.

Harris stuffed a saddlebag with jerked beef, wrapped his horse's hooves in strips of blanket to muffle the noise, and slipped out of camp in the middle of the night. He cautiously walked his horse around the Indian encampment and then headed northwest. The ride seemed to go on forever.

"Seconds became minutes, minutes lengthened themselves into hours, hours were interminable spaces marked off one from the other by an arm getting numb," Harris recalled later. "[Sometimes I] came across a creek which had to be waded, and this gave me momentary rest and a break in the monotony of effort. . . . I can remember seconds when at the top of some ridge I was acutely conscious of a cool breeze and star-strewn skies and the vague outline of prairie ridges; but soon I was again merged in the jog, jog, jog, jog."

After four days of hard riding Harris finally reached Fort Dodge, and with 20 troopers in tow began the long ride back to his friends. They found them sitting dejectedly in camp with most of the cattle gone. The Indians had stampeded the herd at dawn the previous morning and made off with all the cattle except 600 head. With the troopers riding escort, Reece and his cowboys drove the remnants of their herd north to Wichita.

There they lost Charlie, the young cowboy whose good looks

had always made him popular with the girls. Charlie, Bent, and Harris had visited a saloon where Charlie insisted upon playing cards. The action went against him, and he lost heavily. Charlie accused the dealer of cheating. The two squared off across the big table. The dealer pulled a large revolver out of a drawer and fired, just as the cowboy knocked out the overhead light, plunging the area into darkness. The three cowboys fled the saloon and rode hurriedly out of town. An hour later Charlie reined in his horse and fell to the ground. The other cowboys knelt beside him and saw that he was bleeding heavily.

"I'm finished," Charlie whispered in a weak voice. "I want you to send my money to my mother in Pleasant Hill, Missouri."

"Are you badly hurt?" Harris asked quietly.

"He drilled me through the stomach," the wounded man replied. "I'm done."

Charlie lifted himself up.

"Good-bye, boys," he said, and died.

The young Harris broke into tears at the death of his companion for the past 15 months. The cowboys arranged for a proper burial back in Wichita. Then they drove the herd to Kansas City and sold them in a depressed market for $10 a head. It was there Harris learned that his older brother William had come to America and established himself in nearby Lawrence, Kansas, as a real-estate broker. The likelihood is that despite all his bravado, the young Harris was homesick for English faces and speech and especially for his family. A few days later he boarded a train and began the next chapter of his stay in America.

7

Lawrence in 1872 was a Western town whose fine new banks and offices building belied a bloody history of raids and lynchings by pro- and antislavery bands from Missouri. Ten years earlier a band of Missouri guerrilla fighters, led by William Quantrill, had ridden into town one morning and murdered 150 unsuspecting citizens. The old Abolitionist fever had since died down and been replaced by an intellectual fervor symbolized by the newly established University of Kansas, which stood apart, on a hill above the city.

Harris made his journey to Lawrence on a hot summer day and found his brother waiting for him at the Eldridge House Hotel. The two brothers surveyed each other. Willie had developed into a handsome young man of 25 with a dark face, small mustache, and jet-black goatee. "America is the greatest country in the world," he told Harris enthusiastically. "Any young man who works can make money here. If I had a little capital I'd be a rich man in a very few years. It's some capital I need, nothing more." At Willie's urging, Harris loaned him $1,000. "One can buy real estate here to pay fifty percent a year," his brother advised him. "The country is just beginning to be developed."

Harris moved into a boardinghouse for $4 a week. Within a few days he met a man who was to affect him profoundly—Byron C. Smith, a professor of Greek at the nearby university and an outspoken socialist. "To think of you as a cowboy is impossible," Smith told him at their first meeting. "Fancy a cowboy knowing books of Virgil and poems of Swinburne by heart. It's absurd. You must give your brains a chance and study."

Harris quickly fell under the influence of this man's luminous eyes and shining spirit. "Smith led me, as Virgil led Dante, into the ideal world which surrounds our earth as with illuminable spaces of purple sky, wind-swept and star-blown," he recalled in *My Life and Loves*. But Smith was more than his intellectual mentor. He became the father Harris never had.

Harris enrolled as a student at the University of Lawrence and for the first time tried his hand at disciplined study. Under Smith's patient supervision, he took up philosophy, literature, and the visual arts. That Smith lavished so much time and energy on this shabbily dressed outcast speaks well of him.

University of Kansas records show that Harris attended classes without working toward a specific degree. There is no record that he completed any of his courses.

A fellow student left behind her description of Harris at this time: "James Harris was a brilliant youth with a remarkable power of absorbing knowledge. He was a great reader and an eloquent, fascinating talker. He was self-confident and sometimes showed an extraordinary youth's lack of respect for the opinions of others and this I think won him dislike."

Unlike his fellow students, Harris was always flush with cash. He lived well. And he loved well. In Lawrence he gave the sensualist in him full play. In later years he spoke of himself at this time as "a rattlesnake striking at everything that moves, even the blades of grass." By his own account in *My Life and Loves* he had affairs with five different women during this period in his life. One of these, when Harris worked at a Lawrence saloon, was Lorna Mayhew, the passionate wife of his employer. She was a woman of 30, with a tall, slender figure and large blue-gray eyes. On numerous occasions he slipped discreetly into her home for afternoon sessions of uninhibited sex.

"Of course, it is manifest that my liaison with Mrs. Mayhew had little or nothing to do with love," Harris admitted later in *My Life and Loves*. "It was demoniac youthful sex-urge in me and much the same hunger in her, and as soon as the desire was satisfied my judgment of her was as impartial, cool as if she had been indifferent to me. But with her I think there was a certain attachment and considerable tenderness. In intimate relations between the sexes it is rare indeed that the man gives as much to love as the woman."

In 1873, stock speculation, overly rapid expansion of the agricultural West, and a worldwide drop in commodity prices brought on a depression that lasted three years. The resulting panic wiped out the fragile real-estate empire of Harris's brother Willie. He had speculated recklessly, run up a huge debt, and then watched in despair as his $100,000 in paper profits swiftly melted away, leaving him a ruined man.

Harris quarreled with the university—he insisted in his memoirs that it had to do with its policy of enforced chapel—and decided to study law. He joined the office of a friendly attorney in Lawrence and on June 22, 1875, was admitted to the bar. Because he had been advised that his British accent would hurt him with local juries, he set about to cultivate a Western accent, forcing himself to speak in the slower enunciation and drawl of the prairies.

In time the restlessness that had long been an essential part of his spirit seized him once again. His mentor Smith had long since departed Lawrence. Before Smith left, Harris promised that he would seek a Continental education and an intellectual career.

One of his last acts before departing America was to change his name from James Thomas to Frank. "Now for the first time, when about 19 years of age, I came to self-consciousness as Frank Harris and began to deal with life in my own way and under this name, Frank," he wrote later in *My Life and Loves*. The new name, with its suggestions of candor and integrity, was the most obvious external sign of a profound inward change that had come over him during his years in America. He would never again be purely European in his outlook. The vastness of the plains, the intensity of the cattle drives, the energy of Chicago and New York, all would remain with him until his death.

"My months on the trail had marked my very being," Harris wrote years later. "It made a workman of me, and above all, it taught me that tense resolution, will power, was the most important factor of success in life."

Chapter

◊ 8 ◊

Oscar Wilde:
Wilde in the American Streets

January 2, 1882, aboard the steamship *Arizona* in New York harbor. A group of eager reporters crowds its decks, excitedly interviewing a tall Irishman with shoulder-length hair. He is dressed outlandishly in a bottle-green fur-lined overcoat, yellow kid gloves, and round sealskin cap. A reporter scribbles furiously in a notebook: "Face utterly devoid of color—like putty—eyes bright and quick—face oval, long chin—doesn't look like a Du Maurier model—more like an athlete—instead of having a small, delicate hand only fit to caress a lily, his fingers are long and when doubled up would form a fist that would hit a hard knock." The Irishman admits to having been "disappointed with the Atlantic Ocean."

The reporters trail behind the new arrival as he makes his way briskly through customs. "Have you anything to declare?" the blue-clad inspector asks the visitor.

"Nothing but my genius," he replies.

And thus Oscar Wilde began his American tour. At the height of his fame as the leading representative of the Aesthetic Movement (he had defined *aesthetics* for a New York reporter as "the science of the beautiful") and an aspiring poet and playwright, Wilde was famous for his clever wit, extravagant opinions, and extreme style of dress. Now he was in New York City, soon to embark on a lengthy tour of the States that would prove witty, unorthodox, and unrivaled in American history. Here was the leading British snob, an effete poseur of highly refined sensibilities, lecturing American audiences from Boston to

Leadville on the principles of aesthetics and becoming a popular celebrity in the process. At the same time Wilde found himself growing inordinately fond of Americans. A less likely love match could scarcely be imagined.

A man with a prodigious appetite for life, Wilde sought to gather as many experiences as possible. "I want to eat of the fruit of all the trees in the garden of the world," he once said. He lived a life of excess and in the end, that destroyed him. "Oscar Wilde walked towards catastrophe like Oedipus, blind and clear-sighted," one contemporary wrote shortly after his death in 1900.

Few Victorians generated more controversy. Wilde achieved contemporary fame with a series of brilliant social comedies laced throughout with sharp verbal wit and shocking paradoxes; a short novel, *The Picture of Dorian Gray*, and some highly derivative poetry. But he found a more permanent niche in social history as a martyr in the cause for sexual freedom after he was tried in 1895 for homosexuality and sentenced to two years in prison at hard labor. The case exposed the hypocrisy of British society, much as the Dreyfus scandal the preceding year had exposed anti-Semitism in French society.

"The story of Oscar Wilde has usually been told in terms of *hubris*—Oscar as the child of the gods, lavishly endowed with every talent except that of restraint, whom they destroyed because that's the kind of thing gods do," observed his biographer Sheridan Morley. "In fact, there was a more prosaic explanation of Wilde's theatrical triumphs and of his social collapse: he was a child not of the gods but of the Victorians, and his tragedy was that he allowed himself to remain one. Like all children he failed to recognize or to estimate the moment at which the grown-ups would stop laughing. Like Peter Pan . . . he refused to age or to take stock of his surroundings and for that the Victorians broke him."

Oscar Fingall O'Flahertie Wills Wilde was born in Dublin on October 16, 1854. His mother thought the names "grand, misty, and Ossianic." An adult Wilde disagreed. He abandoned three of his names by the time he was 30, saying: "A name which is destined to be in everybody's mouth must not be too long. It becomes so expensive in the advertisements."

The young Wilde attended Trinity College, Dublin, where his success in classical studies won him a scholarship to Magdalen College in Oxford. A good student, he nonetheless professed contempt for formal education. "Nothing that is worth knowing can be taught," he once said. At Oxford he soon won a reputation for his brilliant conversation and studied eccentricities in dress and manner of living. In dress, he favored the bold check suits then in fashion. He filled his rooms with blue and white china made fashionable by the Pre-Raphaelites, which provoked his celebrated quip: "Oh, that I could live up to my blue china!" (The remark was later reported to the shocked vicar of St. Mary's Church, who used it to open a sermon deploring the heathenism he saw creeping over Oxford.) A close friend from Oxford, Bouncer Ward, remembered Wilde fondly in later years:

> How brilliant and radiant he could be! How playful and charming! How his moods varied and how he revelled in inconsistency! The whim of the moment was his acknowledged dictator. One can see now, reading his character by the light of his later life, the beginnings of those tendencies which led to his destruction. There was the love of pose, the desire for self-realisation, the egotism, but they seemed foibles rather than faults, and his frank regret or laugh at his own expense robbed them of blame and took away offense.

Wilde's sexual preferences at college appear to have been perfectly normal. "I am just going out to bring an *exquisitely pretty girl* to afternoon service in the Cathedral," he gushed in a letter to a friend in 1876. "She is just seventeen with the *most perfectly beautiful face I ever saw and not a sixpence of money*." He fell in love with two girls and deplored homosexual behavior as shocking on the occasions that he encountered it.

Nor was Wilde the limp-wristed namby-pamby of the popular imagination. Once a group of athletes decided to "rag" him in his room and smash his precious blue china. They proved no match for the burly, six-foot Wilde, who was waiting for them. He easily tossed three down the stairs. Then he picked their leader up, carried him bodily back to his room, and buried him under a pile of his own furniture. "When the debris of tables, sofas, chairs, and pictures had been raised to the height of a respectable mausoleum, Wilde invited the now admiring crowd to sample the victim's cellar," another student recalled later. The ragging ended with the athletes, happily drunk on their leader's expensive liqueurs and wines, sitting at Wilde's feet and listening to his stories.

Wilde studied under Walter Pater and John Ruskin, made trips to Italy and Greece, and wrote poems, some of which he sold to magazines. His father died in 1876 and left him a small property worth £4,000. After graduating with honors from Oxford, Wilde determined to move to London to join his mother and brother. In the summer of 1878 a friend asked him about his ambitions. Wilde thought a moment and then answered: "God knows. I won't be an Oxford don anyhow. I'll be a poet, a writer, a dramatist. Somehow or other I'll be famous, and if not famous, I'll be notorious. Or perhaps I'll lead a life of pleasure for a time and then—who knows?— rest and do nothing."

His thoughts proved remarkably prophetic.

2

In the autumn of 1879 Wilde and an artist friend settled into an apartment between the Strand and the Embankment on the edge of London's theater district. The witty paradoxes, brash affectations, and skills as a raconteur which had served him so well at Oxford quickly gained him access to the most privileged bastions of London society. "To get into Society nowadays one has either to feed people or shock people—that is all," he once observed.

Lacking the funds for the first option, he chose the second and became the perfect party guest. His clever epigrams were the talk of the town. "Give me the luxuries and I can dispense with the necessities" was one of his favorites. Another was "I can resist everything but temptation." A shrewd self-publicist with an eye for the headlines, Wilde knew that in the staid confines of Victorian society such observations would quickly gain him notoriety. Once when he was out walking, he overheard a man mumble as he passed, "There goes that bloody fool Oscar Wilde." Wilde remarked cheerfully to his companion, "It's extraordinary how soon one gets known in London."

(As one of Wilde's biographers regretted, "One of the greatest tragedies—well, misfortunes really, but something about Oscar encourages one to exaggerate—of Wilde's life was that he and television missed each other by fifty years. If ever a man was made for the instant fame of the [talk] show it was surely Oscar.")

Wilde thus became our first modern celebrity, known not for what he had done but famous simply for being famous. He had no solid achievements of any sort on which to base his reputation. But he had quickly discovered that those who praise passionately are generally welcomed guests. He possessed to the fullest what his friend Frank Harris later called "the gift of enthusiastic admiration," and it served him well in the salons of London. No one praised more effusively than he. Scarcely a bitter word escaped him. (Wilde won over the actress Sarah Bernhardt by meeting her boat at the Dover docks, his arms full of lilies, shouting, "Long live Sarah, Long live the Goddess.")

In the matter of dress, Wilde's adopted motto was "Nothing succeeds like excess." He affected velvet coats edged with braid, knee breeches, black silk stockings, and flowing pale green neckties. He wore strange flowers—gilded lilies, sunflowers, and green cornflowers—on his coat lapels. He studied diction to perfect his mastery of the spoken word. And he adopted a new role, the languid dandy. In the words of his biographer Philippe Jullian, "he would take a cab in order to cross a street and would lean on the arm of a friend to cross the room; the sight of a badly furnished house took away his strength and he wondered if he was strong enough to stand the sight of a masterpiece." On one occasion a hostess asked an apparently exhausted Wilde how he had spent his day. "I was working on the proof of one of my poems all the morning and took out a comma," he replied. "In the afternoon I put it back again."

Arguably the finest British playwright of his century, Wilde made his life into his greatest theatrical production. "Would you like to know the great drama of my life?" Wilde asked André Gide in 1895. "It's that I've put my genius into my life; I've put only my talent into my works." And in this one-man show he did it all, serving as actor, playwright, director, press agent, costume designer, and prop man. (The one flaw in an otherwise perfect production was Wilde's badly stained teeth; he always covered his mouth when he laughed.)

Frank Harris met the young Wilde at this time. "He looked like a Roman Emperor of the Decadence," Harris wrote later in *Contemporary Portraits*. "He was over six-feet in height, and both broad and thick-set. . . . He wore a great green scarab ring on one finger. He was overdressed rather than well dressed. His clothes fitted him too tightly; he was too stout. . . . At this time he was a superb talker, more brilliant than any I have ever heard in England, but nothing like what he became later in life."

Wilde slipped easily into the theatrical scene, befriending such actresses of the day as Ellen Terry, Sarah Bernhardt, and Lillie Langtry. One of the most popular actresses of her day, the "Jersey Lily" counted among her admirers both the Prince of Wales and the aging prime minister William Gladstone. Wilde, too, fell hopelessly in love with the beautiful and talented 28-year-old actress. They became fast friends. At the conclusion of his American tour in 1882, he told a group of reporters, "I would rather have discovered Mrs. Langtry than have discovered America. Her beauty is in outline perfectly modeled. She will be a beauty at eighty-five. Yes, it was for such a lady that Troy was destroyed and well might it be destroyed for such a woman."

(The general public, which today thinks of Wilde's sexual orientation as exclusively homosexual, may find such adoration perplexing. But the fact is that for much of his life women exerted a strong attraction for him. And few remember today that in 1884 he fell in love with a daughter of a distinguished Irish barrister. "I am going to be married to a beautiful girl called Constance Lloyd, a grave, slight, violet-eyed little Artemis with great coils of heavy brown hair . . . and wonderful ivory hands which draw music from the piano so sweet that the birds stop singing to listen to her," a love-stricken Wilde wrote to a friend. They married on May 29. Constance went on to bear him two sons. She died in 1898, the year after Wilde's release from prison.)

Calling himself a "Professor of Aesthetics and a Critic of Art," Wilde soon established himself in the public eye as the most flamboyant spokesman for the Aesthetic Movement, a loose grouping of artists and reformers whose heterodox ideas on art and socialistic ideals generated considerable controversy in 1880s England. They scorned the Victorian middle-class way of life and the hideousness of the industrial age. The Aesthetes deplored the products of mass production and demanded a return to the handicrafts and cottage industries of an earlier age wherein, they argued, true art lay. They rallied around the motto "Art for Art's Sake" and espoused a creed based on sensitivity, unrestrained emotions, and a freer flow of natural instincts. Although not a founder of the movement, Wilde quickly became, in the words of one biographer, "a convenient vehicle for its advertisement."

In 1881 Wilde's reputation rested solely upon the outrageous poses he affected in public. He had written one play, *Vera,* but could not get it produced. His slim volume of verse, *Poems,* privately printed, had received hostile reviews. His early attempts at journalism had met with little success. He had mortgaged to the hilt the small piece of property in Dublin he had inherited from his father. There was little ready cash to put against the heavy expenses of being Oscar Wilde. Then something happened to save him. On April 23 Richard D'Oyly Carte's opera company opened a

production of William Gilbert and Arthur Sullivan's new work
Patience. The opera satirized Aestheticism. And the character of
Reginald Bunthorne, the Fleshy Poet

> *"A most intense young man,*
> *A soulful-eyed young man,*
> *An ultra-poetical, super-aesthetical*
> *Out-of-the-way young man,"*

was widely perceived as a caricature of Wilde.

Patience was an immediate hit and played to a packed house in
London for more than a year before going on tour. Wilde himself
attended a performance as a guest of D'Oyle Carte. "A fierce
clamour of screams, yells, and hisses which descended from the
Gallery signalled the arrival of Mr. Oscar Wilde himself," wrote a
critic from *The Era* who observed the scene. "There with the
sacred daffodil stood the exponent of uncut hair, Ajax-like,
defying the Gods."

Wilde sat good-naturedly through the opera and heard the cast
sing the popular view of him and his activities:

> *Though the Philistines may jostle,*
> *You will rank as an apostle*
> *In the high aesthetic band,*
> *If you walk down Piccadilly*
> *With a poppy or a lily*
> *In your medieval hand.*
> *And everyone will say,*
> *As you walk your flowery way,*
> *"If he's content with a vegetable love*
> *Which would certainly not suit me,*
> *Why, what a most particularly pure young man*
> *This pure young man must be."*

As Wilde's biographer Sheridan Morley has observed: "Oscar himself at this time, indeed at all times, was far from the poetic buffoon . . . dramatized by Gilbert. The point about his behaviour was not that he did in fact walk down Piccadilly with a lily in his hand but that he made people believe it was the kind of thing he and he alone would do—in itself a far more satisfying achievement, since it established a reputation based on fantasy, one which could be trimmed and adapted and reconstructed to suit the prevailing winds of any given season."

In September 1881 an American production of *Patience* opened in New York. D'Oyly Carte, the wily London producer and stage manager who had first brought Gilbert and Sullivan together, decided that something needed to be done to introduce the American public to the Aesthetic Movement so that they might better appreciate the play's satire. He quickly saw a solution. What better way to promote the play than to send the original Bunthorne to New York with a sunflower in his buttonhole and a lily in his hand and have him lecture Americans on the principles of aesthetics?

Colonel W. F. Morse, the New York manager of *Patience*, cabled Wilde an invitation: Would he visit America to deliver a series of lectures in advance of the touring company. Wilde promptly wired back: "Yes, if offer good." Morse promised all his expenses plus one-third of the gate receipts. Wilde accepted immediately, eager for the opportunity to visit America and hopeful, too, that he might find a producer for his own play *Vera*. A few days before his departure he received a telegram from a New York editor offering him the enormous sum of $100 for a 20-line poem on the sunflower or lily. On Christmas Eve 1881 he sailed on the Cunard liner *Arizona* for America.

3

Rumors abounded among New Yorkers regarding the Irishman who was coming to visit them. Was it true that he ate flowers?

Did he really look like a hothouse tropical plant? New Yorkers finally got the chance to see for themselves. After a day in quarantine, Wilde—with a sunflower firmly affixed to his coat lapel disembarked from the *Arizona* on January 3 and checked into a two-room suite in the Grand Hotel at the corner of Broadway and Thirty-first, in the heart of the city's theatrical district.

Colonel Morse had watched with considerable satisfaction as enormous curiosity in Wilde built among Americans. This came as no surprise to the astute showman and manager. The freak show, he knew, was as much an American institution as Mom's homemade apple pie. P.T. Barnum, the country's best-known showman, had bought a shaved monkey head stuck on a fish tail, called it the "Feejee Mermaid," and made a tidy $30,000 within a year; from this and other curiosities, he had built a $4,000,000 fortune.

Freak shows, circuses, and dime museums, all of which catered to the American craving for "curiosities," flourished in the final quarter of the nineteenth century. (In England Queen Victoria was very much of a freak fancier herself, having granted audiences to the midget Tom Thumb and "The Two-Headed Nightingale," a pair of black Siamese twins who had been born into slavery in North Carolina.) Some freaks achieved a success as celebrities equal to the greatest names of the day in the theater and sports.

Americans eagerly shelled out hundreds of thousands of dollars every year to view such celebrated curiosities as John Hanson Craig, who at 907 pounds was "The Heaviest Man Alive"; Myrtle Corbin, the four-legged woman from Texas; Jo Jo, "The Man with a Dog's Head," who usually sold out his 23 daily shows; and Fanny Mills, who billed herself as "The Ohio Big Foot Girl" and wore size 30 shoes, which required three goatskins per pair. And in January 1882 just around the corner from Wilde's Grand Hotel the popular Miss Lizzie Sturgeon, who had been born armless, skillfully played a piano with her bare toes for the curious patrons of a dime museum.

One of Wilde's first tasks was a visit to the studio of the celebrated New York photographer Sarony. Colonel Morse explained to the Irishman that Americans were inordinately fond of collecting pictures of both the famous and infamous, which they often included in albums along with those of their families and friends. He pointed out that such pictures were an important form of advertising. And yes, Colonel Morse insisted, Charles Dickens himself had sat for such pictures on several occasions. (During the 1880s the Bowery photographer Charles Eisenmann specialized in portraits of the famous dime-museum freaks, whose admiring fans bought thousands of these hauntingly beautiful pictures.) Carrying a white cane and wearing a great fur-lined coat, the six-foot Wilde towered over the diminutive Sarony. "A picturesque subject, indeed!" cried the photographer as he eagerly snapped away.

Wilde spent the week before his first lecture exploring New York, in 1882 a city of some 1 million people. His hosts proudly showed off the Brooklyn Bridge nearing completion and already being called the "Eighth Wonder of the World." He quickly decided that "America is the noisiest country that ever existed." But the applications of science in the daily lives of Americans thoroughly impressed him. Thomas Edison was producing 1,000 electric lamps a day at his plant in New Jersey. Ugly telephone poles and lines were being strung the length of the city's streets. Locomotives roared overhead on elevated tracks. Advertisements proclaiming the healthful properties of electricity filled American magazines and newspapers: "Dr. Scott's Electric Corset . . . will ward off disease, improve the elegance of a woman's figure, make the muscles and tissues more plastic and yielding and mold the figure to any desired form without tight lacing. $3." Men wore electric belts guaranteed to restore diminshing virility.

Within 48 hours of Wilde's arrival in New York, he found himself buried beneath an avalanche of invitations to teas, dinners, parties, receptions, and dances. He soon was "on view" morning, noon, and night. Wilde good-naturedly played his part to the hilt, dressing in the style he had made so famous in London, striking his typical languid poses, and "salt and peppering" his conversation with a profusion of witty epigrams. A reporter from the *New York Tribune* studied him closely and wrote later:

> The most striking thing about the poet's appearance is his height, which is several inches over six feet, and the next thing to attract attention is his hair, which is of a dark brown color, and falls down upon his shoulder. . . . The complexion, instead of being the rosy hue so common in Englishmen, is so utterly devoid of color that it can only be said to resemble putty. His eyes are blue, or a light grey, and instead of being "dreamy" as some of his admirers have imagined them to be, they are bright and quick—not at all like those of one given to perpetual musing on the ineffably beautiful and true. . . . One of the peculiarities of his speech is that he accents almost at regular intervals without regard to the sense, perhaps as a result of an effort to be rhythmic in conversation as well as in verse.

In New York, as in London, women made the greatest fuss over Wilde. At every event Wilde was mobbed by crowds of adoring women, many of whom dressed in costumes they thought suitably "aesthetic." He quickly won them over with his clever wit and lavish praise. At one gathering he raised his hand to his forehead and slumped against a chair as if stricken. "I am on the edge of a nervous breakdown," he cried. "America reminds me of one of Edgar Allan Poe's exquisite poems because it is full of belles." The ladies screamed in delight and pelted him with flowers.

As art historian Philippe Jullian has observed, Wilde's visit coincided with major changes in the status and role of women in American society. "In this hurly-burly Oscar would have been completely lost without the women who were now coming to the fore in Society, whereas a generation earlier house-keeping had occupied the time and thoughts of all women except the very rich, and Calvinistic modesty had kept them to their family circle," he has stated. "At the time that Oscar arrived in the United States there was a great number of very rich people, and modesty by then was merely a barrier protecting the established social sphere of the new rich—the men, all of whom worked, left their wives alone far more than was usual in Europe. The women felt it was their mission to civilize the inhabitants of the United States, and grouped themselves into philanthropic or artistic societies . . . and they bore witness to [a great] appetite for culture and fashion." These women of a new generation were to give their enthusiastic support to Wilde and his message of aestheticism as he traveled across America.

One evening several prominent gentlemen, jealous of Wilde's success with the ladies, took the Irishman to a stag dinner at Brown's Chop House on Broadway determined to get him drunk and then make a fool of him. They consumed a prodigious amount of whiskey and soda along with the oysters, chops, cheeses, and other foodstuffs. When the party finally broke up in the early morning hours, they were all drunk—except Wilde, who graciously helped the others down the stairs to the waiting hansom cabs. "Would you like an escort to your hotel?" the group's leader asked Wilde. "No thanks," he politely replied. "It's a wonderful night for a stroll." And with that he went off with a steady gait, leaving behind his American hosts dumbfounded in their drunken stupor.

On the evening of January 7 Wilde attended a performance of the New York production of *Patience,* appearing at the theater in his velvet coat and black stockings with a scarlet silk handkerchief conspicuously displayed. A few minutes later the actor playing Bunthorne came on the stage dressed in almost the identical costume. "Caricature is the tribute mediocrity pays to genius," Wilde later told a group of reporters in the lobby.

Two nights later Wilde delivered his lecture, "The English Renaissance," to a packed Chickering Hall. One reporter noted: "Everybody known in New York society seemed to be there—staid matrons, pretty women, a charming array of fair and 'rapturous maidens,' business men, figures well known in conservative clubs, and, leaning against the back wall of the parquet, many aesthetic and pallid young men in dress suits and banged hair."

Wilde quickly set about educating his audience in his principles of aesthetics. "You have heard . . . of two flowers called, erroneously, . . . the food of aesthetic young men," he told them. "Well, let me tell you that the reason we love the lily and sunflower is not, in spite of what Mr. Gilbert may tell you, for any vegetable fashion at all. It is because these two lovely flowers are, in England, the two most perfect models of design. They are the most naturally adopted for decorative art. The gaudy leonine beauty of the one, the precious loveliness of the other, give to the artist the most nearly perfect joy."

Wilde continued: "It is not increased moral sense your literature needs. Indeed we should never talk of a moral or an immoral poem. Poems are either well written or badly written. That is all. A good work aims at the purely artistic effect. Love art for its own sake and all things you need will be added to it."

Wilde complimented his American hosts: "It is perhaps to you that we turn to perfect this great movement of ours. There is something Hellenic in your air, something that has a quicker breath of the joy and power of Elizabeth's England about it than our ancient civilization can give us. You are young. No hungry generations tread you down. . . . The past does not mock you with the ruins of a beauty the secret of whose creation you have lost."

Wilde was ecstatic at his reception. "The hall had an audience larger and more wonderful than Dickens ever had," he wrote to a friend. "I was recalled and applauded and am now treated like the Royal Boy." His first lecture reaped more than $1,000 in box-office receipts, a sum that greatly pleased Colonel Morse. The national publicity had been tremendous. Stories on the lecture appeared on the front pages of newspapers across the land. Some were scornful. "Wilde is a twittering sparrow come to fill his maw with insects," snapped the *Chicago Tribune*. Many were favorable. The *Cincinnati Enquirer* insisted: "The stranger among us is a young apostle of beauty against a decaying age of trade and swap."

Wilde was now the toast of New York. "I am torn to bits by Society," he wrote boastfully to a friend in England. "Immense receptions, wonderful dinners, crowds wait for my carriage. I wave a gloved hand and an ivory cane and they cheer. . . . Rooms are hung with white lilies for me everywhere." He hired two secretaries: "One to write my autograph and answer the hundreds of letters that come begging for it. Another, whose hair is brown, to send locks of his own hair to the young ladies who write asking for mine; he is rapidly becoming bald."

Wilde was optimistic about the positive effect additional lectures might have on the state of the arts in America: "I have something to say to the American people, something that I know will be the beginning of a great movement here."

Even discounting his own natural tendancy to exaggerate, Wilde did enjoy an enormous success in New York. His popularity, in turn, reflected the wave of Anglomania that had swept over America in the preceding decade. In 1874, New York socialite Jennie Jerome, the daughter of a Wall Street broker, married Lord Randolph Churchill. Five years later Americans were pleased by the tremendous reception accorded former president and Mrs. U.S Grant when they visited London. English fashions had become the rage. One manufacturer started a popular fad with a line of eyeglasses that promised to give its wearers "a strong British stare."

On January 11 D'Oyly Carte arrived in New York and was immediately asked by reporters about his "Bunthorne in the flesh."

"A clever young man," he told them. "I think I shall send him around the country."

4

On January 16 Wilde boarded a ferryboat for the trip across the Hudson at the start of his trip to Philadelphia. He cut a conspicuous figure in his olive-green and otter fur-trimmed overcoat. "There he is," the crowd on the dock murmured. "See him. That's Oscar Wilde." In New Jersey Wilde's party boarded a train.

The Irishman was impressed by both the luxuriousness of his Pullman accommodations and the speed at which they traveled. But he was put off by the hustling commercialism he saw around him. "Romeo and Juliet would have had no time for lyrical pathos in America because they would have been preoccupied with catching trains," he complained.

A reporter for the *Philadelphia Press* conducted a lengthy interview with Wilde for much of the train ride. "Why does not science, instead of troubling itself about sunspots, . . . busy itself with drainage and sanitary engineering?" Wilde asked. "Why does it not clean the streets and free the rivers from pollution? Why, in England there is scarcely a river which at some point is not polluted; and the flowers are all withering on the banks!"

Wilde expressed his hopes for what the Aesthetic Movement might accomplish in America: "The two classes we must directly work upon are the handicraftsmen and the artists. . . . And the handicraftsmen must be directed by the artists; and the artists must be inspired with true designs. It is only through these classes that we can work." He insisted at every turn that people fill their lives with things of beauty and fight against their "unlovely, hard, repulsive surroundings."

But Wilde had arrived 20 years too late with his message. As social historians Lloyd Lewis and Henry Justin Smith have pointed out: "America [in the 1880s] was interested no longer in the workman who took raw materials and, with his own hands, brought forth a finished article. Piecework at machines, production in large, standardized quantities, swift, quick competition were the new gods of industry. . . . A man could now turn to a machine that would let him do in a day what it had taken twenty yesterdays to do with his hands, but in the victory he had sacrificed most if not all of whatever artistic pleasure he had taken in his work."

Wilde lectured twice in Philadelphia, each time to capacity crowds numbering more than 1,000. Both times he found the audiences unsympathetic to his themes. "My hearers were so cold I several times thought of stopping and saying, 'You don't like this, and there is no use of my going on,'" he complained afterward.

Wilde took advantage of the occasion to pay a visit on his favorite American poet, Walt Whitman. "Perhaps he is not widely read in England," he told a reporter. "But England never appreciates a poet until he is dead." In 1873 Whitman had suffered a severe stroke of paralysis and moved into his brother's home in Camden, New Jersey. In 1881 he had published a revised and expanded edition of *Leaves of Grass*. But a Boston district attorney, objecting to some poems about prostitutes, had classified the book of verse as "obscene literature" and ordered the publisher to cease distribution.

Wilde could not help but be impressed by the bearded Whitman, who looked much older than his 63 years and as remote as Michelangelo's Moses. "May I call you Oscar?" Whitman asked. "I'd like that very much," Wilde replied. The two men sipped a bottle of elderberry wine and talked at length about the London literary scene. "Yes, Mr. Wilde came to see me this afternoon," Whitman told reporters later. "I took him to my den where we had a jolly time. I think he was glad to get away from lecturing and fashionable society and spend time with an 'old rough.' We had a very happy time together. . . . I was glad to have him with me, for his youthful health, enthusiasm, and buoyancy are refreshing."

After Philadelphia Wilde went to Washington, where he met with the novelist Henry James, who was in the capital for a brief visit, and the Secretary of War, Robert Lincoln, the only living son of the former president. The Irishman took a tour of the city's parks, which were filled with a seemingly endless number of statues of military heroes. "Washington has too many bronze generals," he complained. Wilde's visit provoked a cartoon in the *Washington Post* comparing him to "The Wild Man of Borneo," which he found particularly painful. Later he was to remark with bitterness how astounded he had been by "the powers of journalistic venom in America," a complaint heard frequently from other British travelers.

Wilde's visit coincided with the close of one of most the sensational trials in Washington's history. On July 2, 1881, Charles Guiteau, a disgruntled office-seeker, shot James Garfield just four months after he had become president. Garfield lingered through the summer and died on September 19. Guiteau's trial began on November 14. The chief issue was his sanity, for he proudly admitted shooting the president. God told him to do it, he said, to heal the breach in the Republican Party caused by Garfield's quarrel with Senator Roscoe Conkling of New York. "The Deity furnished the money with which I bought the pistol," he asserted. Guiteau insisted upon conducting much of his defense: "On July 25th, the physicians announced, 'The President is not fatally shot.' My bullet was not fatal. Garfield's death was caused by malpractice. I was only inspired to *shoot* the President. The doctors finished the work."

In a performance that mixed wit, irreverence, and cunning, Guiteau turned the courtroom into a circus. He mocked the judge and insulted his attorney, who was also his brother-in-law. He distributed scores of autographed photographs of himself to the crowds of women who eagerly mobbed him, and once brought the trial to a halt by screaming, "I have seven or eight hundred letters from sympathizers, many from ladies, expressing their sympathies and prayers for my acquittal."

As the trial slowly drew to a close, most observers bet on a death verdict. The president of a Philadelphia-based firm manufacturing refrigerated railroad cars approached Guiteau's relatives with the proposition that after the assassin had been hanged, his body be quickly frozen and then exhibited across country, his heirs receiving half the proceeds.

On January 28 Wilde completed a lecture in Albany, New York, and boarded a train for Boston, the Athens of America and the Olympus of American culture, fearful of the sort of reception he might find there. For two decades before the Civil War, Boston evangelists had preached an antislavery message with a zealous fervor unmatched by abolitionists elsewhere. In 1882 a later generation of reformers was waging energetic crusades against tobacco and liquor throughout the New England states. The legislature of Connecticut debated a bill that would have prohibited all smoking in the state capitol building. *The Primer of Politeness* urged its young readers to consider that the man who from the age of 20 on smoked eight ten-cent cigars a week for 40 years would have squandered $8,311 in actual out of pocket costs and accrued interest.

The temperance people were even more emphatic about the evils of drink. A Boston preacher thundered from his pulpit: "There are 1,000,000 drunkards in this country; 100,000 are annually sent to prison, and 200,000 children each year thrown on the world, victims of the Red Dragon. Officials say eighty-five percent of all criminals owe their fall to drink." The Centennial Exposition of 1876 had exhibited the world's first soda fountain, and by 1882 temperance leaders in Boston and elsewhere were advocating this "purely American institution" as a healthful alternative to the neighborhood saloon.

Soon after his arrival in Boston, Wilde found himself the target of zealous reformers. A local critic denounced his published poems as immoral and called upon local society to ostracize him. The Irishman shot back: "If one wants to realize what English Puritanism is, much can be found in Boston and Massachusetts. We have got rid of it. America still preserves it, to be, I hope, a short-lived curiosity."

Wilde quickly arranged meetings with local luminaries, including Oliver Wendell Holmes, Henry Wadsworth Longfellow, and Julia Ward Howe, the author of "The Battle Hymn of the Republic." As he prepared for his lecture in Boston's Music Hall, he received word that Harvard undergraduates had bought up the first several rows of seats and intended to appear dressed in velvet coats and knee breaches in ridicule of him. Wilde outfoxed them by showing up in formal evening dress. He glided to the lecture stand and coolly surveyed the Harvard boys monopolizing the front rows. "I

see about me the signs of an aesthetic movement," he began. "As
I look about me, I am impelled for the first time to breathe a fervent
prayer, 'Save me from my disciples.'" The *Boston Transcript*
noted with approval the next day, "Mr. Wilde achieved a real triumph,
and it was his by right of conquest, by force of being a
gentleman, in the truest sense of the word."

In spite of occasional harassments, Wilde was sincerely
impressed with the courtesies extended him by average citizens.
"The American man may not be humorous," he told his British
friends later, "but he is certainly humane. He tries to be pleasant
to every stranger who lands on his shores. He has a healthy freedom
from all antiquated prejudices, regards introductions as a
foolish relic of medieval etiquette, and makes every chance visitor
feel that he is the favored guest of a great nation."

Back in New York Wilde learned the interest in him was so
great that D'Oyly Carte's office had booked him for an extended
tour of the Midwest. "I like the excitement of lecturing," Wilde
confided to a reporter, "but I hate traveling. I hate punctuality,
and I hate time-tables." His itinerary took him through numerous
cities in upstate New York. While in Buffalo he visited Niagara
Falls, the mecca for honeymooners. He observed the hideous commercialism
of the scene—the numerous souvenir stands, the
raucous pitch men, the shell-games, the predatory photographers—and
remarked: "Every American bride is taken there, and
the sight of that stupendous waterfall must be one of the earliest,
if not the keenest, disappointments in American married life."

Wilde spent the next day exploring. With a guide, he donned a
raincoat to go under the falls. The freezing cold had created an
impressive winter landscape of ice bridges and enormous crystal
festoons of frozen spray. The Irishman's initial cynicism gave way
to enthusiastic admiration. He later confessed to reporters: "It
was not until I stood beneath the Falls at Table Rock that I realized
the majestic splendor and strength of the physical force in
nature here. The sight was far beyond what I had seen in Europe.
It seems a sort of embodiment of Pantheism." And he wrote in his

guest album at his hotel: "The roar of these waters is like the roar when the mighty wave of democracy breaks on shores where kings lie couched in ease."

The abundance of "ready money" also left Wilde awestruck. "A short time before I came to America, [Prime Minister William] Gladstone said to me that from the United States would come at once the greatest danger and the greatest good to civilization," he told a reporter. "The greatest danger is the vast accumulation of capital, and the greatest good is the perfect simplicity of American politics. . . . The personal control of capital, with the power it gives over labor and life, has only appeared in modern American life. We have as yet nothing like it in England. We call a man rich over there when he owns a share of Scotland, or a county or so. But he doesn't have such control of ready money as does an American capitalist."

America in 1882 was awash in "ready money," reflecting the economic transformations that had begun during the Civil War. These changes represented an expansion and extension of the first industrial revolution, marked by the application of machine power, in constantly enlarged units, to new processes and in new regions. Although a series of bank failures in 1873 had developed into a depression that had resulted in the collapse of 50,000 businesses, the economy had recovered by the late 1870s and was booming in 1882. This recovery was enriched by successive inventions such as electric lights, halftone, and continuous-roll printing, the telephone, and—most appropriately—the cash register.

Transportation was the key to the American boom. In 1865 America boasted 35,000 miles of steam railroad; that number had more than tripled by the 1880s. As historian Samuel Eliot Morison noted: "In the 1870's the refrigerator car, first used to carry freshly slaughtered beef from Chicago to the Eastern cities, was adapted for the transportation of fruit and vegetables, which eventually enabled the products of California to undersell those of Eastern truck gardeners." The new generation of railroad tycoons accumulated wealth that was fabulous beyond the dreams of most European businessmen. Jay Gould slept in a $25,000 bed; J.

Pierpont Morgan traveled in a $100,000 private rail car; and Collis Huntington built a $2,000,000 Manhattan mansion.

Mark Twain called the period "The Gilded Age," and the label stuck. This continued to be a time of corruption on a massive scale in both the public and private spheres, of market manipulations, stock-waterings, and monopolies that spread wreckage, panics, and scandals across the land. The federal government waited until 1887 before moving to regulate the railroads and break up trusts. As social historians Lloyd Lewis and Henry Justin Smith have observed:

> Oscar Wilde had come upon an America which was developing a new Manifest Destiny. In the old civilization America had seemed destined to become the one place in the world where the common man was supreme, where the farmer and artisan were independent, captains of their soul, masters of their fate. That romantic dream was now gone, and it was manifest to some that America was destined to be the one place in the world where the business man was supreme—dignified and honored as in no other age or nation—the business man, set free to climb and rule.

As Wilde left Utica, he casually remarked to a reporter, "You call America a country, but I call it a w-o-r-l-d." That observation became one of his favorites, and he repeated it often, always knowing that it would make the newspapers the next day. From upstate New York he took the train straight through to Chicago, arriving on February 10. The next day one of the big Chicago papers carried the headline:

SAINT OSCAR DE WILDE

ARRIVES, LILIES AND

ALL, IN CHICAGO

Chicago in 1882 was one of America's most dynamic cities. When Wilde arrived in the Windy City on that blustery winter day, little evidence of the terrible fire remained. Great Lakes trade and rail connections had transformed a sprawling grain and live-stock center into a thriving metropolis of more than half a million people. Vast quantities of iron ore and cheap coal flowed to smelters in Chicago where the first American steel rails were rolled in 1865.

Wilde quickly fell into a hectic social routine. He spewed forth epigrams like sparks struck from Chicago-made steel: "Life without industry is barren, and industry without art is barbarism," and "One production of Michaelangelo is worth a hundred by Edison." Still, the number of telephones in Chicago impressed him. A transplanted British businessman told him how he had saved $8,000 and a great deal of time and effort in only one year using the new device that Alexander Graham Bell had invented just six years before.

Wilde had tired of his lecture on the English Renaissance. He quickly worked up a new one, "The Decorative Arts," in which he discussed home furnishings, civic beauty, and related subjects. He gave the lecture in Central Music Hall to a packed crowd of 2,500 people. *The Chicago Times* sniped in a critical review that they had paid the stiff $1 admission "to see a two-headed Australian 'what-is-it' who would talk Greek or Choctaw." Wilde retaliated, saying, "I will not reprove the wicked and imaginative editor because I know that the conscience of an editor is purely decorative."

In his lecture Wilde elaborated on some of his major themes. "No machine-made ornaments should be tolerated," he told his audience. "They are all bad, worthless, ugly. People should not mistake the means of civilization for the end. The steam engine and the telephone depend entirely for their value on the use to which they are put."

Overall, Wilde was immensely pleased with his success. He wrote home to a friend: "In Chicago I lectured last Monday to 2,500 people!—a great sympathetic, electric people who cheered and applauded and gave me a sense of serene power." He was incredulous at the money his lectures brought in. In Chicago he had received as his share $1,000 for an hour's work. In the smaller cities his take was smaller but never less than $60. "I could lecture from now till the day of doom if I had the strength and time to do it," he wrote a friend. "The East has been horrid in the newspapers, but the West is very good and simple. I have a sort of triumphal progress, live like a sybarite, and travel like a god."

After Chicago Wilde embarked on an exhausting tour of a dozen cities in Ohio, Michigan, Kentucky, Missouri, and Wisconsin. In Cleveland he told his audience: "You in America don't want that we should look upon you as a mere collection of money-making merchants. You would like to influence the civilization of Europe. You are ambitious and should be so; but the only way you can influence us is by producing noble art and a noble civilization."

A reporter in Cleveland asked Wilde to characterize the major American cities he had visited thus far. The Irishman answered: "I find New York brilliant and cosmopolitan; Philadelphia, literary; Baltimore, pleasant; Washington, intellectual; Boston, more like Oxford than any [other] city you have. The people in Chicago I find simple and strong and without any foolish prejudices that have influenced Eastern America."

In the smaller cities Wilde found fewer amenities and cruder comforts. Like so many British visitors before him, he was repulsed by the American habit of spitting incessantly in public. "America is one long expectoration," he complained caustically.

In Cincinnati Wilde had strong competition from a large religious revival that filled the streets with multitudes singing,

> *"Oh, wondrous bliss! oh, joy sublime!*
> *I've Jesus with me all the time."*

He toured the downtown area and found the buildings drab beyond belief. "I wonder that criminals do not plead the ugliness of your city as an excuse for their crimes," he told several shocked Cincinnati officials.

In a heavy, cold rain Wilde climbed to the top of Mt. Adams to visit Rookwood Pottery, which would soon establish an international reputation as the premiere American art pottery. Founded by Maria Longworth Nichols on Thanksgiving Day in 1880, Rookwood attracted an inordinate amount of attention in the national press from the beginning because it was run by a woman at a time when there were only a handful of female entrepreneurs in the country. Few business ventures in the late nineteenth century were more suffused with idealism than Rookwood Pottery where, it was hoped, the profits would be used to develop a higher art form. Wilde toured the facility, met its community of artists, and gave his blessing to the enterprise.

Whereas Mrs. Trollope had hoped to redeem America by making it well-mannered, Wilde sought to redeem it by making it stylish and artistic. "I [have] found everywhere I went bad wall papers, horribly designed and colorful carpets, and that old offender, the horse-hair sofa, whose stolid look of indifference is always so depressing," he told audiences. "I found meaningless chandeliers and machine-made furniture . . . which creaked dismally under the ubiquitous interviewer."

If the domestic furnishings repelled him, Wilde grew to respect his hosts. "In America there is no opening for a fool," he later told his friends in London. "They expect brains, even from a boot-black, and get them. . . . There is no such thing as a stupid American. Many Americans are horrid, vulgar, intrusive, and impertinent, just as many English people are also; but stupidity is not one of their national vices."

After Wilde's lecture in Louisville, a middle-aged woman "with a sweet, gentle manner and a most musical voice" approached him and introduced herself as Mrs. Philip Speed, a niece of John Keats, the poet whom the Aesthetics claimed as the founder of their movement. Her father, Keats's younger brother, had emigrated to Kentucky in 1818. Wilde visited her home the next day and spent several hours reading the poet's letters to her father. A few weeks later she sent him the manuscript of Keats's "Sonnet on Blue," which he had quoted in his lecture. A grateful Wilde wrote from Omaha: "What you have given me is more golden than gold, more precious than any treasure this great country could yield me, though the land be a network of railways, and each city a harbour for the galleys of the world. . . . Since my boyhood I have loved none better than your marvelous kinsman, that godlike boy, the real Adonis of our age."

In Indianapolis Wilde's hosts introduced him to a new American craze, ice cream. He was not impressed. "Mr. Wilde promptly placed the small of his back in the seat of his chair and spooned in the ice cream with the languor of a debilitated duck," noted a disappointed writer for *The Saturday Review*. "Perhaps ice cream disagrees with him."

Wilde's party by now included both a secretary and a valet, an enormous trunk, hatbox, dressing case, and portmanteau. "With what incumbrances one travels!" he complained in a letter to Julia Ward Howe. "What would Thoreau have said to my hat box! Or Emerson to the size of my trunk, which is Cyclopean!"

In St. Louis Wilde wired Colonel Morse to order two coats, specifying that they be "beautiful; tight velvet doublet, with large flowered sleeves and little ruffs of cambric coming up from under the collar." He thought they would excite "a great sensation." He also demanded two pairs of gray silk stockings because "they were dreadfully disappointed in Cincinnati at my not wearing knee breeches." Wilde had long since come to appreciate that his wardrobe was his scripture; for many in his audiences what he had to say in his lectures was less important than what he wore while presenting them.

The newspapers in St. Louis were full of stories about Charles Guiteau. The case had finally gone to the jury, which took just 30 minutes to render a guilty verdict. The assassin fired his attorney and announced to the press that henceforth he would handle his own appeals. "I have the public with me," he boasted. "I could make $50,000 next winter lecturing if I could get out of this." A Missouri rope maker urged Washington officials to use reliable St.

Louis hemp rope on execution day, while a city tailor offered to supply a black death mask of his own design.

Back in Chicago, Wilde learned that D'Oyly Carte's New York office had booked him into a tour of the West between March 22 and April 15. Soon he was on a train traveling across the Great Plains toward Omaha. "I don't know where I am," he confessed in a letter to a friend. "Somewhere in the middle of coyotes and cañons: one is a 'ravine' and the other a 'fox.' I don't know which, but I think they change about. I have met miners. They are big-booted, red-shirted, yellow-bearded and delightful ruffians."

Ahead loomed the Rocky Mountains. Wilde was about to experience the West and the greatest adventures thus far on his tour.

5

In the West Wilde found a society more tolerant of his eccentricities. The egalitarian bias of the frontier tradition valued such traits as personal courage, physical prowess, and the ability to drink a quart of whiskey or to lose all one's capital on the turn of a card without the quiver of a muscle. These, rather than rank and wealth, often determined a man's place in the fluid world of the boomtowns. One man might boast of a larger spread or more money in the bank, yet if his less-fortunate neighbor could out-shoot or outride him, then in the eyes of many people the one was as good as the other.

Even Wilde's shoulder-length hair, which had provoked so much waspish comment on the Eastern seaboard, carried entirely different connotations in the West. There long hair was a badge of distinction proudly worn by brave men like George Armstrong Custer, Wild Bill Hickok, and Buffalo Bill Cody, whose exploits loomed larger than life in the popular imagination. (A reporter in Denver saw Wilde dressed in a wide-brimmed hat and long coat and noted that he looked "not unlike a Texas Ranger who had struck it rich.")

Wilde's next stop was San Francisco, which he reached after a lengthy train ride from Omaha across the plains and mountains. San Francisco, perhaps more than any other U.S. city, was the perfect setting for Wilde. In a letter home to a friend, he rhapsodized lyrically:

> I was four days in the train. At first, grey, gaunt desolate plains, as colourless as waste land by the sea, with now and then scampering herds of bright red antelopes and heavy shambling buffaloes, . . . and screaming vultures like gnats high up in the air, then up the Sierra Nevadas, the snow-capped mountains shining like shields of polished silver in that vault of blue flame we call the sky, and deep cañons full of pine trees, and so for four days, and at last from the chill of the mountains down into eternal summer here, groves of orange trees in fruits and flower, green fields, and purple hills, a very Italy, without its art.

Wilde fell in love with California. The census of 1880 had counted a population of 870,000; but only one in 20 of these had actually been born in the state. "The enjoyment of life is a prominent purpose of California society," a report based on the census figures concluded. "The prevalent mode of living is luxurious; and the habits are expensive. In no place is society more free and cordial and ready to give a friendly reception to a stranger than in California. In no part of the world is the individual more free from restraint. High wages, migratory habits, and bachelor life are not favorable to the maintenance of stiff moral rules among men."

San Francisco gave Wilde a warm welcome. "The farther West one comes, the more there is to like," Wilde told reporters. "The Western people are much more genial than those of the East." A crowd of 4,000 people met his train at the San Francisco railroad station. He rode in an open carriage drawn by four horses to the Palace Hotel, one of the city's most lavish. The roof on the seven-story-high hotel was studded with unprecedented 2,042 ventilating tubes, one each for every room, every bathroom, and every closet.

San Francisco was the happiest engagement of Wilde's tour. "I'm fêted and entertained to my heart's content," he wrote home enthusiastically. A fashion for sunflowers raged throughout the city. A reporter from a big Salt Lake City paper called it all "silliness" and noted: "Milliner's windows are decked with sunflowers; sunflower buttonhole bouquets are worn; sunflower fans are fashionable in the theaters."

Wilde's hosts took him through Chinatown, which enchanted him. He told a reporter later: "I was delighted with the Chinese quarters. They fascinated me. I wish these people had a quarter in London. I should take pleasure in visiting it often." In Chinatown he discovered further evidence to support his theory that articles for daily use could be made more beautiful. "At the hotel I was obliged to drink my chocolate or coffee out of a cup an inch thick. I enjoyed getting down into the Chinese quarters and sitting in a pretty latticed balcony and drinking my tea out of a cup so dainty and delicate that a lady would handle it with care. Yet this was no expensive place for wealthy people to go to. It was for the common people."

Wilde's first lecture came in the evening of March 27 in Platt's Hall. A reporter for *The Morning Call* described the crowd as "one of the best-dressed, most fashionable, learned, critical, distingué and, in point of fact, the most aesthetic audiences ever assembled . . . a wealth of beauty and a bewilderment of color." A reckless profusion of sunflowers, lilies, primroses, dahlias, and fuchsias decorated the stage. Wearing his celebrated knee breeches, Wilde made his appearance shortly after 8:00. His lecture that evening was one of his most spirited performances; his audience applauded enthusiastically at its conclusion. A second lecture two days later in Oakland went equally well, although reporters noted that women made up the majority of the audience. *The Morning Call* declared, "The young poet has made a palpable hit in San Francisco. It is certainly a fact that he has done better, from a managerial point of view, here than in any other city in the United States."

Then two things occurred that boosted Wilde's stock ever higher in the city. A group of gentlemen invited the Irishman to the exclusive Bohemian Club, intending to get him drunk and have some fun at his expense. Wilde had been through this once before, in New York City. Once again he drank his companions under the table and then walked back alone to his hotel. Word of his capacity to hold his liquor spread rapidly. Wilde was henceforth respected as a "three-bottle man." Impressed Bohemian Club members petitioned him to sit for a portrait to hang on their club wall. He graciously assented.

Soon afterward a second Oscar Wilde story generated banner headlines in the San Francisco newspapers. Several acquaintances took him to the Cliff House where, along with the food, guests enjoyed a spectacular view of the Pacific Ocean breaking against the rocks below. Soon he ended up at the bar, where a game of dollar ante was in progress.

"What is dollar ante?" Wilde asked innocently.

The players explained and invited the Irishman to join them.

"A great sadness fell upon him," one newspaper reported later. "Sometimes an unutterable melancholy would . . . shadow his dreaming eyes, but he said little—only sighed."

Soon it was Wilde's turn to deal. "He caressed the cards gently and distributed them mournfully, like crumbs at communion," the reporter noted. "Everybody went in. The captain took two cards; Fry took one and Oscar one."

The players rapidly escalated the betting. Soon the pot had more than $100 in it.

"The o'ershadowing sky is murky, but I must stay," Wilde announced languidly. "I will—how do you phrase it, call? I will call on you."

The captain uttered a cry of glee and lay down three aces.

"Full house," Fry shouted and started for the pot.

"Tsk-tsk," Wilde murmured and revealed four deuces.

The others were dumfounded.

Wilde collected the money and then slowly rose from the table, saying, "Now that I remember it, gentlemen, we used to indulge in this little recreation at Oxford. Come and take a snifter with me."

Incidents like this were windows into the public character that Wilde had developed so carefully over his months of touring in the States. D'Oyly Carte had originally hired him as a walking promotional stunt to pave the way for Gilbert's Bunthorne. But Wilde's stage persona had evolved in complexity and depth, so that in the end it had little in common with the two-dimensional creation from *Patience*.

On April 8 Wilde boarded a train for the two-day ride to Salt Lake City. The usual crowd of reporters met him at the station. They asked him about his reception in America. "I am more and more astonished and pleased every time I lecture at the courtesy with which I am received by audiences," he told them, in that winning combination of flattery and humility that had become his style. "Among the personal friends I have made in America, there are many who have exacted the promise that I return next year. And so I will when I have got more to say and learnt a better style of saying it."

Wilde visited the great Mormon Tabernacle ("it looked like a soup-kettle") and lectured to a capacity crowd in the opera house ("an enormous affair about the size of Covent Gardens that holds with ease fourteen [Mormon] families"). The reviews were largely favorable. "We should like to see the person in Salt Lake who can fill an hour more entertainingly than Oscar Wilde did on art or any other subject," an editor said in the *Tribune*. Wilde met with John Taylor, the church president, whose seven wives had borne him 34 children. Wilde later decided that polygamy Mormon-style was "most prosaic—how much more poetic to marry one and love many."

Wilde headed for Colorado. The train passed through the Territory of Wyoming about the time when the editor of the Laramie newspaper explained to his readers the etiquette of the napkin: "It is poor taste to put it in your pocket and carry it away. The rule of etiquette is becoming more and more thoroughly established that napkins should be left at the house of the hostess. It should be left beside the plate where it may be easily found by the hostess and returned to the neighbor from whom she borrowed it for the occasion."

Wilde was having such a good time that he good-naturedly accepted the ignorance of art that characterized the frontier mining communities. Indeed, this aspect of the American West yielded some of his most memorable stories. One of his favorites concerned the ex-miner turned art patron who "actually sued the railroad company because the plaster cast of Venus de Milo, which he had imported from Paris, had been delivered minus the arms. And, what is more surprising still, he gained his case and the damages."

When Wilde arrived in Denver, he discovered that the city had been preparing for weeks for his arrival. A great uproar had occurred when the madams of brothels along Holladay Street decorated their houses in the "Aesthetic" style and their girls took to carrying sunflowers. Denver was home to one of the great Western humorists, Eugene Field, a popular columnist for the *Tribune* who once dismissed an actor with the following review: "The Reverend George Miln played *Hamlet* at the Opera House last night. He played it until eleven o'clock."

The mile-high city of Denver was unlike any other Wilde had visited. "Here was a town without a single man who had been born in it," wrote historians Lloyd Lewis and Henry J. Smith. "Practically all the inhabitants had lived in the town less than ten years. In 1871, Denver's population was estimated at less than 5,000 people. In 1882, it had between 35,000 and 65,000 inhabitants, depending upon the time of year estimates were made. The city had an immense floating population, transients who at the first sign of spring left town for the mountains and the mines."

Denver owed its existence to the presence of enormous deposits of silver in the surrounding mountains. Wilde soon met silver king

Horace Tabor, whose extravagant lifestyle made him Colorado's best-known citizen. One hundred peacocks strutted across the grounds of his Denver mansion. In 1878 he was a shopkeeper in the booming Colorado silver camp of Leadville when he "invested" $10 in a grubstake for two down-and-out prospectors. Within a few days the pair struck a fabulously rich vein of silver ore, and their mine started producing $8,000 of bullion a week. Tabor was a millionaire. The mines that he developed, especially the Little Pittsburgh and the Matchless, made Tabor one of the wealthiest and most powerful men in the West. His romance with Baby Doe became the stuff of novels and operas. In 1883, when they married in Washington, D.C., President Chester Arthur and his entire cabinet attended the wedding. Tabor lavished more than $15,000 on the christening of their first daughter. Then came the Crash of 1893. Silver plunged from $1.29 to 50 cents an ounce. And the Tabors suddenly were broke.

But in April 1882 Tabor was at the height of his power and influence. Some of his mines in Leadville were producing more than $100,000 of silver bullion a month. Tabor was eager to meet the visiting Irishman. After all, Wilde was booked into the Tabor Opera House for his lecture and the Windsor Hotel, also Tabor's property, for his nights. Tabor quickly invited Wilde to visit his Matchless Mine in Leadville. The Irishman eagerly accepted, having longed for an opportunity to tour one of the West's most notorious mining towns.

Leadville was proudly known as one of the richest, roughest, and most lawless boomtowns in the West. When Wilde was advised that some toughs had threatened to shoot him or his manager if he set foot in Leadville, he good-naturedly fired back: "Nothing they can do to my traveling manager will intimidate me."

Wilde's visit in Leadville proved a highlight of his tour across America. He was told that on the day before his arrival a vigilante committee had tried and hanged two murderers. On April 13 he lectured in the Tabor Opera House, just two years old and already boasting a reputation as the finest structure of its kind west of the Mississippi River. It seated 880 guests in elegant Andrews patent opera chairs upholstered in scarlet plush. Wilde may have heard the story about a recent production of *Faust*. At the end, when Faust was to descend into Hell amid fire and smoke, elaborate arrangements had been made for the special effects. The singer playing Faust was suspended from ropes so he could be lowered through a trapdoor at the right moment. But the ropes twisted and he could not get down, instead hanging above the smoke and flames of Hell. One of the miners stood up and shouted, "What's the matter? Is Hell so crowded there ain't room for one more?"

Wilde found his audience of miners "very charming and not at all rough. I read them passages from the autobiography of Benvenuto Cellini and they seemed much delighted. I was reproved by my hearers for not having brought him with me. I explained that he had been dead for some little time which elicited the inquiry, 'Who shot him?'"

Later Wilde insisted, "Nothing is more graceful in the world than the broad-brimmed hat of the Rocky Mountain miners." After his lecture he was taken on a tour of Leadville. In a dance saloon he saw a printed notice above a piano: "PLEASE DO NOT SHOOT THE PIANO PLAYER. HE IS DOING HIS BEST." Wilde called it "the only rational method of art criticism I have ever come across." After the lecture Tabor took his guest to an elegant banquet deep in the bowels of the number three shaft in the Matchless Mine. Wilde wrote later:

> The amazement of the miners when they saw that art and appetite could go hand in hand knew no bounds. When I lit a long cigar they cheered until the silver fell in dust from the roof on our plates; and when I quaffed a cocktail without flinching, they unanimously pronounced me in their grand simple way "a bully boy with no glass eye"—artless and spontaneous praise which touched me more than the pompous panegyrics of literary critics ever did or could. Then I opened a new vein, or lode, which with a silver drill I bril-

liantly performed, amidst unanimous applause. The silver
drill was presented to me and the lode named "The Oscar." I
had hoped that in their simple grand way they would have
offered me shares in "The Oscar," but in their artless untu-
tored fashion they did not. Only the silver drill remains as a
memory of my night in Leadville.

Wilde never returned to Leadville, but the miners continued to
speak of him with affection. Years later a miner who had attended
the Matchless Mine banquet told a visitor to the town, "That
Oscar Wilde is some art guy, but he can drink any of us under the
table and afterwards carry us home two at a time."

On Wilde's April 18 arrival in St. Joseph, Missouri, he found
that he had been upstaged by Jesse James, the notorious train rob-
ber, who had been murdered only two weeks before. Hundreds of
sightseers flooded the town to stare at the house in which fellow
gang member Bob Ford had shot his leader in the back of the head
for the reward money. The public looked upon the James brothers
as modern Robin Hoods and accorded them the status of heroes.
A popular story, almost certainly apocryphal, recounted the time
Jesse once lent a poor widow $1,400 shortly before a banker
arrived to foreclose on her house; the outlaw later ambushed the
departing banker and recovered his money.

Interest in the dead outlaw was intense. Soon the whole country was singing:

> Jesse had a wife
> To mourn all her life;
> His children they were brave.
> But the dirty little coward
> Who shot Mr. Howard [Jessie's alias at the time]
> Has laid poor Jesse in his grave.

An embalming establishment in Cincinnati offered the outlaw's
mother $10,000 for her son's body plus a percentage of the

receipts from a cross-country tour. Wilde attended an auction where James's personal effects fetched astronomical prices. "They sold his dust-bin and foot-scraper by public auction, his door-knocker is to be offered for sale this afternoon, the reserve price being about the income of an English bishop," an incredulous Wilde wrote home. "His favorite chromo-lithograph was disposed of at a price which in Europe only an authentic Titian can command." Wilde concluded that "Americans are great hero-worshippers and always take their heroes from the criminal classes."

While touring Kansas, Wilde received a request from the mayor of the nearby town of Griggsville, "Will you lecture us on aestheticism?" He quickly replied by return telegram, "Begin by changing the name of your town." From Topeka he wrote a friend, "The local poet has just called on me with his masterpiece, a sanguinary lyric of 3,000 lines on the Civil War. The most impassioned part thus begins: 'Here Major Simpson battled bravely with his Fifteenth Kansas Cavalry.'"

In Lincoln, Nebraska, Wilde lectured before a group of enthusiastic undergraduates from the local university. Afterward they took him to visit the state prison. He was deeply moved by the "poor odd types of humanity in hideous striped [clothing] making bricks in the sun . . . and the little whitewashed cells, so tragically tidy, but with books in them. In one I found a translation of Dante and a Shelley. Strange and beautiful it seemed to me that the sorrow of a single Florentine in exile should, hundreds of years afterwards, lighten the sorrow of some common prisoner in a modern gaol." (The experience was curiously prophetic; years later Wilde himself would read the whole of Dante's *Divine Comedy* during his stay in Reading Gaol.)

Wilde returned to New York City in early May where he gave another lecture on May 11, using new material he had worked up on his swing through the West. The response convinced D'Oyly Carte that Wilde's attraction as a speaker was far from dimmed. Two more tours were booked, the first to eastern Canada. Then in

July Wilde set out for a three-week swing through the Old South. Friends warned him of the risks to his health in New Orleans, then suffering through an epidemic of yellow fever. Wilde refused to worry. "I think that one who has survived the newspapers is impregnable," he insisted.

The sticky summer heat that suffocated like a wet blanket caused attendance at his lectures to drop off sharply. But Wilde professed himself happy just to be in the South. "I write to you from the beautiful, passionate, ruined South, the land of magnolias and music, of roses and romance; picturesque too in her failure to keep pace with your keen northern pushing intellect; living chiefly on credit and on the memory of some crushing defeats," was how he described it to Julia Ward Howe in Boston.

Throughout the South Wilde found a pervasive melancholy which he attributed to the recent Civil War. Later he joked with friends in Boston: "I was once sitting on the portico of a country house with a young lady admiring the beauty of a limpid stream under the rays of the moon, and I said, 'How beautiful is the moonlight falling on the water!' And she replied, 'It is beautiful indeed, but, oh, Mr. Wilde, you ought to have seen it before the War!'"

Wilde sought out Jefferson Davis, the seventy-four-year-old former president of the Confederacy, at his home in Beauvoir on the Gulf Coast. He was deeply moved by their meeting. "He lives in a very beautiful house by the sea amidst lovely trees," he told a reporter later. "He impressed me very much as a man of the keenest intellect, and a man fairly to be a leader of men on account of a personality that is as simple as it is strong, and an enthusiasm that is as fervent as it is faultless." Wilde made clear that much of his sympathy stemmed from his own Irish partisanship. He went on: "We in Ireland are fighting for the principle of autonomy against empire, for independence against centralization, for the principles for which the South fought."

On the afternoon of July 1 Wilde lectured on domestic furnishings to a small group of women in Mobile. At the same time, in

Washington, D.C., Charles Guiteau was marched from his cell to the prison yard and hanged before a large crowd. The day before, authorities had arrested his sister and charged her with a conspiracy to help her brother commit suicide. The leaves of the flowers she had given him on her last visit proved under examination to have been dusted with arsenic powder. Seconds before the executioner slipped the black death mask over his head, the assassin shouted out his last words: "President Arthur is a coward and an ingrate."

By the end of his Southern tour Wilde had netted more than $6,000 for his own account in six months of lecturing, a sum that established him as one of the top money-makers on the American lecture circuit. He remained in the country several more months. He passed almost two months socializing in the fashionable resorts of the East, lecturing informally on art in the homes of the wealthy. In October Wilde was back in New York City, vainly attempting to mount a local production of his play *Vera*.

Finally, on December 27, almost one year after he first stepped ashore in America, Wilde sailed for England aboard the steamer *Bothnia*. By then he had traveled more than 15,000 miles across America and lectured in 60 cities. And yet the *New York Tribune* reported that on the eve of his departure Wilde had confessed that his "mission to our barbaric shores had been substantially a failure." Clearly, from a financial perspective the tours had been most lucrative. But he had failed to fulfill his original design of stimulating among American craftsmen and industrialists a cult of the beautiful.

Robert Sherard, one of Wilde's closest friends and later his biographer, noted that if the Irishman had failed to change America, America had changed him. His tour had brought Wilde "into contact with some of the most energetic of men, roused his latent energy, sharpened and stimulated him to a degree that made him almost unrecognizable. . . . The dealings he had had with men, the struggles both social and commercial in which he had, in the main, triumphed, had given him an experience which years of life in London might never have afforded."

On his return voyage Wilde decided to drop many of the affectations that had been his signature for the past several years—the velvet coats, knee breeches, long hair, sunflowers, and bizarre mannerisms. "America had taken the nonsense out of him," Sherard recalled in later years. "He arrived in London the conventional nineteenth-century gentleman, quiet in dress and reserved in manner," another contemporary observer reported.

Oscar Wilde and Reginald Bunthorne had parted company forever.

♦ Epilogue ♦

"Perhaps, after all, America has never been discovered," Oscar Wilde wittily observed during his 1882 lecture tour. "I myself would say that it had merely been detected."

If we are to perceive the advantages and disadvantages of life in America and the values it provides—the unceasing hurry, the intense political activity, the sensitivity to public opinion and foreign criticism, the newspapers and the evening television news shows as the food and fuel of daily life, the confidence in the future and in education, the blend of kindness and generosity with hardheaded practicality, the enjoyment of business—then we must see America through the eyes of the outsider, the foreign visitor. Alexis de Tocqueville thought that Americans lived "in the perpetual utterance of self-applause, and there are certain truths which Americans can learn only from strangers."

Now, as then, travelers to America continue to give Americans unique opportunities to see themselves through the eyes of others. "America is like life," English novelist E. M. Forster astutely observed after his 1947 visit here, "because you can find usually find in it what you are looking for."

Today's foreign visitors to America often find themselves struck by the same features of America and Americans that so impressed our eight British travelers in the nineteenth century. To take but one example of the many available, the vast distances that characterize life in this country can both inspire and frighten. "The first thing a foreigner has to take in about America—and it is not something automatically grasped even by all the natives—is the simple size of the place and the often warring variety of life that goes on inside it," Englishman Alistair Cooke once observed. Americans often take for granted the stupendous beauty of the Tetons, the deserts, and Yosemite, which leave many foreign visitors today, especially those from Britain, feeling as though they have come face to face with their maker. But the Polish author Leopold Tyrmand found himself quite intimidated after a visit: "The vastness of this continent makes me think with excessive sympathy of the nice, cozy, secure claustrophobia of Europe."

Tocqueville's metaphor of America as a laboratory for the future, promising either salvation or damnation of mankind, continues to be a common theme of many foreign visitors today. "One comes to America—always, no matter how often—to see the future. It's what life in one's own country will be like five, ten, twenty years from now," an Israeli businessman once told this author.

The more-perceptive visitors to America in the nineteenth century understood that many of the national characteristics they branded as uniquely American were products of the generations of pioneering needed to settle the continent. British author T. H. White after his 1964 visit insisted the foreign traveler to America must never lose sight of this essential fact of American history. "Americans . . . are essentially an *earnest* people," he wrote in *America at Last*. "They have so much love and kindness and are so little blasé. But it is fatal to forget that they are all descended from *people who had the guts not to stay at home*. . . . Americans are the children, in a melting pot, of adventurers who had this one thing in common, that they were individualists who had the courage, initiative, and vigor to break out of the Old World and conquer a continent."

America's strength, thus, lies not in its unity but its diversity. As a chaos of disparate realities, very different from the claustrophobic, centripetal societies of Europe, America alone in the history of the modern world has possessed the ability to revise itself for different people at different times. "The reality of America is selective, optional, fantastic: there is an America for each of us," the modern British scholar Peter Conrad insisted in *Imagining America*. "Because America offers an incarnation of your most recondite and specialized fantasies, in discovering America you are discovering yourself."

British visitors in the nineteenth century, from Frances Trollope to Oscar Wilde, discovered that truth for themselves on their travels through America. In their different ways, they returned to London profoundly changed by their exposure to America's landscapes, people, and ideas. In a very real sense they discovered themselves while discovering America.

✎ Notes for Further Reading ✎

Frances Trollope

Domestic Manners of the Americans is available in several modern reprints. The 1949 edition published by Vintage Books contains a superb appreciation of the book by Donald Smalley. The only reliable biography is Helen Heineman's excellent *Mrs. Trollope: The Triumphant Feminine in the Nineteenth Century*. Ray Billington's *America's Frontier Heritage* brilliantly discusses the multitude of ways the frontier shaped the American character. Glyndon G. Van Deusen's *The Jacksonian Era, 1828–1848* is a solid history of this critical period, while editor George E. Probst in *The Happy Republic: A Reader in Tocqueville's America* brings together numerous insightful documents to form a fresh and unique survey of Jacksonian America.

Fanny Kemble

The finest modern edition of Fanny Kemble's *Journal of a Residence on a Georgian Plantation in 1838–1839* is that edited brilliantly by John A. Scott. His 61-page introduction also succinctly covers the major events of the author's life. Kemble has been fortunate to have several fine biographies written about her. Two excellent ones are Constance Wright's *Fanny Kemble and the Lovely Land* and Dorothy Marshall's *Fanny Kemble*. In *The Terrific Kemble* Eleanor Ransome edited a selection of Kemble most interesting autobiographical writings to create a self-portrait. Louis Filler's *The Crusade Against Slavery, 1830–1869* is an eminently readable history of abolition. Two excellent books on the South are Clement Eaton's *The Growth of Southern Civilization, 1790–1860* and W. J. Cash's *The Mind of the South.*

Interested readers may also want to check out Edward Ball's 1998 book, *Slaves in the Family,* a fine account of his search for the descendants of the people his ancestors kept as slaves. Through six generations his family acquired more than 4,000 slaves and 25 rice plantations in South Carolina, which they operated until the defeat of the Confederacy in 1865. The book also contains a lengthy description of life on a rice plantation from the perspectives of both the owners and their slaves.

Charles Dickens

For a full account of Dickens's 1842 tour of America the reader must supplement his *American Notes* with the third volume of the Pilgrim Edition of *The Letters of Charles Dickens.* Michael Slater's *Dickens on America and the Americans* brings together a wide variety of his writings on America in one handy volume accompanied by an excellent introduction. Edgar Johnson's massive two-volume biography, *Charles Dickens: His Tragedy and Triumph,* continues to be definitive even after all these decades. Sidney P. Moss's study, *Charles Dickens' Quarrel with America* is the fullest documentation of this controversy. The best account of the struggle for an Anglo-American copyright agreement can be found in James J. Barnes's *Authors, Publishers, and Politicians.*

George Ruxton

The major sources for George Ruxton's travels through North America are his two books *Adventures in Mexico and the Rocky Mountains* and *Life in the Far West,* both of which are available from any good library in modern reprints. No biography of the man exists. But in *Ruxton of the Rockies* Clyde and Mae Reed Porter have assembled all available information on his life, including many of his letters, articles, and private papers, and arranged them chronologically to make a kind of autobiography. Jack Schaefer has a chapter on Ruxton in his *Heroes Without Glory: Some Good Men of the Old West*. The handiest introduction to mountain men is Ray Billington's brief but excellent study *The American Frontiersman*. The finest modern history of the mountain man and his era is Bernard DeVoto's *Across the Wide Missouri*. DeVoto's brilliant *The Year of Decision: 1846* is indispensable to anyone seeking an understanding of the impact of the concept of Manifest Destiny on American history. Dale Van Every has informative chapters on the mountain men in *The Final Challenge: The American Frontiers, 1804–1845*. I found David J. Weber's *The Mexican Frontier, 1821–1846* quite useful for its discussion of the American Southwest under Mexican rule.

Richard Burton

The major source for Richard Burton's overland journey is his *City of Saints and Across the Rocky Mountains to California*, available in an excellent modern reprint edited by Fawn M. Brodie. Of the several biographies on Burton, the most reliable are Fawn M. Brodie's *The Devil Drives: A Life of Sir Richard Burton* and Byron Farwell's *Burton: A Biography*. Ralph Moody's *Stagecoach West* provides a broader context in which to place Burton's own journey. Also useful for background are Oscar O. Winther's *The Transportation Frontier: Trans-Mississippi West, 1865–1890* and John D. Unruh's *The Plains Across: The Overland Emigrants and the Trans-Mississippi West, 1840–1860*. Leonard J. Arrington and Davis Bitton's *The Mormon Experience: A History of the Latter-Day Saints* is an excellent introduction to the Mormon church and its history.

William Russell

William Russell's dispatches have been reprinted at various times over the past 30 years. I used *My Civil War Diary*, edited by Fletcher Pratt. Alan Hakinson has written a full biography, *Man of Wars: William Howard Russell of The Times*. Of the several histories of war reporting, the most readable is Philip Knightley's *The First Casualty: From the Crimea to Vietnam, The War Correspondent as Hero, Propagandist, and Myth Maker*. The first chapter examines Russell's contributions to his profession. William C. Davis's *Battle at Bull Run* gives a detailed account of the first battle of the Civil War. The first volume of Bruce Catton's *The Coming Fury* is an eloquent history of the early phase of the conflict.

Frank Harris

The major source for Frank Harris's youthful adventures remains his autobiography, *My Life and Loves*. Much later, he published *My Reminiscences as a Cowboy*. This, however, is more a novel than a factual memoir, and Harris allowed himself considerable freedom to romanticize and exaggerate the incidents from this period of his life. (The 1958 Paramount film *Cowboy*, starring Glenn Ford and Jack Lemmon, followed the book with reasonable fidelity.) No reliable biography of Harris exists. Philippa Pullar's *Frank Harris* suffers grievously from the author's hostility to her subject. Robert B. Pearsall's *Frank Harris* is a solid appraisal of Harris's literary achievements. David McCullough's exhaustive *The Great Bridge* is a fine history of the building of one of America's two most famous bridges. Emmett Dedmon's *Fabulous Chicago: A Great City's History and People* has a useful chapter on the city's catastrophic fire. J. Frank Dobie's brilliant study *The Longhorns* is a classic in the field of Western history.

Oscar Wilde

Lloyd Lewis and Henry Justin Smith's *Oscar Wilde Discovers America* is definitive in its account of the Irishman's odyssey across country. As a model of how social history ought to be written, it cannot be bettered. Of the many biographies available, two of the best are those by Richard Ellman and Sheridan Morley, both titled *Oscar Wilde*. Rupert Hart-Davis's comprehensive *The Letters of Oscar Wilde* is also of great value.

ঙ Bibliography ঙ

Ambrose, Stephen E. *Undaunted Courage: Meriwether Lewis, Thomas Jefferson, and the Opening of the American West*. New York: Simon & Schuster, 1996.

Albert, James W. *Albert's New Mexico Report, 1846–'47*. Albuquerque, NM: Horn & Wallace, 1962.

Allen, John Logan. *Passage Through the Garden: Lewis and Clark and the Image of the American Northwest*. Urbana, IL: University of Illinois Press, 1975.

Anon., "The Late George Ruxton," in *Blackwood's Magazine*, 64 (November 1848), pp. 591–4.

Armstrong, Margaret. *Fanny Kemble: A Passionate Victorian*. New York: The Macmillan Company, 1938.

Arrington, Leonard J. and Davis Bitton. *The Mormon Experience: A History of the Latter-Day Saints*. New York: Alfred A. Knopf, 1979.

Atkins, John B. *The Life of Sir William Howard Russell*. London: John Murray, 1911.

Ball, Edward. *Slaves in the Family*. New York: Farrar, Straus and Giroux, 1998.

Barnes, James J. *Authors, Publishers, and Politicians*. Columbus, OH: Ohio State University Press, 1974.

Berger, Max. *The British Traveller in America, 1836–1869*. New York: Columbia University Press, 1943.

Bethke, Frederick J. *Three Victorian Travel Writers: An Annotated Bibliography of Criticism on Mrs. Frances Milton Trollope, Samuel Butler, and Robert Louis Stevenson*. Boston: G. K. Hall, 1977.

Billington, Ray A. *America's Frontier Heritage*. New York: Holt, Rinehart and Winston, 1966.

_____. *The American Frontiersman*. Oxford, England: Oxford at the Clarendon Press, 1954.

_____. *The Far Western Frontier, 1830–1860*. New York: Harpers & Brothers, 1956.

_____ and Martin Ridge. *Westward Expansion: A History of the American Frontier*. New York: MacMillan Publishing Company, 1982.

Boornstin, Daniel J. *The Americans: The National Experience*. New York: Random House, 1965.

Bowen, Frank C. *A Century of Atlantic Travel, 1830–1930*. Boston: Little, Brown, and Company, 1930.

Brandon, William. *The Men and the Mountain: Fremont's Fourth Expedition*. New York: William Morrow & Company, 1955.

––––––––. "The Wild Freedom of the Mountain Men," in *American Heritage*, VI (August 1955), pp. 4–9.

Brodie, Fawn M. *The Devil Drives: A Life of Sir Richard Burton*. New York: W.W. Norton & Company, 1967.

Burton, Sir Richard. *The City of Saints and Across the Rocky Mountains to California*. Edited by Fawn M. Brodie. New York: Alfred A. Knopf, 1963.

Calhoun, Charles W., editor. *The Guilded Age: Essays on the Origins of Modern America*. Wilmington, DE: Scholarly Resources, 1996.

Cash, W. J. *The Mind of the South*. New York: Alfred A. Knopf, 1941.

Catton, Bruce. *The Centennial History of the Civil War*, Vol. I, *The Coming Fury*. New York: Doubleday & Company, 1961.

Chambrun, Clara Longworth de. *Cincinnati: Story of the Queen City*. New York: Charles Scribner's Sons, 1939.

Chesterton, G. K. *Charles Dickens: A Critical Study*. New York: Dodd Mead & Company, 1906.

Clemens, Samuel L. *Roughing It*. New York: Harper & Brothers, 1959. (First published in 1872.)

Cohen, Patricia Cline. *The Murder of Helen Jewett: The Life and Death of a Prostitute in Nineteenth-Century New York*. New York: Alfred A. Knopf, 1998.

Conrad, Peter. *Imagining America*. New York: Oxford University Press, 1980.

Cross, Helen Reeder. "I Hate America," in *History Today*, 20 (March 1970), pp. 163–73. (On Frances Trollope.)

Crum, Mason. *Gullah: Negro Life in the Carolina Sea Islands*. Durham, NC: Duke University Press, 1940.

Davis, Paul B. "Dickens and the American Press, 1842," in *Dickens Studies*, 4 (March 1968), pp. 32–77.

DeNova, John A., editor. *The Gilded Age and After*. New York: Charles Scribner's Sons, 1972.

Deusen, Glyndon G. Van. *The Jacksonian Era, 1828–1848*. New York: Harper & Brothers, 1959.

DeVoto, Bernard. *Across the Wide Missouri*. Boston: Houghton, Mifflin Company, 1947.

––––––––. *The Year of Decision, 1846*. Boston: Houghton, Mifflin Company, 1961.

Dickens, Charles. *American Notes for General Circulation.* London: Oxford University Press, 1957.

————. *Dickens on America and the Americans.* Edited by Michael Slater. Austin, TX: University of Texas Press, 1978.

————. *The Letters of Charles Dickens.* Volume Three, *1842–1843.* Edited by Madeline House, et al. Oxford, England: Clarendon Press, 1974.

Douglass, Frederick. *Narrative of the Life of Frederick Douglass, An American Slave.* Cambridge, MA: The Belknap Press, 1960.

Eaton, Clement. *The Growth of Southern Civilization, 1790–1860.* New York: Harper & Brothers, 1961.

Ekirch, Arthur A., Jr. *The Decline of American Liberalism.* New York, Atheneum, 1971.

Elliott, Russell R. *History of Nevada.* Lincoln, Nebraska: University of Nebraska Press, 1973.

Evans, J. Martin. *America: The View from Europe.* San Francisco: San Francisco Book Company, 1976.

Farwell, Byron. *Burton.* New York: Holt, Rinehart and Winston, 1963.

Feck, Luke. *Yesterday's Cincinnati.* Miami, FL: E.A. Seeman Publishing, 1977.

Filler, Louis. *The Crusade Against Slavery, 1830–1860.* New York: Harper & Brothers, 1960.

Flanders, Ralph Betts. *Plantation Slavery in Georgia.* Chapel Hill, NC: University of North Carolina Press, 1933.

Fogel, Robert William and Stanley L. Engerman. *Time on the Cross: The Economics of American Negro Slavery.* Boston: Little, Brown and Company, 1974.

Forster, John. *The Life of Charles Dickens.* 2 vols. London: J.M. Dent & Sons, 1966.

Furnas, J. C. *Fanny Kemble: Leading Lady of the Nineteenth-Century Stage.* New York: Dial Press, 1982.

Gaines, Francis Pendleton. *The Southern Plantation: A Study in the Development and the Accuracy of a Tradition.* New York: Columbia University Press, 1924.

Garrard, Lewis H. *Wah-to-Yah and the Taos Trail.* Norman, OK: University of Oklahoma Press, 1955.

Gilbert, Bil [sic]. "Pioneers Made a Lasting Impression on Their Way West," in *Smithsonian,* May 1994, pp. 40–51.

Griffith, Russell A. "Mrs. Trollope and the Queen City," in *The Mississippi Valley Historical Review,* 37 (September 1950), pp. 280–302.

Hale, Richard W. *Sir Richard Burton at Salt Lake City.* Boston: Privately printed, 1930.

Hall, James. *The West: Its Commerce and Navigation*. New York: Burt Franklin, 1970.

Harris, Frank. *My Life and Loves,* John F. Gallagher, editor. New York: Grove Press, 1963. *Oscar Wilde: His Life and Confessions*. 2 vols. New York: Bretano's, 1916.

Hart-Davis, Rupert. *The Letters of Oscar Wilde*. New York: Harcourt, Brace & World, 1962.

Heilman, Robert B. "The New World in Charles Dickens's Writings," in *The Trollopian*, 1 (September 1946), pp. 25–43 and (March 1947), pp. 11–26.

Heineman, Helen. *Frances Trollope*. Boston: Twayne Publishers, 1984.

_____. *Mrs. Trollope: The Triumphant Feminine in the Nineteenth Century*. Athens, Ohio: Ohio University Press, 1979.

Hollon, W. Eugene. *Frontier Violence: Another Look*. New York: Oxford University Press, 1974.

Houtchens, Lawrence H. "Charles Dickens and International Copyright," in *American Literature*, 13 (March 1941), pp. 18–28.

Howe, Daniel W., editor. *Victorian America*. Philadelphia: University of Pennsylvania Press, 1976.

Hulse, James W. *The Nevada Adventure: A History*. Reno, NV: University of Nevada Press, 1965.

Hyde, H. Montgomery. *Oscar Wilde*. London: Metheum, 1975.

Johnson, Claudia D. "That Guilty Third Tier: Prostitution in Nineteenth-Century American Theaters," in *Victorian America*, Daniel W. Howe, editor. Philadelphia: University of Pennsylvania Press, 1976, pp. 111–20.

Johnson, Edgar. *Charles Dickens: His Tragedy and Triumph*. 2 vols. New York: Simon and Schuster, 1952.

Johnson, Johanna. *The Life, Manners, and Travels of Fanny Trollope*. New York: Hawthorn Books, 1978.

Jones, Howard Mumford. *O Strange New World: American Culture, the Formative Years*. New York: Viking Press, 1964.

Jullian, Philippe. *Oscar Wilde*. New York: Viking Press, 1969.

Kemble, Frances Anne. *Fanny: The American Kemble, Her Journals and Unpublished Letters*. Tallahassee, FL: South Pass Press, 1972.

_____. *Journal of a Residence on a Georgian Plantation in 1838–1839*. Edited by John A. Scott. New York: Alfred A. Knopf, 1961.

_____. *Records of a Girlhood*. New York: Henry Holt and Company, 1884.

_____. *The Terrific Kemble: A Victorian Self-Portrait from the Writings of Fanny Kemble*. Edited by Eleanor Ransome. London: Hamish Hamilton, 1978.

Ketchum, Richard, editor. *The American Heritage Book of the Pioneer*

Spirit. New York: American Heritage Publishing Company, 1959.

King, Spencer B. *Georgia Voices: A Documentary History to 1872*. Athens, GA: University of Georgia Press, 1966.

Klein, Benjamin F., editor. *The Ohio River Handbook and Picture Album*. Cincinnati, OH: Young and Klein, Inc., 1969.

Knight, Oliver. *Life and Manners in the Frontier Army*. Norman, OK: University of Oklahoma Press, 1978.

Kronenberger, Louis. *Oscar Wilde*. Boston: Little, Brown and Co., 1976.

Lambert, Neal. *George Frederick Ruxton*. Boise, ID: Boise State University Press, 1974.

Lancaster, Clay. "The Egyptian Hall and Mrs. Trollope's Bazaar," in *Magazine of Art*, 43 (March 1950), pp. 94–112.

Lewis, Lloyd and Henry Justin Smith. *Oscar Wilde Discovers America*. New York: Harcourt, Brace and Company, 1936.

Lewis, Oscar. *San Francisco: Mission to Metropolis*. Berkeley: Howell-North Books, 1966.

Mackenzie, Norman and Jeanne. *Dickens: A Life*. Oxford, England: Oxford University Press, 1979.

McDougall, Walter A. *Promised Land, Crusader State: The American Encounter with the World Since 1776*. Boston: Houghton Mifflin Company. 1997.

Marcy, Randolph B. *The Prairie Traveler: A Handbook for Overland Expeditions*. New York: Harper & Brothers, 1859.

Marshall, Dorothy. *Fanny Kemble*. London: Weidenfeld and Nicolson, 1977.

Mitchell, Michael. *Monsters of the Gilded Age: The Photographs of Charles Eisenmann*. Toronto: Gage, 1979.

Moody, Ralph. *Stagecoach West*. New York: Thomas Y. Crowell Company, 1967.

Morgan, H. Wayne, editor. *The Gilded Age*. Syracuse, NY: Syracuse University Press, 1970.

Morison, Samuel Eliot. *The Oxford History of the American People*. New York: Oxford University Press, 1965.

Morley, Sheridan. *Oscar Wilde*. London: Weidenfeld and Nicolson, 1976.

Moss, Sidney P. *Charles Dickens' Quarrel with America*. Troy, NY: The Whitson Publishing Company, 1984.

Mulder, William and A. Russell Mortensen, editors. *Among the Mormons: Historical Accounts by Contemporary Observers*. New York: Alfred A. Knopf, 1958.

Munro, J. "Ruxton of the Rocky Mountains," in *Good Words, 34* (August 1893), pp. 547–51.

National Geographic Society. *We Americans*. Washington, DC, 1975.

National Park Service. *Soldier Brave: Indian and Military Affairs in the*

Trans-Mississippi West, Including a Guide to Historic Sites and Landmarks. Vol. XII in The National Survey of Historic Sites and Buildings. New York: Harper & Row, 1963.

Nelson, Harland S. *Charles Dickens.* Boston: Twayne Publishers, 1981.

Nevins, Allan, Editor. *Americans Through British Eyes.* New York: Oxford University Press, 1948.

Olmsted, Frederick Law. *The Cotton Kingdom: A Traveller's Observations on Cotton and Slavery in the American Slave States.* Edited by Arthur M. Schlesinger. New York: Alfred A. Knopf, 1970.

Osterweis, Rollins G. *Romanticism and Nationalism in the Old South.* New Haven: Yale University Press, 1949.

Pachter, Marc, Editor. *Abroad in America: Visitors to the New Nation, 1776–1914.* Washington, DC: Smithsonian Institution, 1976.

Paul, Rodman Wilson. *Mining Frontiers of the Far West, 1848–1880.* New York: Holt, Rinehart and Winston, 1963.

Payne, Edward F. *Dickens' Days in Boston.* Boston: Houghton Mifflin Company, 1927.

Pearson, Hesketh. *The Life of Oscar Wilde.* London: Methuen & Company, 1946.

Peters, Arthur King. *Seven Trails West.* New York: Abbeville Press, 1996.

Piercy, Frederick Hawkins. *Route from Liverpool to Great Salt Lake.* Edited by Fawn Brodie. Cambridge: Harvard University Press, 1962.

Porter, Clyde and Mae Reed. *Ruxton of the Rockies.* Edited by Leroy R. Hafen. Norman, OK: University of Oklahoma Press, 1950.

Probst, George E., editor. *The Happy Republic: A Reader in Tocqueville's America.* New York: Harper Torchbooks, 1962.

Putnam, George. "Four Months with Charles Dickens," in *Atlantic Monthly,* 26 (October 1870), pp. 476–82.

Rapson, Richard L. *Britons View America: Travel Commentary, 1860–1935.* Seattle: University of Washington Press, 1971.

Remini, Robert V. *Andrew Jackson.* New York: Twayne Publishers, 1966.

Riegel, Robert E. *America Moves West.* New York: Henry Holt and Company, 1956.

Root, Frank A. and William E. Connelley. *The Overland Stage to California.* Topeka, KS: Privately printed, 1901.

Rosa, Joseph G. *Age of the Gunfighter: Men and Weapons on the Frontier, 1840–1900.* New York: Smithmark Publishers, 1993.

_____. *They Called Him Wild Bill: The Life and Adventures of James Butler Hickok.* Norman, OK: University of Oklahoma Press, 1964.

Rosenberg, Carroll Smith. "Beauty, the Beast, and the Militant Woman: A Case Study in Sex Roles and Social Stress in Jacksonian America," in *American Quarterly,* 23 (October 1971), pp. 562–584.

Ruth, Kent. *Great Day in the West: Forts, Posts, and Rendezvous Beyond the Mississippi.* Norman, OK: University of Oklahoma Press, 1963.

Ruxton, George Frederick. *Adventures in Mexico and the Rocky Mountains.* Edited by Horace Kephart. Oyster Bay, NY: Nelson Doubleday, 1915.

————. *Life in the Far West.* Edited by Leroy R. Hafen. Norman, OK: University of Oklahoma Press, 1951.

Sadleir, Michael. *Trollope: A Commentary.* London: Constable & Company, 1947.

Sandoz, Mari. *Love Song to the Plains.* New York: Harpers & Brothers, 1961.

Schaefer, Jack. *Heroes without Glory: Some Goodmen* [sic] *of the Old West.* Boston: Houghton Mifflin Company, 1965. (Chapter on George Ruxton.)

Schlesinger, Arthur M. *The Age of Jackson.* Boston: Little, Brown and Company, 1953.

Slotkin, Richard. *The Fatal Environment: The Myth of the Frontier in the Age of Industrialization, 1800–1890.* New York: Atheneum, 1985.

————. *Gunfighter Nation: The Myth of the Frontier in Twentieth-Century America.* New York: Atheneum, 1992.

————. *Regeneration Through Violence: The Mythology of the American Frontier, 1600–1860.* Middleton, CT: Wesleyan Univeristy Press, 1973.

Smalley, Donald, editor. "Mrs. Trollope in America," in Frances Trollope, *Domestic Manners of the Americans.* New York: Vintage Books, 1949.

Smith, Henry Nash. *The Virgin Land: The American West as Symbol and Myth.* Cambridge: Harvard University Press, 1950.

Stone, Harry. "Dickens' Use of HIs American Experiences in *Martin Chuzzlewit,*" in *Publications of Modern Language Association.*, 72 (June 1957), pp. 464–78.

Sutherland, Bruce. "George Frederick Ruxton in North America," in *Southwest Review*, 30 (Autumn 1944), pp. 86–91.

Taylor, Philip A. M. *Expectations Westward: The Mormons and the Emigration of Their British Converts in the Nineteenth Century.* Ithaca, NY: Cornell University Press, 1966.

Trollope, Anthony. *An Autobiography.* Oxford, England: Oxford University Press, 1980.

Trollope, Frances. *Domestic Manners of the Americans.* London: The Folio Society, 1974.

Trollope, Thomas Adolphus. *What I Remember.* London: William Kimber, 1973.

Tucker, Louis Leonard. "Cincinnati: Athens of the West, 1830–1861," in

Ohio History, 75 (Winter 1966), pp. 11–25. (On Frances Trollope.)

Tuckerman, Henry T. *America and Her Commentators.* New York: Antiquarian Press, 1961. (First published in 1864.)

Tyler, Alice Felt. *Freedom's Ferment: Phases of American Social History from the Colonial Period to the Outbreak of the Civil War.* New York: Harper Torchbooks, 1944.

United States Department of the Interior. *Exploring the American West, 1803–1879.* Washington, DC: Division of Publications, National Park Service, 1982.

Unruh, John D. *The Plains Across: The Overland Emigrants and the Trans-Mississippi West, 1840–60.* Urbana, IL: University of Ilinois Press, 1979.

Van Every, Dale. *Ark of Empire: The American Frontier, 1784–1803.* New York: William Morrow and Company, 1963.

_____. *The Final Challenge: The American Frontier, 1804–1845.* New York: William Morrow and Company, 1964.

Voelker, Frederick E. "Ruxton of the Rocky Mountains," in *Bulletin of the Missouri Historical Society*, 5 (January 1949), pp. 86–90.

Walker, Don D. "The Mountain Man as Literary Hero," in *Western American Literature*, I (Spring 1966), pp. 15–25.

Weber, David J. *The Mexican Frontier, 1821–1846: The American Southwest Under Mexico.* Albuquerque, New Mexico: University of New Mexico Press, 1982.

Welter, Barbara. "The Cult of True Womanhood, 1820–1860," in *American Quarterly*, 18 (Summer 1966), pp. 151–174.

Wesick, Jane Louise. *The English Traveller in America, 1785–1835.* New York: Columbia University Press, 1922.

Wills, Garry. *John Wayne's America: The Politics of Celebrity.* New York: Simon & Schuster, 1997.

Wilson, Angus. *The World of Charles Dickens.* London: Martin Secker & Warburg, 1970.

Winther, Oscar O. *The Transportation Frontier: Trans-Mississippi West, 1865–1890.* New York: Holt, Rinehart and Winston, 1964.

Wright, Constance. *Fanny Kemble and the Lovely Land.* New York: Dodd, Mead & Company, 1972.

ॐ About the Author ॐ

James C. Simmons is the author of thirteen books and more than 500 magazine articles on travel, history, biography, and wildlife. Raised in Cincinnati, he received his bachelor's degree from Miami University, Ohio, and a doctorate in nineteenth-century British literature from the University of California at Berkeley. Before becoming a freelance writer, he taught courses on British and American literature at Boston University and San Diego State University. His book, *Americans: The View from Abroad*, won first prize as Best Travel Book of 1990 in the presitigious Lowell Thomas Competition of Travel Journalism. He also writes privately commissioned life, family, and corporate histories. He lives in San Diego.

❦ Index ❧